# The Making of NO, NO, NANETTE

# The Making Of

## By Don Dunn

THE CITADEL PRESS

Secaucus, New Jersey

For M. J.

## ACKNOWLEDGEMENTS

In writing *The Making of No, No, Nanette*, a number of books were drawn upon for research, and several warrant special mention. *Producing on Broadway* by Donald C. Farber (DBS Publications, Inc.) was of immense help. Highly valuable also were *The Season* by William Goldman (Harcourt, Brace, Jovanovich), *The Immortal Jolson* by Pearl Sieben (Frederick Fell, Inc.), and *The World of Musical Comedy* by Stanley Green (A.S. Barnes & Co.). The encyclopedic *Theater World* series (now published by Crown) similarly rates a bow of thanks, as does Abel Green and Joe Laurie Jr.'s *Show Biz from Vaude to Video* (Henry Holt & Co.). A salute, too, to Fred Allen's *Much Ado About Me*, Fred Astaire's *Steps in Time*, Brooks Atkinson's *Broadway*, Daniel Blum's *Pictorial History of the American Theater*, Bernard Rosenberg and Harry Silverstein's *The Real Tinsel*, Harris Lewine's *Good-bye to All That*, and Jerry Stagg's *The Brothers Shubert*.

In addition, a number of institutions provided valuable assistance, and deserve considerable credit—

The Research Library of the Performing Arts at Lincoln Center, whose voluminous collection includes an amazing labor of love, *Jolsonography*, by the late David Jay.

The New York City Public Library, whose mammoth files of *The New York Times, New York Herald Tribune*, and *Variety* were of immense value.

The Museum of Modern Art, whose film-art files and retrospective showing, *The Roots of the American Musical Film*, could not have been more helpful or better timed. (Thanks, Lillian Gerard and Mark Segal.)

The Tower Isle Hotel, Jamaica, W.I., which materialized a typewriter in a moment of crisis.

General Electric Co. and its advertising agency, N. W. Ayer & Son, Inc., which provided a tape recorder in a similar instance.

Sardi's, "the" theatrical restaurant where so many of the interviews for this book were conducted. (Thanks, Vincent, Jimmy, and Martin.)

Warner Bros. Music for permission to quote selected lyrics from "Tea For Two" (© 1924), "I Want to Be Happy" (© 1924), "Too Many Rings Around Rosie" (© 1924), and "Peach on the Beach" (© 1925), by Vincent Youmans-Irving Caesar. Original copyrights by Harms, Inc. Copyrights renewed, all rights reserved.

The Memory Shop, New York, for its fine historical photographs.

*The New Yorker* magazine.

The city of Atlantic City, N.J., and its Mayor, William T. Somers, along with Vincent Catalano, James Kerley, George and Richard Fetter, and Elliott Ryan.

Which brings us around to the *people* who really made everything that follows this acknowledgement possible. My thanks to:

Mr. and Mrs. Harvey A. Vien of Tavares, Florida, who offered much assistance;

Floracita, Chris, Paul, Elena, and Carrie Dunn, who hopefully will understand;

John Scott, of Young & Rubicam, Inc., who laughed in the right places;

Anne Colamosca, Grant Compton, Janice Corday, Frances Favre, Judith Figueroa, Tessie Mantzoros, Robert McAuley, Jomary Moseley, Sally Powell, Stewart Ramsey, and Marcella Rosene of *Business Week* who contributed valiant efforts—and Lew Young, Elliott Bernstein, Phil Osborne, John Berry, Jack Pluenneke and the other members of the staff who provided an occasional breathing space or word of encouragement;

Mrs. Helen A. Plumbridge, who knows her contribution cannot be sufficiently acknowledged in mere words;

Fran Simmons, who typed most of the final manuscript, and the painstaking Eileen Brand, who edited it;

Allan Wilson, who never pushed, and who offered wisdom and understanding;

*And* Loni Zoe Ackerman, Dr. Martin Ackerman, *Audience* magazine, James Awe, Busby and Etta Berkeley, Valerie Bettis, Rose Bigman, Joretta Bohannon, Dr. Barry Brooks of Winthrop, Mass., Lt. Col. Richard L. Bryan, U.S.D.A., Irving Caesar, Ted Cappy, David Cheifetz (of Globe Signs), David Chimay, Alexander Cohen, Kevin Daly, Buster Davis, Gale Demarest, Carole Demas, Raoul Pène du Bois, Jimmy Durante, Sammy Fain, Clay Felker (*New York* magazine), Michael Flanagan, Sy Friedman (Zodiac Photos), Tyler Gatchell, Charles Gaynor, Faith Geer, Maribeth Gilbert, Martin Gross (Nostalgia Book Club), Terry Hall, Ruby Keeler, Patsy Kelly, Goldie Kleiner, Miles Kreuger, Gil Lamb, Floria Lasky, Abe Lastfogel, Carolyn Leigh, Guy Livingston, Joanne Lotsko, John and Sharon Lowe, Jim Maher, Ann Ray Martin, Frank McHugh, Grace McKeefe, John McKeefe, Jim Mennen, David Merrick, Max Meth, Joe Moore, Joe Morgan, Peter Neufeld, Mary Ann Niles, John Roach, Arthur Rubin, Mrs. Vera Rubin, Joe Russell, Wini Shaw, Hiram Sherman, Burt Shevelove, Toots Shor, Pearl Sieben, John Slagle, Louis Sobol, Gary Stevens, Monica Tiller, K. C. Townsend, Paul Truss, Bobby Van, Irvin Warwick, Gertrude White, Walter Winchell, and Daryll F. Zanuck.

Particular credit, however, must go to three people who worked to make a dream into a reality, and my thanks to them—

Harry Rigby, Cyma Rubin, Sam Rubin

DONALD H. DUNN

*November 3, 1971*

6

# The Making of NO, NO, NANETTE

**1** On the ninth floor of a gleaming mid-Manhattan skyscraper, the conference rooms of the American Arbitration Association wait every weekday morning in crisp, efficient expectation. Shortly after ten o'clock, each of the sparsely furnished rooms fills with angry combatants of modern industry. In one, labor leaders lean forward in the soft-cushioned, black leather chairs and pound their fists on the thick mahogany table as they quarrel with a company president over a salary hike. In another, elected city officials meet with striking firemen to iron out a new pension plan. In still another, the partners in a bankrupt business divide their few remaining assets.

> "Nostalgia? Good heavens, I never thought about Nostalgia. It sounds like the name of a cheap perfume."
>
> HARRY RIGBY

Soundproofed, and with heavy draperies and Venetian blinds that can close out the city's pulsebeat completely, the rooms are highly functional. A table, some chairs, a wall phone, a signal light that warns away intruders, everything in somber brown and neutral beige—the message is clear: "This is serious . . . *real* . . . *Business*."

On occasion, though, the make-believe business of Show-business finds its way along the stretch of tile-floor hall, past the large modern paintings on the walls, and through one of the heavy doors. It did so in the spring of last year when the two people who had given birth to the blockbuster revival of *No, No, Nanette* faced each other across a table and—like divorced parents battling for custody of an only child—began to quarrel bitterly over whose show it really was.

As the trio of impassive judges turned their heads back and forth to follow testimony from first one side and then the other, they could have been watching a tennis match.

*In the far court:* Mrs. Cyma Rubin, the "producer" of *No, No, Nanette*. Divorced, remarried, in her mid-forties, she wears her long black hair pulled tightly against her head and wound into a prim knot at the back. Her taste in clothes —expensive clothes—runs to the Bendel look, all straight lines and slender; in midi-skirt or longer lengths, and in

9

dark wine-reds, suede browns, and blacks. Despite a hawkish nose and wide mouth that sometimes is an angry line beneath it, Cyma (pronounced See-ma) is not an unattractive woman—partly, perhaps, because of her large and impressive brown eyes that burn with a fierce intensity of their own. Nevertheless, when she speaks—loudly and with machine-gun rapidity—it is apparent that she is all business, a lady to be reckoned with.

*In the near court:* Harry Rigby, once identified as the "co-producer" of *No, No, Nanette,* and now precisely what he has been for the last few years—a near penniless Broadway gadfly with more ideas than business sense. He is tall, angular as a scarecrow, with longish gray hair that swirls above a deeply furrowed forehead. Nervously, he chews his thumbnail or waves his expressive hands in gestures that might indicate either glee or desperation. His voice is a high-pitched whine that frequently turns into a giggle. Fiftyish, a bachelor, witty and charming, Harry is typically one of New York's "theater people."

As the days and weeks of argument and rebuttal wore on, the three members of the arbitration panel shuffled their papers and sought to answer a basic question:

Was Mrs. Cyma Rubin, wife of multimillionaire Sam Rubin, acting within her legal rights when she "fired" Harry Rigby and took his name off the posters and programs for *No, No, Nanette?*

It was a simple question, one that might more simply come down to: Who gets the credit for a hit?

And, perhaps much more important, who gets the profits?

Plenty of profits. The guess is that *No, No, Nanette* will return between three and five million dollars to the people who put up approximately $600,000 to get the show on.

And who are those people?

Just one man. Samuel Rubin.

Can he use three million dollars? Well, why not? He certainly knows what to do with that kind of money. Founder and president of Fabergé, the company that sells all those perfumes and men's toiletries, Sam sold out in 1963 to new

**10**

owners. His price? Only $26 million, plus $10 million more payable six months later to the Samuel Rubin Foundation. Now, gray-haired at sixty-nine, but energetic, Sam lives in comfortable retirement and busies himself with pet charities and philanthropic projects.

His foundation gives away a million dollars a year. Here, $50,000 to the New York Shakespeare Festival. There, $50,-000 a year for ten years to Gian Carlo Menotti's Festival of Two Worlds. On one hand, a new residence hall for foreign students at New York University Medical Center gets a contribution. On the other hand, money goes to Leopold Stokowski's American Symphony, of which Sam is president.

Now, Sam Rubin may find that *No, No, Nanette* is pouring in money faster than he can give it away. Since the show opened on Broadway, January 19, 1971, at the 46th Street Theater, it has "gone clean" at every performance, eight times a week. That means every available seat in the theater has been sold—at prices that reach $12 for orchestra tickets during the week and $15 on weekends. And there are usually thirty people who pay $5 apiece for standing room. Squeezed side by side, leaning on a ledge behind the last row of seats, they enable *No, No, Nanette* to take in several hundred dollars over its capacity weekly gross. That, by the way, is $107,000.

The whopping amount gets split up several ways. The theater owners get nearly $30,000 a week for rent and to cover the expenses of the box-office help, ushers, doormen, and managerial employees. Perhaps $50,000 a week more goes out to pay for the show itself—salaries of the cast, the orchestra, and the backstage crews; cleaning of costumes; purchase of supplies and properties; royalties to music companies, the directors, choreographers, and other "creative" people; and so on. What is left is profit.

In the case of *No, No, Nanette*, the production is estimated to be making a profit above $25,000 a week. That's $100,000 a month. Over $1.2 million a year.

All of which means that the initial investment—Sam's $600,000—was returned in about six months. From then on, everything that came in was gravy. And the gravy will be pouring in for a long time to come. A half-year after it paid back its cost, *No, No, Nanette* had an advance sale of almost $1 million—and Broadway scalpers were busily selling orchestra tickets for $25 and more. *Nanette* was on everyone's "must see" list.

When newlyweds Tricia and Edward Cox invited Mom and Dad Nixon to New York for dinner and a show, what show did they attend? *No, No, Nanette,* of course. And when moon voyager Alan Shepard and his fellow astronauts came down to earth, where did New York Mayor John Lindsay show them off? At *Nanette.* When Lyndon Johnson came to town, he saw *Nanette.* And so did the Duke and Duchess of Windsor. And Ann-Margret. And Jack Benny. And—well, name the celebrity, and you can almost bet that he or she has seen the show.

But what turned the 1971 version of an antique and creaking 1924 musical comedy into a modern money machine was the eagerness with which it was grabbed, embraced, and held by hundreds and thousands of people who are not celebrities. They can be called part of "the Silent Majority" or "the Middle Americans," or simply "*Nanette* lovers." Most of them are elderly—in their late forties or fifties, if not older. Their fervent willingness to listen once more to the "big" song hits in *No, No, Nanette*—"Tea for Two" and "I Want to Be Happy"—zoomed the show's original-cast recording onto *Variety*'s list of the fifty best-selling record albums across the country, and kept it there for months. (Sales of record albums, by the way, also provide profits to a musical's producers. So do road companies. And European companies. And amateur productions. And films.)

The fact that *No, No, Nanette* found and captured a huge audience—or was captured by it—is almost a miracle, and a large one, at that. On Broadway, the odds are tilted so sharply against a producer and investors making back the cost of a production, much less coming up with a profit, that showbusiness is frequently used as a tax loss by overly wealthy people.

12

During the 1969-70 theatrical season, for example, backers poured $12.5 million into thirty-two new plays and musicals on Broadway, and into fifty-eight smaller ones Off-Broadway. And, according to the New York attorney general's office, the investors came out on the short end by $1.4 million. In 1970-71, when *No, No, Nanette* opened, it was in competition with eleven other new musicals. Eight closed after running only a few days or weeks. Two lasted several months, or just long enough to give the performers hope that they might stay off the unemployment lines for an entire season. Only one other musical had a slight chance to go into the black-ink columns along with *No, No, Nanette*. As a further indication of the odds against success, two of last season's big-budget musicals closed out of town and poured about $1.5 million down the drain.

But *No, No, Nanette* made it. It beat the odds. It not only leaped like a healthy thoroughbred over the usual Broadway hurdles, but did it while carrying extra weight. Producer David Merrick, who has made himself a millionaire several times over by knowing how to turn out hits like *Hello, Dolly* and *Promises, Promises* on a fairly consistent basis, admits he was skeptical when he first heard about the revival of the 1924 musical. "I predicted a three-week run," he says. Then he adds, "I shrugged and said, 'Another one of those lunatic projects.'" Merrick and other theatrical veterans had reasons for their doubt.

*Who is this bored, rich woman?* they wondered. This Cyma Rubin, who has never produced a show before. This perfect example of the dilettante.

*Is she serious about starring Ruby Keeler?* A sixty-year-old dancing grandmother who once—yes, once—was a star of stage and screen, but who hasn't put on her tap shoes for three decades.

*And Harry Rigby?* Yes, he knows his way around Broadway. He should. He's been producing on and off since 1951. But he's never had a hit.

Wait a minute, that isn't all. Are the producers really going to hire *Busby Berkeley?* To direct? A seventy-five-year-old man who bases his dance patterns on military drill

**13**

maneuvers that he learned 'way back in World War I!

And *Patsy Kelly* is their comedienne? Sure, she was funny once—but now when her name is dropped into a conversation, it usually brings a gasp and the embarrassed rejoinder, "Is she still around? I thought she was. . . ."

And is it true that Mrs. Rubin has a *daughter* who—naturally—dances and sings, who will have a featured part in the show?

You've *got* to be kidding.

Besides, argued the Broadway experts, there is no place in the theater in 1971 for an old-fashioned musical with a juvenile plot and songs that talk of baking a sugar-cake "for me to take for all the boys to see." At $15 a ticket, audiences want more. They want big stars, like Lauren Bacall in *Applause,* or Katharine Hepburn in *Coco,* or Danny Kaye in *Two by Two.* And they want relevance, like *The Me Nobody Knows,* with its portrait of slum life, or *The Rothschilds,* that sings of the Jews' indomitable zest for freedom. Or they want nudity—a dash of it here, as in *Hair,* or a lot of it there, as in *Oh! Calcutta!*

But *No, No, Nanette?* No stars? No relevance? No nudity?

Not a chance.

Still, it happened. What the Broadway regulars could not foresee, and what carried *No, No, Nanette* along with it, was a tidal wave of Nostalgia. It began sweeping across the country a few years ago when television stations and movie theaters found that old movies attracted audiences if they were grouped as "A Humphrey Bogart Festival" or "Garbo in Retrospect." The wave grew as radio stations began playing old recordings of *The Shadow* and *Big Town.* Comic books dug from attics and basements suddenly commanded high prices. Mickey Mouse watches appeared on wrists that once sported the latest electronic Timex or Accutron. A Nostalgia Book Club signed up thousands of members. Record companies began cleaning up with reissues of old favorites by Tommy Dorsey, Harry James, and Benny Goodman.

**14**

Even while sociologists were studying the trend, it grew faster and faster. Fashion designers, searching for something to make people forget the midi-skirt debacle, came up with hot pants—and paid their respect to the bib-top shorts Ruby Keeler danced in when she was making those 1930 movie musicals. First, *Liberty* magazine, which had died twenty years earlier, was revived as "the nostalgia magazine" and offered people the opportunity to read (or reread) original 1935 articles about Shirley Temple and the Dionne quintuplets. Then, *The Saturday Evening Post* reappeared to take additional sentimental readers back several decades into time.

Reproductions of old Sears, Roebuck and Montgomery Ward catalogues were bought by hundreds of thousands of people who smiled at the ads for $2 shirts and $12 stereopticons. Tiffany lamps were bid to sky-high prices at antique auctions. Old Coca-Cola signs, priced at $100, were snapped up as wall decorations. A picture of Donald Duck printed on the front of a $1 T-shirt could raise the shirt's price to $5. Pen-makers Parker and Sheaffer, which concentrated for years on sleek, slim ballpoints, sold replicas of their bulky, leaky models from the 1920s. National advertisers—Hertz, Arrow shirts, Canada Dry, among them—began running ads that looked as if they could have appeared in the original issue of *Liberty* that posed the question, "Can Hitler Conquer America?"

*No, No, Nanette* hit the Broadway stage virtually at the peak of the nostalgia craze. It *was* the peak. More than any old magazine, or old lampshade, or old song, *Nanette* possessed the power to transport people backward in time. It could carry them to an earlier day, a nicer day—a day when the air was clean, and young men wore neckties, and orange juice was fresh, and a skeptical maiden would turn aside her boyfriend's compliments with "Banana oil!" rather than "Bullshit!"

The impact of *Nanette* on the Broadway theater was immediate. It was powerful enough to cause one of the "big bands" still touring with the dance arrangements of the

1930s and 1940s to take a full-page ad in *Variety*. The ad
carried a simple headline:

NOSTALGIA IS BOX-OFFICE!

But there were philosophers and pundits and critics who
scorned the trend, who said that people with 1971 problems
would not solve them by trying to escape into the past.
"Those audiences are made up of emotional cripples,"
snorted Broadway Producer Alexander Cohen. And showman Merrick added that it wouldn't last, that "Nostalgia is
already dated, and if they come up with any more revivals
like *Nanette*, they will fail."

Undaunted, one producer had already laid plans to bring
back *On the Town*, fresh from the 1940s. And Harry Rigby
(when he wasn't busy at the arbitration proceedings that
might reinstate him as *Nanette*'s co-producer) was dreaming about a revival of *Irene*, the musical that introduced
"Alice Blue Gown" in 1919, five years before the original
*No, No, Nanette* reached the stage.

The original *No, No, Nanette*?

Perhaps, as the audiences in the 46th Street Theater do
each evening in New York, it is possible to free the mind . . .
to move backward in time . . . and see where it all began.

**2** "Irving!"

Irving Caesar was leaning casually against the heavy stone wall of the building when the voice cut through the sunny March afternoon, and he looked up with a start. Across 48th Street, picking his way past sleek, new 1924 roadsters and huge, dusty taxis, came Otto Harbach. Caesar watched him approach, thinking the older man with his near-white hair and steel-rimmed glasses still looked more like the college English professor he had once been than Broadway's most prolific lyric writer.

> "If Frazee had ever been sober, and had seen how bad the show was, we would have closed out of town."
>
> IRVING CAESAR

Harbach thrust out his hand. "Irving, my boy, surely you have more important things to do than prop up the Friars Club."

The short, stocky Caesar shuffled his feet in momentary embarrassment. Ordinarily he was cocky—after all, he had written "Swanee" with George Gershwin in 1919, and it had been the biggest song in the country—but now, at twenty-nine, he still was a kid when it came to talking to the fifty-one-year-old master.

"Actually, Otto," he said with a weak grin, "I'm a little ashamed to tell you. I'm waiting for the afternoon poker game to start upstairs."

The older man shook his head in mock dismay. "Irving, Irving," he said, "how much are you losing?"

Caesar shrugged. "Not much. Fifty—all right, a hundred a week."

Now Harbach rolled his eyes upward. He put his arm around the younger man's shoulders, and turned him away from the building. "Your fellow Friars are not treating you gently," he said. "Besides, we have business. Come take a walk with me."

Caesar saw that Harbach had something on his mind, but he walked along Broadway in silence until he could not hold back the question.

"Problems, Otto?"

17

"A little one, Irving. I'm working on a new show for Frazee. The songs are nearly finished, but—"

"Who's doing the music?" Caesar interrupted.

"Vincent Youmans."

Caesar whistled softly. "Think you can top *Wildflower*?"

Harbach shrugged. "Who knows, Irving? That was last year. All I know now is if we don't come up with a number for Anna Wheaton, she is going to be a very angry young star. She hates a couple of things Youmans and I already wrote for her—"

"And you're asking me to help out?" Irving Caesar would not have admitted it, but he felt flattered.

The older man smiled over his shoulder as he began climbing the steps to a musty rehearsal hall. "It's better than letting you lose all your money at poker. Besides, you work fast, I hear. And you had a nice song or two in that *Jack and Jill* revue thing last year."

Caesar grinned. "I didn't think you noticed them."

"Oh, I always notice other writers' songs in a show that has my numbers too." He stepped aside to let Caesar through the frosted glass-paneled door. "The others give the audiences something to measure my lyrics against. They make mine look better."

For an instant, Harbach struggled to keep a straight face, but then he chuckled softly and Caesar realized that the usually modest writer was joking. A second later, they were weaving their way through the ragged lines of chorus girls, actors, and dancers toward the antique upright in the corner.

Vincent Youmans, handsome, boyish at twenty-six, his delicate fingers resting lightly on the keyboard, stared glumly into space as he listened to the attractive blonde woman at his side.

"I'm sorry, Mr. Youmans," she said petulantly, "but it just isn't fast enough for us to dance to. And if you play it faster, we can't sing it. The kind of thing we need—"

"The kind of thing we need, Miss Wheaton," Harbach interrupted, "is a new lyricist. And I've got the young man. My friend Mr. Caesar is going to fix things right up. Right,

Irving?" He turned to the composer. "Vincent, you know Irving?"

Youmans nodded. "I've heard of him," he said warily. " 'Swanee' and all that." His voice took on a cutting edge. "I've also heard that he likes to write melodies for the composers he works with."

"Wait a minute," Caesar said quickly. "Maybe I've put the names of some ginks who did piano arrangements for me on some of my songs, but I'd never even breathe a tune to a *real* composer. Like Gershwin. Or you—"

Youmans stared at the fast-talking young man from the Lower East Side, then reached out a hand. "Okay. Great to have you aboard—so long as we know who writes the words and who writes the music."

Anna Wheaton smiled happily as Harbach began filling Caesar in on the kind of number she needed. The show, he explained, was called *No, No, Nanette*. The plot came from a 1919 story called *His Lady Friends*, by May Edington. Millionaire producer Harry H. Frazee had asked two playwrights—Frank Mandel and Emil Nyitray—to turn it into a farce entitled *My Lady Friends* for popular character actor Clifton Crawford. The show had been a huge success on Broadway, and on tour. Audiences chuckled warmly at the tale of a wealthy Bible merchant who struggled to free himself from the clutches of three young gold diggers before his wife and his innocent ward, Nanette, got wise to him.

After Frazee had milked as much as possible from the play across the country, he had ordered Mandel to turn it into a musical. The writer, who had worked with Harbach on *Mary* in 1920, suggested teaming with him again. Frazee agreed at once, since Harbach had written the producer's first big musical hit, *Madame Sherry*, in 1910. Now, with the young composer, Vincent Youmans, Harbach promised to come up with another hit.

Suddenly, the dust-laden air of the rehearsal hall was shattered by a bellow from the door.

"What's going on here? Why is everybody standing around? I'm paying you people to put a show together!" Shouting as he moved quickly past the scurrying perform-

19

ers, H. H. Frazee brought his portly frame to the group huddled in the corner. He pushed his round face close to Harbach's.

"What are you sonsabitches up to?"

Calmly, while Youmans busied himself with soft arpeggios as a background, Harbach explained that he was trying to speed the appearance of the Muses. He introduced Caesar.

Frazee was aghast. "Another writer?" he shouted. "Another writer!" He leaned down and began fumbling in the heavy leather satchel on the floor at his side. A bottle of bourbon and a glass appeared. "I bought a story by one writer, a play by two more, then hired three for this show—and now a new one!" He filled the glass and tossed down the liquor at a gulp. "You!" he said, waving the empty glass at Harbach. "You pay him out of your share. This show's already costing me a fortune."

Harbach nodded.

Frazee blinked in surprise, then shook Caesar's hand. "All right, it's a deal. Want a drink on it, kid?" He pulled a second glass from the satchel and had it filled before Caesar could reply. "Here."

The younger man took the drink and, as if in imitation, tossed it down without flinching.

"Hey," Frazee said admiringly, "it's about time we got someone around here who can keep up with me." He poured another pair of drinks. "Irving, I like you. I don't give a damn if you can write songs. You now have a special job. This satchel, here. You see to it that it's always filled with a couple bottles of the best hooch you can find. And you carry it for me. Right?"

Caesar grinned. He clinked his glass against Frazee's and they drained them simultaneously.

"All righ' now," Frazee muttered. "You sonsabitches get to work."

That evening, inside a fifteen-minute stretch, Caesar and Youmans wrote a song for Anna Wheaton's second-act spot. "You Can Dance with Any Girl at All" not only pleased the beautiful performer, but brought a new request.

"Irving," said Harbach, "Donegan's unhappy with the seaside number. Now he wants a lyric from you."

Caesar glanced across the rehearsal room and watched comic dancer Francis X. Donegan prancing with six chorines before a polished mirror. "He's jealous that Wheaton got a new song."

Harbach nodded. "Of course. But I'm not crazy about the sea number myself. And, look, I just don't have time to work on it. I knocked myself out getting *Kid Boots* ready for Cantor a few months ago—you know what a perfectionist Ziegfeld is. And I'm already working with Oscar Hammerstein and Rudolf Friml on *Rose-Marie* for next September. How about you hanging on and helping keep these egotistical actors happy? I think I can get you half a percent of the gross."

"It beats losing at poker," said Caesar, grinning. "Just one question: Is Frazee as tight as he says?"

Harbach laughed. "How do you think millionaires get to be millionaires? They don't give it away, Irving. Come on, I'll tell you about him."

Over a beer at Dinty Moore's, the writer sketched in the amazing career of the producer. Frazee had first been an usher at a theater in his hometown of Peoria, Illinois, and then an advance publicity man for a touring troupe of actors. At twenty-two, he scraped together enough money to put on a play called *Uncle Josh Perkins*. In the next five years he produced several other plays and musicals that did well at the box office.

"I met him in 1910," said Harbach. "He was about thirty then, and one of the producers on *Madame Sherry*."

"Frazee was in on that?" said Caesar with a whistle. "Hey, I remember. You and Hoscha wrote that song—you know—" He snapped his fingers and began singing loudly, "Ev'ry little movement has a *meeeaning* all its *owwnnn* . . ."

Harbach held up a hand to silence him. "Come on, Irving, I'm modest, remember?" Then he added with a grin, "Besides, I've had so many hits that we'll be here all afternoon if you start singing them."

"Sorry," Irving replied. "I'll make up for it by paying the check."

The two men walked back to the rehearsal hall, pausing to watch a tiny plane spewing white smoke at ten thousand feet to spell "Lucky Strike" three miles long. "That brand's way ahead of Murad now," said Caesar. "So are Chesterfield and Camels. But they won't none of 'em get rich off me." To prove his point, he lit a long, black cigar.

Harbach continued Frazee's achievements. The producer had become interested in sports when he took two prize fighters, heavyweight champion James J. Jeffries and former champ "Gentleman Jim" Corbett, on tour as actors in a play called *Ready Money*. The show drew mobs in New York, Chicago, and London. Then, in 1916, Frazee bought the Boston Red Sox baseball club for $400,000.

"And he started selling off the players," Caesar said. "I'm not a ball fan myself—the track and the poker table are my vices—but I remember the stink he raised."

"That's right," Harbach nodded. "One by one, he sold the best men. Why, four years ago, when Babe Ruth was just starting to look great, Frazee got $125,000 from the Yankees for him. That was the highest price any player went for. And on top of that, they personally loaned Frazee $370,000—and I'll bet he never pays it back."

Caesar shook his head in admiration.

"You must have read the stories last year," Harbach went on. "Frazee sold the whole Boston club to a syndicate for one-and-a-half million dollars. Not a bad little profit, eh? Now he owns three theaters in New York and a couple in Chicago that are pouring in the rent."

"No wonder that stuff in the bag is high-priced hooch."

Under the studio's huge light bulbs hanging in dirty gray globes, Frazee was watching a pretty young blonde practice a pirouette. "Irving," he said in loud welcome, "you're just in time. Pour Miss Cleveland a drink." As Caesar went to the inexhaustible satchel, Frazee beamed at the young girl.

"She's my new find," he said. "Picked her right out of a stock company in Boston. She can act. She can sing. She can dance. When those yokels out front get a load of her as Nanette, she'll be a big star. You watch."

In the next few weeks as the show headed for its opening at the Garrick Theater in Detroit, Caesar and Youmans busily rewrote much of the musical's score. Late one afternoon they were working at the piano in Youmans' apartment when Caesar looked out the window. The sun was sinking swiftly behind the Manhattan towers.

"Listen, Vincent, we're not going to come up with anything else today."

Youmans continued to kibitz at the keyboard. "You want to take a nap, don't you, Ceez? So you'll be able to outdrink everybody at the party tonight."

"Party?" Caesar asked. "Is there a party tonight?"

Youmans laughed. "You've been waiting since noon for Bea Lillie and Gertie Lawrence to drop the curtain on *Charlot's Revue* and come whistling by here. They've done it every Wednesday night for months."

"Oh, yeah. But I thought today was Tuesday," Caesar pretended. "Is it really Wednesday already? My, my. Maybe I'd better take a nap at that."

Youmans picked out a few notes. "You'd better—if you plan to sing your usual ten choruses of 'Swanee'. Honestly, Ceez, you should have been a performer instead of a writer. I know at least one person who thinks you sing better than Jolson himself."

"Yeh? Who's that?"

"Irving Caesar," replied Youmans. Then, chuckling, he watched his partner stretch out on the couch.

"Hell," said Caesar, as he started to drift off, "I don't know why I even bother to go to these parties. The girls are only interested in you guys that play the piano. We poor eggs who tinker around with words get no attention at all."

"That's true," agreed Youmans. "*Unless* you sing them at the top of your voice."

Caesar groaned and pulled a sofa pillow over his eyes to shut out the fading sunlight. In the still air, the tinkling piano lulled him to sleep in seconds.

23

It seemed only an instant later that he felt a tug at his arm. "Ceez, wake up," a distant voice was saying. "Wake up and listen to this."

"Huh? Whazzat?" he said without opening his eyes.

"I've got a tune. Listen to it."

"Vincent, lemme alone. I'll listen later. Tomorrow—" He felt himself drifting off again, but the tug at his sleeve was persistent.

"Will you listen to this? It's so simple it's great," Youmans pleaded. "Come on."

Wearily, Caesar opened his eyes. Outside the blackness was speckled with lights in distant apartments. He swung himself upright on the sofa and put his head in his hands, squeezing his eyes shut and then opening them rapidly to shake off the drowsiness. Youmans began playing brightly.

"Not so loud, Vincent. Not so loud."

"It'll wake you up, Ceez. Now listen." He hummed along with the insistent melody. *"Dee—da-dee—da-dee—da-dee . . . da-dee—da-dum—da-dee—da-dum."*

Caesar listened a moment, then stretched his arms wide. "It's very nice," he said. "I'd better go and shave."

"Wait a minute. Put words to it. We can use it."

"Put words to it? Now? Aw, come on, we've got a party to go to. You think I'm a machine? I'll work on it tomorrow."

Youmans did not move from the piano. His hands stroked the keys to keep the melody going, over and over. "Come on, Ceez, you work fast. We did 'You Can Dance' in fifteen minutes. What'd it take us on 'Too Many Rings Around Rosie'? A half-hour?"

"Twenty minutes, and you know it. I did 'Swanee' with Gershwin in fifteen, too. But I'm half-asleep. I'm not even thinking straight."

"Give a try, anyway. Listen. *Dee—da-dee—da-dee—da-dum!*" . . . .

Caesar waved a hand. "All right, all right, anything to stop you from singing. I'll put some dummy words to the tune so I can remember it in the morning. Then I'll work on it. Play it again, a little slower."

Youmans obligingly dropped the tempo. Caesar thought for a second and began nodding his head in rhythm. He rubbed the tip of his broad nose and pursed his heavy lips.

"How's this?" he asked. "Just picture you . . . upon my knee, just tea for two . . . and two for tea."

Youmans was expressionless. "Perfect, perfect," he said. "Go on."

Caesar shrugged and scratched behind his right ear. "Okay. Tea for two, and two for tea, right? Then, Just me for you . . . and you for me, alone!"

The music continued to pour from the piano. "Great, Ceez. It fits. Keep it up. Keep going."

Caesar yawned. "That's enough, Vincent. I'll remember it. Come on, let's get ready."

The composer did not move. "No, no, finish it. Just add to that."

"Add to *what?*" asked Caesar. "That's just a *dummy.* The words don't even make sense. How can they be having tea if the girl's sitting on his lap? I'll change 'em tomorrow, get something better."

Youmans insisted until, finally, Caesar realized they would not leave for the party until the song was finished.

"All right," he said, giving in, "but I can't go on with monosyllables. Pick it up a little." As Youmans played faster, he began racing drowsily through rhymes: "Nobody near us, to see us or hear us, no friends or relations on weekend vacations. . . ."

In minutes, the song was finished. Caesar headed for the bathroom to shave. "I hope you're happy, Vincent," he said. "The girls'll be here and we'll probably be late." He stopped in the doorway and turned. "But you know how you can make it up to me?"

Youmans grinned boyishly up from the piano and took the pencil he had been using to note the music from between his teeth. "Yes," he said. "Yes, *you* may sing the song at the party tonight. Sing it all night long if you want to."

Caesar waved a thick hand at him. "You read my mind. We've been working together too much." He stepped into the

25

bathroom and turned on the hot water. Behind him, Youmans said something he couldn't quite hear.

"Whazzat?" Caesar shouted, his face bent low over the basin.

"I said, 'Don't say anything to Frazee.' "

Caesar stepped to the door, his face dripping. "What?"

"I said, don't tell Frazee. The song is too good for him. We'll sell it to somebody else for another show. Harbach and I already turned out a whole score for *Nanette,* and I'm doing half of it over with you. For what I'll make off this show, why should I knock myself out? We can sell this new one to Ziegfeld or Hammerstein."

"You're a businessman, Vincent. Sneaky, but a businessman. Mum's the word."

Several days later, at a particularly ragged rehearsal on a gray, windy day, the young ingenue, Phyllis Cleveland, sat dispiritedly in a corner of the gloomy hall. Edward Royce, the show's director, paced the wooden floor, trying unsuccessfully to come up with an idea for a "different" dance movement. Behind his slender figure, sixteen tired chorus girls and eight boys shifted their feet impatiently.

As Caesar and Youmans came in from the street, they immediately sensed trouble.

"What's wrong, Teddy?" Youmans asked. "You look bushed."

"It's nothing, nothing at all," said the director with a fluttering of his hands. "I've staged some of the greatest musicals in the history of the theater, that's all—and now, at my prime, I am drained. Empty. Dry. That's all." Sadly, dramatically, he moved out of the hall in floating, dancelike steps.

"It hasn't been a good day, Mr. Youmans," Phyllis Cleveland said. "The rain outside, the blues number we're working on—and the fact we open in two weeks. It's getting us all down, I guess."

Caesar looked at the tired, pretty girl. "Hey," he said, "want some cheering up?" He turned to Youmans. "Let's do the new song for the kids."

26

Youmans fairly flew to the piano. He touched the keys lightly, and then said, "One thing, everybody. This number's not for *Nanette*. It's for the next show Ceez and I work on. This is a preview."

As the chorus gathered around the upright, Caesar began singing. By the time he had finished the song, the girls and boys knew the melody and were ready to do a second chorus with him. Applause and shouts of delight brought a third rendition, and it was only when Caesar threw back his head for a big finish that he saw H. H. Frazee standing in the doorway.

"Mr. Frazee!" one of the chorus girls squealed as she turned to see why Caesar had choked off the last notes. "Mr. Frazee, isn't it wonderful?"

Frazee blinked slowly several times. Damp with rain, he held tightly to his satchel as he started slowly toward the group. His step was unsteady. "Isn't *what* wonderful?" he growled.

"The song, their new song," said the girl. Caesar and Youmans reached simultaneously to silence her, but it was too late.

"Song? I came here to see Royce's new dance, not to hear songs." He looked around, trying to focus his red-rimmed eyes. "Where is Royce?"

"He'll be right back," a chorus boy said.

"Should be here when the producer comes," growled Frazee half to himself. "I'm the goddam producer. Should be here." He focused on Caesar. "Little Irving, you were supposed to call me this morning. I had to drink without you."

Caesar muttered an apology and started to move away from the piano.

"'S'all right, we can drink this afternoon." He blinked, waiting. "Well, let's hear it," he said finally. "Let's hear your goddam song."

Youmans spoke swiftly. "It's nothing, Harry. Just a throwaway."

Frazee's face began to grow redder. "I'm the goddamn producer and when I say let's hear your song, let's hear it!"

Youmans poised his fingers obediently over the keys and put them down an octave too high. "Sing it, Ceez," he said with a wink, and Caesar began singing hesitantly in a flat, unemotional voice. The chorus girls frowned at the weird rendition. It was impossible to sing along.

When it was over, Caesar shrugged and spread his hands wide. "I told you it was nothing," Youmans said.

Frazee rocked unsteadily on his heels. "Sounds all right to me," he mumbled. "L'il Irving, let's go have a drink."

He turned away. Behind him, Youmans and Caesar quickly shook hands. Frazee reached the door, nearly bumping into Royce, who was hurrying in.

"Mr. Frazee, I've got it. I've got it!"

Frazee shoved past him. "Keep it," he growled. "I'll see it later." Over his shoulder as he stomped down the steps, he called, "Irving! Bring the bag!"

\* \* \*

Opening night in Detroit on Monday, April 21, 1924, was a nervous affair. Frazee had chartered a train to move the cast, technicians, scenery, and costumes from New York to the Garrick Theater over the weekend. The trip was tiring, and an all-day rehearsal Sunday did not help things. Tempers were short by Monday afternoon when a dress rehearsal was performed for the cast of *Innocent Eyes*, the Shuberts' new musical that was en route from Chicago to the Winter Garden on Broadway. The Romberg show was a big one—with 16 scenes, 24 songs, 600 costumes, and more than 120 people in the cast—and the performers politely applauded *Nanette*, but obviously found it unimpressive. It had just 3 scenes, some 15 songs, and a cast of only 34, including the 16 chorus girls and 8 boys.

Detroit citizens, given their chance to buy tickets to *Innocent Eyes*, playing at the Shubert Theater and already acclaimed "the biggest success of the season," or the unheralded *No, No, Nanette*, chose the former.

"We'll have a full house for opening night," the theater manager said to Frazee just before the curtain went up, "but for the rest of the week we'll die."

"The hell we will," Frazee snapped. "I won't have it!"

Backstage, Royce gave last-minute instructions to vaudeville comedian "Skeets" Gallagher, who played the role of Jimmy Smith, the aging Lothario.

"For heaven's sake, Skeets, if you forget your lines," urged Royce, "just wait for the prompter to give them to you. Don't start doing those vaudeville routines of yours."

"I know how to get laughs," said the worried comic.

Royce shook his head angrily. "Nobody said you don't. But this is a show with a story—and with characters that the audience has to believe in. Your laughs have to come from the kind of person you are, not from a joke you tell about two Irishmen."

The slender comedienne, Georgia O'Ramey, who played the part of a devil-may-care maid, pushed her way through a crowd of chorus girls. She tugged a heavy vacuum cleaner onstage. "Georgia," Royce called over the blare of the overture out front, "get that thing way out in the center. I want them to see you the minute the curtain goes up." In reply, the actress blew him a kiss and pretended to stumble comically over the trailing vacuum cord.

Royce giggled and turned to Gallagher. "See what I mean? You leave the broad comedy to her. Tonight you are mild, bumbling Jimmy Smith."

Frazee suddenly was onstage. "Let's go, let's go, goddammit! I'm spending $50,000 to put this show on and you're all standing around. Good luck everybody. Now, let's go! Where's Irving? Where's my bag?"

Royce shooed the producer offstage just as the gold curtain slid upward. Out front, fashionably dressed flappers in cloche hats and fox scarfs sat next to escorts trying to look like John Gilbert in their evening tails. A ripple of applause saluted the set showing the living room in the Smiths' home, and when Georgia O'Ramey was spotted swinging her vacuum like a broom, there was a breeze of laughter.

After a long, long gestation period, *No, No, Nanette* was born.

* * *

At noon the next day, Frazee woke up groggily in his Statler Hotel room and squinted at the production staff gathered around his bed. When he spoke, his gravel voice seemed to grate more than usual.

"All right, you sonsabitches, what went wrong?"

"Didn't you see the show, Mr. Frazee?" asked the timorous Royce.

Frazee made a face. "I saw part of the first act. That was enough. It was a better show when it was *My Lady Friends.* I went over to the Oriole Terrace and had a drink." He licked his lips. "Irving, open a can of juice."

Caesar went to the case of sauerkraut juice shipped from New York and punctured a can. Frazee tilted his head back, screwing up his eyes as he drained the liquid. "Best damn stuff for a hangover ever," he said as he wiped his mouth with a rough hand. "Tastes so terrible, 's got to be great."

The others waited in silence until their irascible producer had finished his morning routine. They knew what would come next.

"All right, Irving. Time for a l'il Black Velvet. A l'il hair of the dog, eh?" Caesar mixed the champagne sitting on ice at the producer's bedside with some stout. He poured two glasses, touched his to Frazee's, and they each drank thirstily.

Frazee smiled. He sat back and seemed to relax. "Okay, what kind of reviews did we get?"

"Not too bad," said Harbach. He took some strips of newspaper from his pocket. "The *News* says 'an engaging entertainment, mildly amusing, pleasing to the eye, and very melodious.' And Len Shaw says it's 'infinitely better than the original . . . always amusing story that is vastly funnier now . . . should prove a long and remunerative cruise across the sea of popularity.' "

"And our little star got excellent notices," said Royce. " 'Miss Cleveland is fair and fleet of foot. If hers is a still small voice when it comes to singing, it has purity of tone and much promise.' "

"Hell," growled Frazee. " 'Still small voice,' my foot! I

was in the back of the house and couldn't hear a word she said."

"She was nervous, Harry," said Harbach.

"What the hell's she got to be nervous about? It's *my* $50,000. I guess Gallagher was nervous, too, eh? That's why he started telling those stale vaudeville gags as soon as he got onstage! And Donegan kept grinning so much he looked like a sign in Times Square."

Royce coughed softly. "Everybody was a little shaky, Mr. Frazee. It will improve tonight."

"It better," Frazee said as he tilted the champagne bottle. "It just damn well better."

But it didn't.

Only a few hundred people sat in the hot Garrick Theater that night and the songs and jokes echoed ominously off nearly two thousand empty seats. A block away, a packed house cheered Mistinguett and Cecil Lean in *Innocent Eyes*. *Nanette*, a lightweight farce that all too obviously lacked excitement, color, or—yes—sex, seemed about to float away on the warm breeze that blew fitfully off the river.

Things went no better the following night, and an angry Frazee ordered his songwriters to his room. "Find out what he wants, Ceez," said Youmans the next morning, tired from a long stretch of copying music. He turned over and pulled the covers to his face. Alone, Irving Caesar went to beard the lion in his den.

"The yellow cowards are afraid to face me, huh?" Frazee said fiercely, half-lifting his rotund bulk from his bed. "Only L'il Irving has the nerve, hmm?"

"It's nine o'clock in the morning," Caesar explained. "We all had a late night last night, remember?"

"No," Frazee snapped. "I don't remember. And I don't want to. 'at's why I drink—so's I won't remember. So's I won't remember people remindin' me what a stinker I got over there at the Garrick. Get the juice."

Once the routine was over, Frazee leveled a finger at the songwriter. "Look, I got a reputation at stake here. Since I started producin' shows, Irving, I've had hits. Some big ones, and some l'il ones, but *hits*. I am not going to change now."

"We're working on it," Caesar said quickly. "Royce is fixing up the dances. Youmans and I have tightened the songs. The whole cast is—"

Frazee cut him off with a wave of his thick hand. "I don't care what the rest of 'em are doing. I'm telling you this: I want a hit song. Clifton Crawford used to do a great one in the second act of the play. Something about sunshine—"

Caesar instantly picked up the familiar melody: " 'I wanta spread a little sunshine, I wanta drive away all care . . .' "

"That's it, that's the one," growled Frazee. " 'Spreading Sunshine.' Now, look, if you and that sonuvabitch piano player don't give me a song like that for this show, I'm gonna get McCarthy and Tierney out here. They'll give me one!"

"Aw, wait a minute," Caesar protested. "Joe McCarthy and Harry Tierney may have a big show in *Kid Boots*, but they can't turn out a hit on order. Hell, what did they get out of *Irene* except 'Alice Blue Gown'?"

"I don't give a damn what they got. You guys give me a big song by tomorrow, or I get on the phone to New York."

In his room, Caesar picked up the telephone and called Youmans. A sleepy voice answered at the other end, but the composer woke quickly when the ultimatum was delivered. "I'm too tired to walk over to the theater," Youmans said. "Let's meet downstairs in the dining room. There's a piano there."

Fifteen minutes later, Youmans sat frowning at the keyboard. His own heavy drinking and the first stages of the tuberculosis that would end his Broadway career at thirty-three—and his life at forty-seven—were starting to wear him down. "What kind of song does he want, now?" he asked.

Caesar paced fitfully behind him, weaving his way among the dinner tables. "Something like 'Spreading Sunshine.' You know, one of those meaningless little numbers about everybody being happy."

Youmans nodded. " 'I want to spread a little sunshine,' " he sang under his breath.

"Right," said Caesar. "I want to spread sunshine. I want to spread joy. I want to be happy."

The composer looked up. "Hey," he said. "I want to be happy." He touched the keys and picked out six notes. As he did, Caesar sang, " 'I want—to be—happy.' " He looked at Youmans, a smile starting across his face.

"I want to be happy—but I can't be happy—till I make you happy, too!"

The words and the music came almost simultaneously now. It was as if the composer and the wordsmith were trying to outrace each other. Caesar sang louder. Youmans forgot his weariness and pounded out the melody with greater fervor. And suddenly the waiters who were setting the tables for a Rotarian luncheon began humming the song. Some joined in the lyrics. Others whistled the tune.

"My God, Vincent," Caesar said in awe, "we've got a hit and we're not even out of the dining room!"

Youmans smiled. "Let's see McCarthy and Tierney do that." He brought his hands down in a crashing chord for a final fillip. "Let's just see 'em do that!"

Frazee wanted the new song put into the show immediately, but Royce convinced him that too many other things needed fixing, first. "Give us a little time, Mr. Frazee," the director pleaded. "We have to redo the whole 'Chase of the Fox' number, and Gallagher's 'Santa Claus' song just isn't going over."

"Put 'I Want to Be Happy' in and take out 'Santa Claus,' " Frazee growled.

The director pursed his lips. "I will, I will," he said, "But give me time. We'll fix it next week in Cincinnati."

"That means we'll draw nothing but flies there, too," Frazee said, glowering. "All right, Royce. But if we don't have things right by the time we get to Chicago, you're going to pay."

Cincinnati's reaction to the show on April 27, 1924, was much the same as Detroit's. Again, there were favorable notices for the new offering at the Shubert Theater—"*No, No, Nanette* is a very good musical play and should prove a top-notch warm weather attraction"—and again, the audiences failed to come. Evidently potential customers preferred to spend their theater money to catch the big hit, *Abie's Irish Rose*, in its twelfth and final week at the nearby Cox Theater. Others were saving to see D. W. Griffith's new motion picture, *America*, at the Shubert as soon as *Nanette* moved to Chicago.

Caesar found Frazee the morning after the opening sitting in a hotel barber chair, his face covered with lather. "Irving," he sputtered, "is that 'happy' number going in?"

"Yes, I just left the theater, and they're working on it. You can see it tonight."

Frazee groaned softly as the barber carefully edged a razor around his ear. "I don't have to see it. It's good. When does that other one go in?"

A chill crept over the songwriter. "Other one?" he asked. "What other one?"

"You know, 'Tea for Two.' The one you played back in New York. I liked it."

Caesar stuttered, "But—but—we—Youmans and I—"

"Put it in! Tell Royce to put it in the second act somewhere."

"But, Mr. Frazee. It wasn't even written for the show. It was—"

"You sonsabitches are under contract to me, and anything you write on *my* time goes into *my* show if I say so. Put it in."

Royce began staging the song with the singers and dancers that afternoon.

In the middle of the second act that evening, Caesar stood at the rear of the theater looking down over rows of empty seats to the stage, where the dancers were stepping their way through "Tea for Two" for the benefit of roughly seventy-five customers out front. He sensed someone behind him, perhaps because the aroma of good whiskey drifted sharply to his nostrils.

"Good song," the producer's voice rumbled, "but the show stinks." Frazee put his thumb and forefinger to his nose. "Let's go out and have a drink."

34

A day or so later, Frazee announced a sudden decision:
"I'm going to get rid of Gallagher and Cleveland."

"But Gallagher's coming along," protested Harbach. "And
the girl's adorable onstage."

"Gallagher is nervous as a cat, and that little blonde can't
be heard past the fourth row," growled Frazee. "They're
both *out*."

"Who can you get to replace them?" Youmans asked.

"I already been on the phone. Louise Groody is available
in two weeks. So is Charley Winninger."

Caesar whistled softly. "But Groody's on top right now!
She just did *One Kiss*. And Winninger's been big since *The
Passing Show of 1919*. They'll cost a fortune."

"Damn right. Groody wants $1,750 a week. I said, all
right. Nobody's going to say they can't hear the star of a
Harry Frazee show."

He looked steadily at the writers. There were no objections.

"Okay," Frazee rumbled. "Now L'il Irving and I are
taking a train to New York this afternoon. His dad's sick,
and I've got some business to attend to. Don't you bastards
say anything about Gallagher and Cleveland 'cause I can't
get these other people out until after we open in Chicago."

"But, Mr. Frazee," said Royce incredulously, "what's the
sense of making changes *after* we get the notices in Chicago?"

"Because I'm going to take a hit to New York in June if it
kills me!"

Harbach held up a hand. "Harry, wait a minute," he
began. "You've already spent a lot of money on the show.
Look, we all know it's weak. The boys and I were talking it
over, and we'd like to close down here. Why get blistered in
Chicago? We could rewrite over the summer, and open in
the fall in New York."

Frazee's face purpled. "Why, you yellow-livered cowards," he roared. "Don't tell me what to do with my money!
Now, I got Winninger for you! And Louise Groody will be
out, too! And L'il Irving here and me will be fighting all the

way. You promised me a hit, you yellow bastards, and we're going to have one!" He took a deep breath. "Now get to work."

\* \* \*

When *No, No, Nanette* opened at Chicago's Harris Theater on May 5, 1924, the touring company of the Harbach-Youmans hit, *Wildflower*, was playing its third week in the Illinois city and doing great business. But the big show in town was the Duncan sisters in *Topsy and Eva*, a musical version of *Uncle Tom's Cabin* that sold $22,000 worth of tickets each week—and had been doing it for sixteen weeks.

*Nanette* was unveiled at the theater next door to *Topsy and Eva*, and once more drew pleasant reviews: "a gay libretto, a literate yet not highbrow score, comely costumes and scenery"; "one of those typical sugar-coated bromides going over for what looks like a sweet hit," and so on. But after an opening-night sale of $2,300 worth of tickets, the show sold only $9,000 more for the week's remaining seven performances.

*Variety*, the showbusiness paper, estimated that the production had to sell at least $14,000 worth of tickets in order to break even. "For *No, No, Nanette*," it said, "this second week will be a real test."

The test failed. The show once again grossed a disappointing $11,000. But Frazee ordered his publicity man, a fast-talking promoter named Charles Emerson Cooke, to work. Cooke got the newspapers to run stories saying that the producer believed so strongly in his show that he would not let the vicious Chicago critics kill it. (At least 75 percent of the notices had been favorable, but that fact was ignored.) Frazee was said to be negotiating with several big stars who were eager to play in such a wholesome, charming show.

In its third week, *Nanette* edged up $2,000 from the publicity. The next week, Louise Groody and Charles Winninger arrived, and the show climbed to $15,000 on the flurry of attention. Royce, the director, had other commitments back in New York. Frazee let him go, and then spread the rumor that he had fired the king of musical comedy stagers—and was taking over as director himself. Meanwhile, he hired Sammy Lee—a *Ziegfeld Follies* choreographer—to work with the new stars. Two other performers of note, Muriel Hudson and Bernard Granville, were rushed into the show. The continuing newspaper stories sold more tickets. "Now," said *Variety*, "if he only could improve the matinée business."

The following week, Frazee brought in actress Blanche Ring, a popular favorite with the clubwomen who made up the audience at most theatrical matinées. She replaced Anna Wheaton. Matinées began to sell out.

The changes cost Frazee plenty. By the time the show had played six weeks in Chicago, it had run up a loss of $75,000. But with each cast change, critics were invited back to see the show again. Many came—and improved on their earlier notices. "Worth seeing twice," said one. Audiences who returned to see their favorite performers rapidly caught on to "Tea for Two" and "I Want to Be Happy."

In mid-June, a gigantic medical convention swept into Chicago. Nearly every show in town sold out, and *Nanette* jumped to $20,000 for the week. Then one of the Duncan sisters got into an altercation with some traffic policemen in Cicero, Illinois, and came out with a black eye and assorted bruises. *Topsy and Eva* had to refund money for three performances while the actress nursed her wounds, and the angry theatergoers bought tickets for *Nanette* next door. The sudden surge in business—and the short week for *Topsy* —now made *Nanette* look like Chicago's most popular show. When Frazeee publicized the fact, surprised Chicagoans began wondering what they had missed, and rushed to order seats.

On July 30th, three months after *Nanette* had opened for what was to have been a four-week stay, *Variety* noted, "The musical grows stronger each week." Frazee canceled plans to take it to New York after Labor Day. The show was selling out at $23,000 a week. In New York, the producer knew, customers were flocking to the big revues with plenty of comics, girls, and bare flesh. But strait-laced Chicagoans

37

had turned their backs on such entertainment. They wanted a lightweight romantic story, with bushels of sweetness and light.

After six months in the Windy City, Frazee sent out a second company of *No, No, Nanette* to play Philadelphia and other eastern cities. Another company went out a few weeks later to Los Angeles and the West. A third company hit smaller cities in between. And an English production settled down for a two-year run at London's Palace Theater.

It was forty-nine weeks after the Chicago opening when *Nanette* finally headed for Broadway. Racking up ticket sales of $850,000, it had broken *Topsy and Eva*'s claim as the "longest-running musical in Chicago" by two weeks, and had set a record for consecutive weekly sold-out performances. In New York, *Nanette* played only 321 performances —considerably fewer than the 477 for *Wildflower*, the Youmans hit that preceded it, or 352 for *Hit the Deck*, which followed it. But the short run could be easily excused: Audiences in New York were already so familiar with the show from its Chicago and road success that they did not have to see it on Broadway to enjoy it.

"I Want to Be Happy" became a standard favorite with dance bands everywhere. And another number, destined to be one of the most popular songs of all time (if not *the* most popular), had so much strength that it reached Broadway on its own ahead of *Nanette*. It happened this way: In the 1925 Shuberts' production of *Big Boy*, starring Al Jolson, the script called for one of the onstage performers to demonstrate his piano ability. The actor sat down and played, naturally, the song every pianist was asked to play that year —"Tea for Two." (One reviewer, overlooking such songs in *Big Boy* as "If You Knew Susie" and "It All Depends on You," said the Caesar-Youmans tune was the best in the show.)

All of the authors grew rich from *No, No, Nanette*, but none did as well as H. H. Frazee, who profited by several million dollars. Some of the money, however, was lost two years later when he presented *Yes, Yes, Yvette*—with lyrics and musical suggestions by Irving Caesar. The sequel was a quick failure. Other poor investments and the cost of high living rapidly depleted his fortune.

In 1929, Frazee died in his New York apartment shortly after returning from Europe. The cause was Bright's disease, a kidney ailment made worse by alcohol. A close friend, Mayor Jimmy Walker, gave the official statement to the newspapers on the death of the forty-eight-year-old sportsman-producer.

The *New York Times,* noting that Frazee was "always a generous spender," reported that the value of the estate left to his wife was "not more than $50,000."

**3** Alexander H. Cohen, one of the theater's busiest and most respected showmen, has one all-important requisite for a Broadway producer: "Insanity. You have to be a little bit insane, and so stage-struck that you're willing to spend your existence in a business that's fundamentally constructed by lunatics."

Harry Rigby fits Cohen's description. To a T.

Stage-struck since childhood, he has earned what livelihood he could only from the theater. Has he made enough to live comfortably?

"There's a song in *Follies* by Stephen Sondheim that I relate to very much," he answers. "It says, 'I got through last year, and I'm still here.'"

> "It really doesn't matter if Busby Berkeley did one thing or not on 'No, No, Nanette.' He did it all years ago."
>
> **HARRY RIGBY**

Harry has been getting from one year to the next via showbusiness for more than two decades. The theater is the perfect work place for people like him. It permits—and often encourages—the wildest temper tantrums, the most flamboyant clothes, the most outrageous affectations.

And, occasionally, it allows the greatest dreams to come true. Dreams of money. Fame. Power.

In a way, theater is a permanent childhood.

"I was a problem child," says Harry in a voice that is as feminine as it is masculine, and resembles Phyllis Diller's. "Every two or three weeks I would have to have a new nurse because the old one would leave with a nervous breakdown. And then, *compleeetely* by accident, my parents discovered that when I went to a movie I was very well behaved. After that, they sent me to movies all the time."

Harry's father could well afford to send his son to the movies several times a week during the Depression years of the 1930s. A wealthy Philadelphian, he headed what Harry now euphemistically says was "a public relations company." Howard Rigby specialized in helping political candidates get elected.

By the time he was eight years old, Harry had a regular

Saturday routine. Each morning, his doting mother sent him from their home in Hapsburg outside the city into downtown Philadelphia to catch a movie at a motion picture house. Then he would hurry to a matinée of a play or musical at a theater. "As I grew older, I'd see another picture after the theater, too," Harry says proudly.

At school, his classmates talked of the pictures they had seen. Westerns with Buck Jones and Tom Mix. Gangster dramas with Jimmy Cagney and Edward G. Robinson. Comedies with Laurel and Hardy and Joe Penner. But Harry Rigby talked of the musicals.

Ruby Keeler. Joan Blondell. Fred Astaire and Ginger Rogers. These were his idols.

And at the top of his list was Busby Berkeley, the man who could set a hundred girls in flowing gowns dancing on top of a hundred grand pianos. Or send them splashing in revealing swimsuits through a cascading waterfall. Or pose them virtually nude as human harps.

Why an impressionable young boy was awed by such Berkeley pictures as *42nd Street*, *Gold Diggers of 1933*, and *Footlight Parade* to the degree that, when he saw them again some twenty-five years later, he "remembered" each scene and musical number is something perhaps best left to students of psychology.

"The point is," Harry says, "that I was mad for them."

As the vogue for lavish and star-studded Hollywood musicals faded, so did his interest in pictures. It seemed foolish to go on seeing new films when, simply by closing his eyes, he could envision those dozens of boys and girls dressed in stark black-and-white costumes tap-dancing on endless staircases. The best of Busby Berkeley was locked firmly inside his head.

His interest in the theater grew, however, and in the late 1940s, he stepped in with some friends to take over a struggling summer playhouse at Cape May, New Jersey. Here, he met songwriter Hugh Martin, who had collaborated on *Best Foot Forward* and on Judy Garland's "Trolley Song," among other hits. Martin had a new show he was

**41**

working on for Broadway. Harry liked the idea and the score.

On April 18, 1951, *Make a Wish*, with music and lyrics by Hugh Martin, opened at the Winter Garden. In the cast were Nanette Fabray and Helen Gallagher. The settings and costumes were by Raoul Pène du Bois. Vocal direction was by Buster Davis.

The producer credit read: "Harry Rigby and Jule Styne with Alexander H. Cohen present. . . ."

"Rigby raised a lot of money for *Make a Wish*," Cohen says. The money came from his family and his friends. Harry explains: "You certainly don't get money from your enemies."

There was only one problem with Harry's first Broadway venture.

*Make a Wish* was a bomb.

"I was very inexperienced," says Harry. "I really shouldn't have been the *produuucer*. I should have started out as a stage manager or something."

His father was not unhappy over the show's failure. He wanted his son, says Harry, to "take the 8:05 into the city every day and come home on the 5:10 or whatever, I don't remember those awful numerals."

And when the elder Rigby learned that Harry intended to stay in showbusiness? "Well, he just wasn't very helpful after that," Harry shrugs.

In Broadway parlance, "being helpful" to a producer usually means one thing—coming through with funds to help get a show onstage. Basically, there are two ways to attract investors to a production. The simplest way is to produce a long string of hits, as Harold Prince did with *Pajama Game*, *Damn Yankees*, *Fiddler on the Roof*, *Cabaret*, *Company*, and others he has brought to the stage.

If a producer bombs out, however, with his first show—and continues to come up with duds or near-misses afterward—his job is difficult. He must plead, wheedle, and deal intelligently with hesitant investors. He must charm them, and give a thousand reasons why his next show *can't* miss.

He must explain away past failures with any manner of excuses. If he does his work well, if he gets enough money to put on one more show, it does not really matter if it is a hit or a flop. As William Goldman explains in *The Season*, the producer of a musical that runs a year and loses half of its $500,000 investment can make a tidy $60,000 for himself.

For Harry Rigby it was never easy.

After *Make a Wish*, he used his flamboyant charm and nonstop flow of conversation to woo reluctant backers—many of them, wealthy women. But Harry lacked the calculating mind and promotional guile needed, first, to attract a *lot* of money and, second, to produce a sizable annual income for himself. Although he always was buzzing with ideas for several different projects at one time, it usually took two years to get any one of them onstage.

On December 10, 1953, Michael Grace, Stanley Gilkey, *and* Harry Rigby presented a revue, *John Murray Anderson's Almanac*. The fact that Harry's name appeared at the end of the sequence of producers—rather than first, as it did on *Make a Wish*—is significant. It indicates that his contributions (at least his financial ones) were less than those of Messrs. Grace and Gilkey. The show ran only 229 performances, despite a talent roster that featured Harry Belafonte, Hermione Gingold, Orson Bean, Billy DeWolfe and Polly Bergen. As on *Make a Wish*, Raoul Pène du Bois did the scenery, and Buster Davis was the musical director and vocal arranger. The choreography was by a young man named Donald Saddler.

According to *Theatre World*, the Broadway yearbook, Harry's next production did not take place until February 13, 1959. Then, a "limited engagement" of two short plays starring Judith Evelyn was presented by Milton Cassel and Harry Rigby. The show closed after nineteen performances.

Four years later, when Lewis Allen and Ben Edwards presented Edward Albee's play, *Ballad of the Sad Cafe*, Harry's name was listed as a "production associate" at the tail end of the list of credits. Definitions in the theater are often hard to come by, but one knowledgeable showman says that "production associate" can usually be translated as "gopher." A "gopher" is the assistant who is ordered to "go-fer-a-cuppa-coffee" or "go-fer-the-script-I-left-downtown."

Harry giggles and says, "John Murray Anderson once told me that I had started out at the top of showbusiness and was rapidly working my way down."

Two years later, he had worked his way completely out of the production credits of a new musical, *Half a Sixpence* Originally, as indicated on the front of the jacket on the RCA Victor original-cast recording, the show was presented by "Allen-Hodgdon, Stevens Productions *and* Harry Rigby *with* Harold Fielding." The artwork for the front of the jacket, however, was drawn up in advance of the show's opening. On the back, where the printer could change type at the last moment, the show was said to be presented by "Allen-Hodgdon, Stevens Productions and Harold Fielding." Harry's name was removed for "personal" reasons, he notes, after a "perfectably amicable" mix-up over just whose names should be listed. When the touring company of *Sixpence* went out in 1966, his name was back again, but at the end of the list, following Fielding's.

At this point, Harry was devoting considerable time to a woman named Jane Nusbaum, who was listed on *Half a Sixpence* as associate producer. The relationship—a working one—deepened so that in 1967, when a musical called *Hallelujah, Baby* opened on Broadway, the presentation credits read: "Albert W. Selden and Hal James, Jane C. Nusbaum and Harry Rigby."

(Buster Davis, who had also worked on *Sixpence*, was musical director on *Hallelujah, Baby*. The show was directed by another name to remember: Burt Shevelove.)

Despite the fact that it won a Tony Award as the best musical of the season, *Hallelujah, Baby* was not a success. And, since Harry was one of a group of producers, his chances of making much from the show were considerably reduced. Some of the investment amounts that Harry brought into various productions were so small that he now says, looking back, "I *never* was a money raiser. I contributed the artistic ideas."

That usually was enough for him. Never mind that he wasn't getting rich. He lived simply, in a hotel room with his belongings kept in shopping bags so he could be ready for a quick move to another, cheaper, location if need be. And there was always something to dream about. There was always the show he would produce tomorrow. The big one that might be the hit.

*Tomorrow.*

For years, though, Harry's thoughts of the future were irrevocably linked with his memories of the past.

Those long weekends of movie musicals burned brightly in his mind. Those songs, those dances, those tart-tongued, brass-hard chorus girls with hearts of gold whirled inside his head. In the 1950s, when Manhattan's New Yorker Theater dug the old films out of the vaults and showed them for laughs to youthful sophisticates, Harry Rigby did not laugh.

"I went—and went—and *went*, and sat through them over and over again," he says. "And they were just as good as I'd imagined them to be when I was seven or eight." He even saw a parallel between the way Director Busby Berkeley cut his musical numbers in the 1930s and the "new wave" films that came from France decades later.

"I could write a *huuuge* monograph on that," Harry says with a little chuckle. "I *really* could."

Harry believes that the desire to recapture the magic of his childhood on Broadway was always there, lurking in the back of his mind, while other ideas came and went. Then, in the mid-1960s, the sociological phenomenon called "Camp" appeared on the scene. Despite the efforts of various experts —most notably, writer Susan Sontag—to define Camp and isolate what makes one thing amusingly Camp while a near-identical thing is merely odd or cloying or nostalgic or homosexual in nature, few people could gauge the precise differences.

But one thing was certain: Busby Berkeley and Ruby Keeler were Camp.

On college campuses, particularly, thousands of students smiled as they watched silver screens filled with tap-dancing

Keeler carbons. They applauded lustily when Warner Baxter, playing a slave-driver director in *42nd Street*, told a limp, blasé understudy (Ruby again), "You're going out there a youngster—but you've got to come back a star!" And when the onscreen Ruby accepted any kind of good news—whether Dick Powell's profession of his love, or word that she would star in a big Broadway musical—with a simple, "Gee, that's swell," the audiences screamed their delight.

Harry Rigby cannot explain why the young people in the 1960s enjoyed the old films so much that they lined up to see them. Looking back on the period—with its assassination of beloved political figures, its growing war in Vietnam, its racial strife, its campus violence, and other seemingly insoluble problems—it seems that students took to the old movies as a form of sheer release. The problem put forth in the pictures was usually no more complicated than this: Would the young songwriter get his new musical on stage so that he might marry the young ingenue whose father objected to his daughter marrying a penniless good-for-nothing?

And the Berkeley magic? It generally consisted of taking a couple of dozen attractive girls with limited dancing ability and weaving them into endless patterns. The patterns themselves became the focal point, taking attention from the elementary footwork. One girl doing a timestep was dull in the 1930s; one hundred girls doing a timestep atop pianos became exciting.

In a way, the Berkeley numbers resembled a kaleidoscope's patterns. They were pretty, constantly changing, and entirely without significance. It did not matter if the hundreds of boys and girls danced on top of pianos or on spiral staircases, whether they frolicked through hotel corridors or in a waterfall. One design was as good as another. And, to the viewers, they were pleasant, meaningless timewasters. What could be more relaxing, more enjoyable to the student of the 1960s whose every waking minute was filled with worry, problems, and a search for meaning?

By 1965, the Huntington Hartford Gallery of Modern Art in New York was aware of Berkeley Film Festivals popping up on college campuses everywhere. It scheduled a two-month showing of the director's films, which now were acclaimed as classics. The San Francisco Film Festival that year featured the pictures, and other festivals throughout the United States and Europe also began paying homage to the director.

Harry Rigby could not have been more pleased. It was as if others had suddenly learned to recognize the master artist that he alone had praised for years. Strangely, when the legendary Berkeley came to New York to take part in the museum's festival, Harry did not try to meet him. "I'm really very timid," he explains.

Neither did he attend the museum's screenings of Berkeley's films. He had seen them all, many times, in the living room of a friend who ran a film club for worshiping fans. Harry had even managed to compile his own reel of some of the Berkeley dance routines from various pictures.

Once *Hallelujah, Baby* was on the boards, says Harry, he began thinking about his next project. Taking note of the growing cult of Berkeley fans, he asked a friend to contact the great man in California and see if he would be interested in working on a Broadway show. Word came back that "Buz" was ready, willing, and able. Delighted, Harry forgot his timidity and called Berkeley with an idea.

According to an affidavit filed during the *Nanette* arbitration proceedings by the director, he and Harry had planned to revive a series of successful musicals from the 1920s and 1930s. Among the possibilities were *Good News*, Rodgers and Hart's *Peggy Ann* and *I Married an Angel*, and *No, No, Nanette*. Their first project was to be a show called *Divorce Me, Darling*.

Strictly speaking, *Divorce Me, Darling* was not an old musical. It was written in the 1960s by Sandy Wilson, an English songwriter who had scored a great success in 1953 with *The Boy Friend*. In *Divorce Me, Darling*, Wilson tried to write a "new" musical in the style of the 1930s. He took the same characters—the flappers and their beaux—who had appeared in *The Boy Friend*, and moved them ten years

47

ahead in time to show that their visions of living "happily ever after" just weren't necessarily so. But when it was introduced in London, the new show was turned down by the critics and the public.

Harry had heard from a friend who saw the London production that it would have been a hit if only the author had trimmed the book to make it move along faster. He talked to Wilson, who agreed to revisions, and then to Berkeley about directing *Divorce Me, Darling*. There was also some thought given to reviving *The Boy Friend* and presenting it along with the new show on alternate nights. Harry's latest partner, Jane Nusbaum, was to be allied with him in bringing Berkeley back.

"Buz was *aaaaanxious* to do it," he says. "A lot of people had called him, I *know* they had, but nothing had ever happened."

Just when it looked as if Harry's romantic notion of tying the legendary film director to a modern Broadway musical might turn into reality, two things happened to frustrate it.

One was the opening Off-Broadway of a tiny six-person musical, *Dames at Sea*. An affectionate spoof of all the old Berkeley films rolled into one, it wowed the critics. Now there was the chance that a *real* Berkeley musical might look like a copy. More devastating, however, was a review of *Dames* in the *New York Times* by the paper's powerful critic, Clive Barnes. Calling the show "a winner, a little gem of a musical," Barnes said: *"Dames at Sea* tries to do for the Thirties what *The Boy Friend* tried for the Twenties. But it is much better than *The Boy Friend*, because it is infused by a genuine love and knowledge of the period."

Harry Rigby nearly gagged. If Barnes thought his fellow countryman Wilson had no love of the Twenties or knowledge of it—and *The Boy Friend* had been a long-running *hit* in both England and the United States—what would Barnes think about *Divorce Me, Darling*?

Harry decided that he would have to find a new property.

But he had a bigger worry: Jane Nusbaum, the financial brains behind his current project, had become interested in filmmaking, and, after serving as associate producer of *The Lion in Winter*, had left the stage—and Harry.

Before he could do *anything*, before he could put Busby Berkeley and all those dancing girls to work, Harry Rigby needed a new partner.

Preferably, someone who knew how to get money.

Or, better, had it.

**4** Cyma Rubin not only had money when Harry Rigby met her, but she obviously knew how to get it. Slender, dark, and animated, she had worked hard to get where she is—married to a man who is a millionaire several times over, with a villa in Europe, a town house in Manhattan, and a summer home in a posh Long Island resort area.

The Rubins have their own private collection of African art. As president of the American Symphony, which he started in 1962, Sam Rubin has virtually what amounts to his own "fiddlers three," on a scope that Old King Cole never dreamed of. Naturally, there is a Rolls-Royce, and all the other trappings that wealth can bring.

"Harry can really make a very fine impression. He's a cultured guy, with a poodle. He's a gentleman, and genteel. And if you don't know how crazy he is . . ."

CYMA RUBIN

Brooklyn-born Mrs. Rubin did not come by all this through birth or dumb luck. She is proud of her present position, and takes considerable pleasure in telling just how she reached it.

Her father, she begins, was a manufacturer of shirts when she was born on May 23rd in the late 1920s. His parents, however, had an entirely different background. They had come to this country from Russia—where they had traveled with a circus.

"*Honestly*," she exclaims. "My grandfather was a clown. I remember him as a very warm, funny man. And my grandmother had been a bareback rider." The rigors of circus life and traveling in covered wagons from town to town, coupled with the pogroms taking place in Russia at the time, caused the couple to head for New York with their two young boys. Six other children born to them had died previously; five more were born in the United States.

The eldest granddaughter was given the name of Cyma, which means "wave" or a rippling, curving line, according to Webster. At four, she moved with her parents to Greenville, South Carolina, in the heart of the textile country.

Through some unfortunate business moves—"overexpansion," Cyma calls it—her father lost his money *after* the

Depression. That fact, a psychologist might say, could have a lot to do with forming the drive for wealth, power, and position that young Cyma Saltzman obviously developed. At age ten, back in Brooklyn, she attended Abraham Lincoln High School ("where all very good people graduated from") until 1940, when she was faced with one of her father's two mottoes.

"In this family," he said, "either you go to school or you work—and sometimes you have to do both at the same time." His other words of advice had to do with choosing a school ... or a job ... or a friend: "If you go with fleas, you'll get lousy, no matter where you come from." (Cyma gives a little laugh, and evaluates the line: "Not bad, hmm?")

Financially unable to pay his daughter's way through college, the elder Saltzman said he would cover part of her expense if she went to a vocational school that would equip her to get a job. He believed, Cyma says, that even if a woman marries a man who has money, she can be independent if she has a profession to fall back on. "It was very early, early 'women's lib' kind of talk," she notes.

Cyma decided to study textile engineering at the University of North Carolina. There, she figured to combine her interests in art and design with the practical knowledge that might benefit her father in his struggle to get a new textile business under way. On the campus, she promptly discovered that she was the sole northern, Jewish, female student, and was much sought after by some three thousand males, most of whom she put down for being 4-F in wartime.

Dr. Martin Ackerman, Cyma's first husband, says he remembers his wife telling him that at school she wore greasy overalls and crawled over the intricate textile manufacturing machinery with the male students. Today, immaculately groomed, lunching at Sardi's and chatting with David Merrick and Joshua Logan, Cyma Rubin looks as if she was born with a silver spoon in her mouth.

When she graduated, with a degree that indicated she was qualified to run a textile mill if need be, Cyma spent weeks searching vainly for a job. She found one at $65 a week with a company that acted as a middleman, selling textiles from the factory. In a short while, she decided she could make a living by starting her own company to do the same thing. "I did very well," she says excitedly. "I rented a desk for ten bucks a month, with a telephone, and I had a card printed up. I made $150 a week working three days a week, with no expenses." The business grew as she put her knowledge of dyeing and finishing fabrics to use, and began collecting larger commissions on each step of the textile sales process.

Fairly independent now, Cyma met a young medical student who was doing postgraduate work to become an eye surgeon. At the time, she recalls, "the doctor was making sixty dollars a month, some stupid thing like that." But young love and the old idea that every Jewish daughter should marry a doctor brought about a wedding.

Things did not go well for the newlyweds. Dr. Ackerman ("a very intelligent man") grew upset, Cyma says, over the amount of time that his wife spent working. In addition to running her own business, she had taken over the management of a textile firm owned by a large company. "I was operating a three-ring circus," she states with obvious relish.

"She's an active person," laughs Dr. Ackerman, a large friendly man who today has a successful Park Avenue practice. "She's got a lot on the ball and a real tremendous amount of talent and desire to—well, she's got a lot of drive."

His former wife considers it a good thing that she had ability and drive. "He was doing postgraduate work, and we needed money. I had to make a living. We had an apartment on 20th Street, three rooms which I furnished out of Altman's. Oh, a *smashing* apartment. We still have it. I have *all* the furniture that I've had since—" she changes the subject. "Well, then Loni was born."

The birth of her daughter did not help the troubled marriage. After a three-month leave of absence from her business, Cyma wanted to return to work desperately. "I can't seem to take care of a child," she says. "Three months of it was driving me out of my wits." But, rather than return to the textile business over her husband's objections, she went back to school, "for the fourth time," and graduated as an interior designer.

"I came out at a very good time," she says. "We were now in the 1950s, people had a lot of money, and there was a lot of decorating going on." She remembers being one of the first to suggest that a client paint all the walls of his seven-room apartment white, borrowing the idea from the clean, white look of a French chateau. The "white walls" craze swept New York, and in a short time Cyma Ackerman built up a business that she says was "most fantastic, unbelievable." She decorated homes, and offices, and became color consultant for a year to famed architect Mies van der Rohe.

Much of her success, she thinks, stems not only from the fact that she had a good eye and a thorough technical background, but because "in those days, there were no young women in the field; there were only the old fag decorators."

It is possible that, as the youthful career woman moved in and out of some of the wealthiest homes and apartments in the country, she became increasingly dissatisfied with her marital situation. At any rate, after several trips abroad to gather ideas for assignments to make over three mansions on Philadelphia's Main Line, she decided to get divorced.

Money was no longer a problem, she admits. Her ophthalmologist husband had a practice that did better than $35,000 a year. But the continued friction over who wore the pants in the family had not eased; had grown worse, in fact, when Dr. Ackerman chose to go back into the army temporarily during the Korean War. "He didn't *have* to go," Cyma says matter-of-factly. She shakes her head and adds, "I had a lot of trouble with him."

The marriage had lasted more than ten years while she worked hard, but now the divorcée threw herself even more forcefully into her career. Money was needed, she explains, to keep up a lavish apartment on Central Park South, to send her daughter to private school and to camp every summer.

It wasn't long afterward, Cyma remembers, that she took her daughter for a short vacation in the Hamptons on Long

53

Island, and was asked by a friend to drop in on a cocktail party. At first she refused, afraid that as a recent divorcée, she would be ready bait for vacationing summer bachelors. Finally, when the friends insisted, she gave in.

"I was sitting on a couch," she says, "and some man was talking to me, boring me out of my mind." Then the door opened. Everyone looked up to see a short, yet imposing, barrel-chested man standing there. Behind him, as in a cheap movie, the setting sun threw a golden glow over his thick mane of gray hair, and seemed to frame his figure with a fiery outline. His casual manner and obviously expensive clothes—white linen jacket, black shirt, white tie—gave an impression of power. It was the same kind of effect that Edward G. Robinson produced in *Little Caesar*.

"I excused myself from the bore on the couch on the pretext of wanting to turn on a light," Cyma recalls. "I reached for the lamp switch and, as I touched it, I heard that deep baritone voice behind me.

" 'You needn't do that,' Sam Rubin said. 'I've seen all I want to see.' "

She smiles, thinks the line over for a moment, evaluates it: "Not bad."

The two hit it off immediately. Both had Russian Jewish backgrounds, and although Cyma was more than two decades younger than the perfume magnate, she was all too plainly not a giddy girl. Sam Rubin, who had built his own company up from scratch on a $400 investment, saw that his new acquaintance was a hard-working career woman with a business head on her shoulders and a native intelligence. That was important to him, interested as he was in education, politics, scientific research, and the arts. He was in the process of getting divorced from his first wife, a tall, intellectual woman who serves as director of the Research Institute for the Study of Man. Both his children, a son and a daughter, were grown and already on their own.

When he learned that Cyma was a decorator, Sam asked her to look over a summer home he owned. He called for her the next afternoon in a top-down, black Jaguar convertible. The house needed so much work, she says, that at first she turned down his repeated pleas to make it right. Finally, she gave in. When he liked the results and suggested that she might use her knowledge of design and fashion at his company, Cyma agreed to join Fabergé on a part-time basis. She continued her own business interests, too—right up until the time a few years later when, on two days' notice, she married Sam Rubin.

Almost simultaneously, her husband decided to sell his company and retire, to take things easy with his new bride and pre-teen stepdaughter, and Cyma Rubin had to decide what she wanted from her new life. Her daughter, Loni, was thinking seriously of a showbusiness career—possibly a result of the circus blood that flowed in her veins from her great-grandparents—and she was off on a whirl of singing and dancing lessons. Her husband, Sam, was busy with philanthropic activities, his tennis, and adding to the African art collection that Cyma had begun some years before. What might keep the new Mrs. Rubin occupied?

"I knew one thing," Cyma says flatly. "I wasn't going to be *merely* Mrs. Rubin. That wasn't enough. And the social scene—well, I'd already done that. Being in an evening dress five nights a week can drive anyone crazy."

When octogenarian conductor Leopold Stokowski approached the Rubins about backing a new symphony orchestra for him, Cyma leaped at the idea. "I told Sam I'd like to do it," she says. "People thought we were crazy, that it would take ten million dollars to start an orchestra. But I said, let's try." She set about recruiting other supporters, besides the Rubin Foundation, to provide the first year's budget of $117,000 for six subscription concerts. Benefits were arranged, and financing came in from commerce and industry. Children's concerts and special teen-age performances were scheduled. And, little by little, the American Symphony grew into an important musical structure. By the fall of 1969, it was scheduling as many as thirty-two concerts a season.

"Not bad," says Cyma Rubin, "for something that started without even an office. We did our first planning in the kitchen."

But after nine years of almost single-minded devotion to the American Symphony, Cyma grew restless. Then, early in 1969, inspired by a book by Albert Kahn on Pablo Casals, she thought of a tremendous idea for a benefit: Casals was invited to come from his Riviera home to New York and conduct one hundred cellists playing one of his own compositions. Perhaps the idea also had its origins in Busby Berkeley. At any rate, the concert was exceedingly successful. "We raised $158,000 net," Cyma stresses. "More than has ever been raised for any symphony in a benefit—and unbelievable in view of the stock market falling at the time."

The Casals concert, she thought, made a fitting climax to her fund-raising career. Now it was time for others to step in and take over. She wanted to turn her efforts to another pet interest: the theater.

In *The Season*, William Goldman guesses conservatively that Jewish patrons make up 50 percent of Broadway audiences, and that probably half of the playwrights are Jews. When it comes to musical comedy, Goldman notes, the contribution is even more remarkable. He flatly states, "Without Jews, there simply would have been no musical comedy in America." The author does not delve into how many producers and investors in Broadway plays and musicals are Jewish, but the percentages are high.

As are most Jewish women of wealth and social position, Cyma Rubin is an "avid theatergoer." She says that the stage "has been one of my really great passions." When she decided to get actively involved in theater, she turned somewhere close at hand.

Joseph Papp's New York Shakespeare Festival, which puts on free Shakespearean productions each summer in Central Park and also produces many new and experimental plays and musicals in its own downtown theater, had been the happy recipient of several large grants of money from the Samuel Rubin Foundation. A grateful Papp asked Mrs. Rubin to serve on the board of directors. She agreed, with one condition: "That I would not be just another papier-mâché character." She wanted to work, and furnish ideas.

In an early meeting with the Festival's artistic director,

56

Cyma berated Papp for having sold for a small sum the rights to an experimental rock-musical he had produced for a short run. The show was restaged by its new owners, moved to a Broadway theater, and—with a dash of nudity added and a huge measure of publicity—turned into one of the biggest theatrical events of all time. The name of the show? *Hair*.

For *Hair* producer Michael Butler, authors Gerome Ragni and James Rado, and composer Galt MacDermot, the show made many millions of dollars. But Papp's perpetually starving, easygoing operation, which had started the whole thing, got little.

"You idiot!" Cyma shouted at Papp. "The only way for a cultural, nonprofit endeavor like yours to *survive* is to support yourself financially with force! You must have something *else* that could be commercially successful?"

According to Cyma, Papp said, "I don't know—I'll have to look," and he started going through a huge pile of scripts in his sparsely furnished office. "How about a Black *Hamlet?*" he asked casually.

Cyma took the script he held out. She riffled the pages. "It's an interesting idea," she said. "Not bad. It could be done as a movie."

Papp, short, wiry, with tousled black hair and fiery dark eyes, agreed. "That's right. It would make a good movie. But I can't do it now."

"Well, *I* can't do it," Cyma said quickly. "I don't know anything about it."

Papp thought for a quick second. "We'll have to get somebody. I met a woman who might be interested in working on it with you. She's a producer."

"Oh?"

"Her name's Jane Nusbaum."

Describing herself as "innocent as a lamb," Cyma called Jane Nusbaum, who readily said she would be interested in a film of *Black Hamlet*. But before she could get to it, she had *other* projects. One of them was a musical adaptation of the Gary Cooper-Audrey Hepburn picture, *Love in the Afternoon*. The music might come from unpublished melodies that were found in Vincent Youmans' trunk after his death. In almost no time at all, Sam Rubin had been talked into investing $10,000 in the musical. He did it intelligently though, says Cyma, by putting up the money as a loan against an investment. "That way, if the show was not produced within a year, she was obligated to pay back the money." (The production never came off, but only half the $10,000 was repaid, she adds: "Jane says Harry owes the rest.")

During several meetings with producer Nusbaum, Cyma says she was aware of "a man in the background," but her first real meeting with Harry Rigby took place at a benefit affair in Washington, D.C. "Jane introduced me there to her partner, and he was so witty and charming he could knock you right off your feet," she says with a disbelieving shake of her head.

Harry knew well who Mrs. Cyma Rubin was, however. He had seen her earlier at a backers' audition for a musical that had been written by Jane Nusbaum's mother's rabbi. "*Reeeally,*" laughs Harry. "By her mother's *rabbi!* And it was all about these fifteen *other* rabbis!" He remembers that Cyma arrived late, wearing a riding habit, "looking like Lady Chatterley, or fresh from the horseshow in Madison Square Garden," and carrying a riding crop. "I think she kept time to the music with it," Harry says with a giggle.

When Cyma called the Nusbaum office soon afterward to set up a meeting on *Black Hamlet* with Joe Papp, Harry answered the phone. Remembering him from the Washington party, and from a conversation about finding an agent for her daughter, Cyma made the usual pleasantries and then asked for his partner.

"She's gone to Europe," Harry said. "*Lonnndon.*"

"But we're supposed to meet with Papp. And I need some advice. Harry, would *you* mind. . . . ?"

"No," said Harry Rigby quickly. "I wouldn't mind at all. I'll be right over."

And he was.

**5** It is probably not a coincidence that David Merrick, one of the theater's most successful and wealthiest producers, was once a lawyer. Putting a show onstage, or on film, for that matter, calls as much for legal skill and business ability as for artistic ideas. In Attorney Donald C. Farber's guidebook, *Producing on Broadway*, Farber takes seventy pages to explain some of the intricacies of the basic Dramatists Guild contract, twenty-five pages for the Actors Equity Association contract, and twenty-eight pages for the legalities of setting up a production company.

> "We're going to present the show exactly the way it was done forty-five years ago—but first we're going to rewrite the book."
>
> **CYMA RUBIN**

In addition, there are contracts that must be negotiated with a dozen unions—stagehands, wardrobe, managers and press agents, musicians, scenic designers, and so on. There also are negotiations to be conducted with authors, composers, copyright holders, theater owners, and others.

Small wonder that Cyma Rubin, itching to put on a show, thought she could use some advice.

The arrival of Harry Rigby at the time seemed perfect. Trailing a list of theatrical credits from the very recent *Hallelujah, Baby* to *Make a Wish* more than fifteen years earlier, Harry swept into Joe Papp's office, folded his long, fluttering arms, and nodded enthusiastically as Cyma and Papp talked up *Black Hamlet*.

With Harry came a friend, a fast-talking public relations man who had theatrical interests. He, too, loved the idea for the film. It would be *marrrvelous!* If only James Earl Jones, or someone like him, with all that . . . *vitality* . . . could be Hamlet! *Marrrvelllous!*

Someone suggested using an old prison as Castle Elsinore, and someone suggested shooting the picture on Ellis Island in New York harbor, and suddenly Cyma and Harry and Joe —"he was wearing Hamlet's cape, I could have killed him," laughs Cyma—were running, like children, through Ellis Island's old buildings.

"I'm so enthusiastic about the whole thing," Cyma says later, "that I'm practically floating."

But she did not like Ellis Island. She phoned Papp the next morning, just before leaving for a brief European jaunt, and told him so. "It's simply all wrong," she said positively.

On the other end of the phone, the busy Papp sighed. "You sound just like a producer."

"I don't know what a producer sounds like, but I know it's all wrong."

Papp already was putting down the receiver. "Give me a call when you get back from Europe."

A few weeks later, the call came. The New York Shakespeare Festival had opened a new play, *No Place to Be Somebody*, and Papp asked his newest board member to see it. Maybe something could be done with it . . .

"Sam didn't want to go," Cyma says, "so I called Harry." The two had become close by now, to the point that she had hired his public relations friend to do some work for the American Symphony. "We both loved the play," Cyma recalls, "and thought it had tremendous possibilities as a film."

But when she mentioned casually to Papp that "if I had someone to help, I'd make a picture out of it myself," the Festival director curtly remarked that the show was not for sale.

To those who know Papp—who understand how, almost single-handedly and with single-minded devotion, he scrounged and fought and wheedled for twenty years to build the New York Shakespeare Festival into a huge, respected organization—it is not surprising that he thought it best to continue on his own independent way.

His way, however, was not Cyma's. In her fierce, fighting fashion, she possibly determined that if she couldn't join him, she would beat him.

"Sam," she said, one night soon afterward, "what would you think if I started some kind of small repertory company to put on some plays and musicals?"

Refreshed from an afternoon of tennis and a short nap before dinner, her husband smiled amiably. "What do you have in mind? And how much would it cost?"

Cyma spoke quickly. "Not much. I'd like to get together with some creative people. We'd present shows—new ones and revivals that are important to our culture. You know, we'd give the artistic types their head and see what happens."

Sam looked at his younger, energetic wife. He nodded. "How would you get started?"

"Oh, I'd have to find somebody who knows people. Maybe Harry Rigby knows someone. I'll give him a call."

"*Welllll*," said Harry when he heard what Cyma wanted, "I'll have to think about it."

It was a day or two later, Cyma remembers, that Harry's friend, the public relations man, called her, and said he had heard she was looking for someone to help form a production company.

"That's right. I don't want to tie myself down with a lot of details. Sam and I might want to pick up some afternoon and go to France, or—"

"Can I make a suggestion? Why not work with Harry?"

Cyma resisted the idea at first, saying she did not want to come between the Nusbaum-Rigby partnership. But when she was told that Harry intended to leave anyway, and that Jane Nusbaum did not plan to return from abroad, she agreed to talk to Harry about it.

Bubbling with excitement, bursting with enthusiasm, Harry talked . . . and talked . . . of his past successes and his present plans. Contacts? People? He knew them all. He knew the best. Hadn't he worked with great names, great talents, great friends? And right now, at this very moment, he was talking to the living legend, Busby Berkeley *himself*, about doing a show.

Cyma was enraptured, and shrewd enough to see the commercial possibilities. After all, hadn't she herself once built a very successful Fabergé promotion around fashions of the 1930s? And she had put together a 1930s-style benefit for the Symphony, too. Now, when everyone was talking about longer skirt lengths, and when those old movies with Bogart and Harlow and Garbo were all the rage, there probably would be great interest in a Busby Berkeley show—a musical, with all that old-fashioned atmosphere clinging to it. If something could be done quickly, now, in mid-1969, wouldn't everyone be surprised at what Cyma Rubin could do once she put her mind to it!

Harry Rigby agreed. *Completely.* There were just a few small problems that he would have to work out first. Now that no money was coming in from his partnership with Jane Nusbaum, he was going to have difficulties. The hotel bill—expenses . . .

"Well, just wait a minute now," Cyma said, and began to mull over the situation. "We'll *have* to have an office of some kind." The days when she planned a symphony orchestra across a kitchen table were fun, yes, but that certainly was not *professional.* "What if I found a little town house and furnished it?"

"Then I could live there and we could use it as an office, too! What a *graaand* idea." Harry clapped his hands in delight.

A quick search turned up a small, cozy place on 17th street. An expenditure of $5,000 turned it into a highly livable apartment and office. Cyma brought in furniture from the Rubin country house in the Hamptons—

And a new theatrical producing team was born. Informally. Loosely. But born.

At first there was talk about having a *new* musical written for Berkeley to work with. "My idea," says Harry, "was to use the Busby Berkeley girls as a kind of commentary, an ironic commentary, on the period. The form would be a little bit like *Oh, What a Lovely War.*" That show, a success of a few seasons earlier, used the songs and costumes of the first World War to point up the folly of the militaristic spirit of the time.

To script their period piece, the production team hired an unusual choice of writer—known primarily for a best-seller about juvenile delinquency and a series of detective stories. His script, says Harry, "was just *awwwful.*"

In his home at Palm Desert, California, Busby Berkeley took a phone call from Harry Rigby—whom he had never met—and learned that the latest plans to present an original show had been scrapped. What did he think, he was asked, about directing one of the other shows that had been previously discussed? Specifically, Vincent Youmans' *No, No, Nanette.*

Berkeley, who had once directed a local production of the 1924 musical, agreed that the old hit still had a lot going for it.

The road leading to Broadway suddenly was opened.

Except for a few obstacles.

The rights to the musical had to be obtained from several sources. All of the original authors, except one, had died, but their heirs and estates would have to be cut in for a percentage of any profits. Three motion picture versions of the musical had been made, and it had to be determined what rights had been sold to Hollywood. A production crew—musical director, choreographer, etc.—had to be assembled.

And, of course, the lengthy, wordy, unwieldy 1924 script had to be trimmed and modernized for 1970 audiences.

On October 6, 1969, Cyma wrote, from her expensive town house just off Central Park in New York's East 60s:

Dear Mr. Berkeley:

Just a word to let you know that Harry and I are working at the plan to present *No, No, Nanette* this season if possible. We have met with all the parties involved and are attempting to acquire the rights. If and when this takes place, we will immediately send you a contract as the director and choreographer of the production.

I deeply appreciate the interest and assistance you have given us thus far and I am looking forward to meeting you and I hope to have the pleasure of working with you.

I will keep you informed as the project progresses.

Kindest regards,
Cyma Rubin

And, from his modest pink-stucco ranch home in Palm Desert's heat, Berkeley replied:

Dear Cyma Rubin;
  It was so nice to receive your letter . . . .
  I had imagined that you were in the midst of getting the rights cleared—that's why Harry didn't call me as he said he would or get off "that" letter he has promised me. But with it all I think he's a great guy and I am very fond of him—and incidentally I think he's a damn good showman. So give the old b-----d my best.
  I too am waiting to meet you Cyma and I feel working with you will be, shall we say, a most "happy marriage. . . ."
                              Warm regards,
                              Busby Berkeley

From the very beginning, there seemed little doubt who would be the musical director on *No, No, Nanette*. Buster Davis, a short, red-haired, quiet-spoken musical genius given to wearing dark glasses indoors as well as out, had worked on almost every show that Harry Rigby had anything to do with over the years. *Hallelujah, Baby, Make a Wish, Almanac, Half a Sixpence* used his talents, and the tireless craftsman also had *Gentlemen Prefer Blondes, Funny Girl,* and *Bells Are Ringing* among more than twenty-five Broadway musical credits.

As to the script revisions, the answer seemed equally simple. Charles Gaynor, who had done the hilarious 1920s-style *Gladiola Girl* sketch for Carol Channing in *Lend an Ear,* was a close friend of Harry's. Surely he could tighten up the original Mandel-Harbach book of *No, No, Nanette.* So what if Gaynor had written virtually nothing since *Lend an Ear* in 1948? No matter. Harry got a copy of the antique script to him.

Things were moving faster now. But hold on, weren't there a lot of beautiful Youmans melodies that had never been published? Cyma remembered that her husband had invested in a musical that was going to use old Youmans tunes left in his trunk. That show had never been produced, but maybe some of that wonderful music could be worked

**64**

into the score of *No, No, Nanette*, along with the composer's great "Tea for Two" and "I Want to Be Happy." Gaynor thought so, and agreed to write the lyrics.

In November, Cyma wrote Busby Berkeley once more:

> Dear Mr. Berkeley,
> Just to let you know that we are into the final stages of closing contracts on *Nanette* and have sent along a proposal to [your agent] for you.
> Harry is beside himself with anxiety and thus far all reports are very enthusiastic on the revival.
> We will be getting together in the next few weeks just as soon as the last ends are tied. In the meantime, please begin to clear your calendar because we're all going to be very busy—soon.
> Harry says that he is flattered by your compliments and sends his love.
>
> Me too,<br>Cyma

Some nine weeks later, Berkeley replied, noting that he had thought he answered earlier, but "due to some oversight I evidently had not." He wrote:

> Harry called me on the phone Sunday night, had a lovely talk and we are taking care of the contract ourselves. [My agent] no longer represents me. Harry and I talk the same language and we get along great, so we do not need a third or outside party.
> Expect to receive the new contract from Harry within the next few days as soon as his lawyer has drawn it up.
> Can't wait to meet you and jump back into harness once again. It will be a lot of hard work, but I'm sure it will all be very much worthwhile.
>
> Most sincerely,<br>Buz

The show appeared to be coming along so well that Rubin & Rigby Productions, Ltd., as the operation was known, began to think about the future. What would Harry and Cyma do next, after *Nanette?* Harry's brief role as a penguin in *Pound*, a movie made by Director Robert Downey (of *Putney Swope* fame) led to the discovery that Downey was working on the script of a western film to be called *Greaser's Palace,* and the rights were picked up by a stroke of Mrs. Rubin's pen on a checkbook.

The film would come later. But in February, 1970, when Busby Berkeley signed a directorial agreement with Rubin & Rigby Productions, Ltd., Harry was not dreaming of movies. His own private dream was so near to realization that he could hardly keep from laughing out loud.

*Laughing* as he sat on Cyma Rubin's furniture in the house that Cyma Rubin was paying for.

*Laughing* as he fixed a drink with the liquor bought with Cyma Rubin's paychecks.

*Laughing* as he jetted from coast to coast on plane tickets bought with Cyma Rubin's expense money.

His dream—a Busby Berkeley musical—was coming alive.

Busby Berkeley!

Busby Berkeley!

*And, yes, oh my god, yes*—Ruby Keeler, too!

**6** Mrs. John Homer Lowe did not want to star in a Broadway musical.

That was a fact, plain and simple. Never mind that Mrs. John Homer Lowe once had been Ruby Keeler, tap-dancing darling of millions of Americans struggling their way through the Depression. For twenty-eight years she had been Mrs. John H. Lowe, wife, mother, and now grandmother—and she did not want to star in a Broadway musical.

When Harry and Berkeley held their first telephone conversations, Berkeley recalls, the name Ruby Keeler came up. It was a passing reference, perhaps something as casual on the director's part as, "Say, it might be fun to work with Ruby again." But Berkeley, who had kept in touch with many of the old "Berkeley girls," and who had shown off his favorite leading lady at film festivals in San Francisco, New York, and London, was sure of one thing:

> "We had a star who hadn't been on a Broadway stage for forty-one years, and a comedienne who had been away for thirty-eight. It was something to think about."
>
> **BURT SHEVELOVE**

Mrs. John H. Lowe did not want to star in a Broadway musical.

But that had been before February 11, 1969. On that date, the girl who had once been Ruby Keeler and who had become Mrs. Lowe, wife, mother, and grandmother, added the saddest of designations to her name.

Widow.

And the expansive California homes that she had lived in with her husband—expensive, comfortable homes in Van Nuys, Balboa Island, and Santa Ana—had turned into a quiet apartment in Corona Del Mar. The children—three girls, a son, and an adopted son—who had made the house come alive with noise and energy were gone . . . at school, married, with the army in Vietnam.

All right, perhaps Ruby *didn't* have as much to do as she had just a few years earlier. But there was still plenty to keep her occupied. There was her golf, for example. She loved it, and played daily, letting the California sun weather the taut skin on her soft-sculptured face and still-shapely legs, and streak silver flashes through her gray-blonde hair. And there were telephone calls to her married daughters, to hear the latest about the grandchildren. And there was Mass on Sunday. And, oh, there was—oh, so *much* to do.

Not as much as before, however, when John was alive.

But star in a musical? On Broadway?

And yet, here was Busby Berkeley calling her and saying that he was going to direct *No, No, Nanette*. Berkeley—almost seventy-five years old—directing a musical on Broadway! But he *wanted* to do it, she knew. For years he had been sitting and dreaming and talking about one more chance, one last bow in the spotlight. And now he was getting it.

But not her, not Ruby Keeler Lowe. Why, she could hardly remember when she had danced last. There were those times she had gone to the high school where the kids were working on a show and taught them a step. And she had done a brief routine on Jerry Lewis' television show— when was that, about 1966?—just for laughs, to prove she was still able to do it. And with the surge of interest in the Berkeley films, she had been a guest on *Mike Douglas* and *Merv Griffin*, and if the hosts asked nicely, and the audience insisted, she would stand up and tap through a few bars of "Tea for Two."

But she last danced on a stage, with an orchestra and rehearsals and everything, in—*good heavens, was it that long ago?*—1950. Then, old-movie fan Ken Murray brought the cast of his weekly TV series to the Roxy Theater in New York for a two-week vaudeville stand. *Nearly twenty years ago.* Why, she couldn't even remember if she had been any good.

She had been. If Ruby Keeler had ever been involved enough emotionally with her theatrical career to read her press notices and paste them into a scrapbook, she might have seen in *Variety:*

Murray's ace lure on this show is Ruby Keeler, the former tapstering Warner musical star, long since in retirement, if one can call rearing five kids any sort of retirement. Miss Keeler still dances. And from the mezz one can get a good flash of those still-slim gams and chassis. Maybe the terps aren't what they used to be, but that's not of prime importance on this show. Nostalgia is creating the big payoff. This Keeler date is the result of her appearance on the Murray video show several weeks ago.

Maybe, Ruby recalled, maybe her performance had been all right. At least she didn't remember getting booed off the stage. Things probably had gone a little better 'way back then than in 1968, when, hoping to take her mind off her husband's illness, she agreed to a three-week acting role in a Chicago stock production. Then, in the part of a tipsy witch in *Bell, Book and Candle,* she drew from one reviewer: "She reads her lines in a fine, clear voice, as if she were being very careful not to make anyone laugh out loud." The problem, of course, was that the play was a comedy—and it was no sin to make the audience laugh out loud.

Ruby Keeler Lowe had not really wanted to do the play. She had not seen the film, and did not know the character she agreed to portray. "I thought it might be a mother part, with kids, something very simple . . ." she told a *Chicago Tribune* interviewer. When it was over, she fled to California.

And now Buz and some strange people were asking her to do this musical.

She said no to Busby Berkeley. Politely, but firmly.

"Yes, Buz, you're right, it might be fun, but—Yes, Mr. Rigby sounds like a nice man. I know—but—I appreciate them thinking of me. It's very nice of them, but—"

And she agreed to look at the script.

Incredulously, laughing, she told her children about those crazy people in New York who wanted her—their mother, their children's grandmother—to be in their musical. *Wasn't that just too funny?*

The kids didn't think so. *Take it, mom,* they said. *What do you have to lose?*

"We didn't want her to turn into a golf widow," says John

**69**

H. Lowe III, just back from overseas and out of the army, ruggedly handsome, like his father, and solidly sure of himself. "We thought the show would give her something to do."

Ruby read the script. It was long and long-winded. The part they wanted her to play—the philanderer's wife, Mrs. Jimmy Smith, foster mother to Nanette—was a straight acting role. And acting had never been Ruby Keeler's strong suit.

Suddenly, Harry Rigby—winging in on Cyma Rubin's plane ticket—was there, in California, persuading her to take the part. Amusing her. Charming her. Insisting he needed her.

"But, Mr. Rigby, I'm a dancer. And this part doesn't have any dances."

"We'll put them in for you," Harry said.

"But it's all acting, and—"

"You'll have songs, too." He turned to Charles Gaynor, who had flown out with him. "Tell her, Charlie."

"I'm writing a duet for you and your 'husband' in the show. It's to a wonderful new Youmans melody."

"But—" Ruby Keeler Lowe looked at them, at the hope shining in Harry's eyes. She looked around at the apartment that would be empty once these fey and fanciful creatures were gone. She sighed and shook the short-cropped hair that had looked so black onscreen in all those 1930s films. Then she turned to the strangers looking expectantly, pleadingly, at her.

"Well," she said, without emotion, without enthusiasm, "I . . . guess . . . I could . . . try it."

But Mrs. John H. Lowe did *not* want to star in a Broadway musical.

\* \* \*

The other players in *No, No, Nanette* came easier.

In some cases, much easier.

\* \* \*

"The last year or two has been pretty slow," says a blowsy, graying Patsy Kelly, looking every one of her sixty years. "Let's see. I had one line in that new TV series, *Bare-*

*foot in the Park,* the colored version . . . And I did some day-time game shows . . . A couple of pictures I was up for just haven't gotten off the ground. I don't know if money is tight or what.

"The work has been kind of in-between. A few days here, and then something else a month or two later. I made some TV pilots, but—"

The Irish eyes twinkle suddenly, and the tired voice takes on the comic rasp it had in dozens of pictures in the Thirties and Forties: "Why, I made so many pilots, I could start my own airline."

Patsy Kelly, the tart-tongued, hard-as-nails kid from Brooklyn, is getting back into shape. After seventeen years without a film role between 1943 and 1960, and only bits in six pictures since then, she's not going to blow this job. For weeks, ever since agent Gloria Safier called her in Holly-wood to tell her she would talk to Harry Rigby about the role of Pauline the Maid, Patsy's been on a crash diet. Now that the body is as ready as it's going to be, she is sharpen-ing her tongue.

A stranger stops her in a hotel lobby and says he loved her in all those films with Judy Garland and Jean Harlow and Gary Cooper. "Thanks," snaps Patsy, "but that was my mother." The stranger walks on, laughing, and Patsy is glad the old wisecracks still work. She knows that other actresses auditioned for the part, and that she came close to not get-ting it. She used to say she played so many maids in movies "they hired me 'cause I had a uniform that fit," and now Patsy knows the line doesn't ring true. She needs new uni-forms, larger ones.

So what if nobody is going to pay her the kind of money she got on Broadway in the old days? The year 1931, when she was with Al Jolson in *Wonder Bar,* is a long time ago. And '32, when she left for Hollywood after starring with Clifton Webb in *Flying Colors,* isn't much nearer. When she was making big money anyway, she spent it. She took care of her friends. And when things got tough, her friends took care of her.

71

Now, many of them are gone. The lovely Thelma Todd, the buoyant Pert Kelton, the indestructible Tallulah. "Every other thing I say seems to be 'God bless,'" says Patsy, bemused. And the money they're offering is enough.

Besides—most of all—the hard-drinking, fun-loving, wise-cracking little Irish comedienne knows just one thing. How to get laughs.

It is more than a job. It is her life.

* * *

For the part of Lucille Early, the sophisticated and wealthy friend who first tells Mrs. Smith about her husband's roving eye, Helen Gallagher seemed an unlikely choice. Throughout most of her career—including Harry Rigby's *Make a Wish* in 1951—she played a variety of tough, brassy broads. There was Ado Annie in *Oklahoma!*, Miss Adelaide in *Guys and Dolls*, a stripper in *Pal Joey*, a dance-hall tramp in *Sweet Charity*.

This would be a new kind of part for her, and she is cautious. She says that she found the script they gave her to read "depressing." But it would be rewritten, she was promised. And the roles offered to her *are* coming less and less frequently these days. After all, she stopped *High Button Shoes* with a comic tango in 1947—twenty-three years ago! —and she hit star billing, too early, in *Hazel Flagg* in 1952.

"I was shy," Helen says, "and it was hard to cope with that much success so young." She coped, all right. She coped by becoming hard-as-nails, by telling people how she wanted things to be onstage, by fighting for it every step of the way. Stars can get away with it. But for nearly a decade now, it was all featured billing, and stock, and replacing other performers, and selling soap on TV. Helen Gallagher was no longer a star, and Helen Gallagher knew it.

She knew it when she went on dozens of times for an ill Gwen Verdon in *Sweet Charity*, and heard people scurry out of the theater for refunds when the loudspeaker broadcast the ominous news: "Ladies and gentlemen, your attention, please. At tonight's performance, the role of Charity will be played by Helen Gallagher." It's tough for a performer to stand backstage and hear an audience groan with disappointment. And Helen heard it. Then, she had gone into a disastrous show, *Cry for Us All*, which ran a week, and although she had gotten good notices from the critics, the somber, downbeat musical had depressed her.

She was ready for something different, something sticky and sweet and light. Maybe it was time for her to be someone else onstage, and backstage, too. The tough little tart with the big voice and the "I'm a star" attitude—maybe she should be played down. Maybe Helen Gallagher should just do her job, take her direction, and hope that this *Nanette* thing ran long enough to pay the bills and keep her in front of some applauding people.

Maybe. At any rate, she'd try it.

\* \* \*

In 1968, Bobby Van was asked by Harry Rigby to consider a role in *Hallelujah, Baby*, but he turned it down. This time he is ready to talk.

As slim and lithe in his early forties as when he worked on TV's *Show of Shows* and in a dozen MGM pictures some fifteen years ago, Bobby is well aware that there are few parts these days for a song-and-dance man. The breed itself is dying.

"A lot of good dancers went into choreography," he says with boyish seriousness. "There's Bobby Fosse. Gene Nelson became a director. Gower Champion. There's very few of us left. Donald O'Connor. And Astaire, a little bit. Gene Kelly works now and then, besides directing.

"And myself."

When Metro stopped making big Technicolor musicals, and the calls for film work came infrequently, Bobby tried the choreographic route, too. He did the dances for a Miss America pageant, a TV commercial or two, a couple of Jerry Lewis slapstick films. And there were occasional guest shots on TV variety programs.

"But why hire a song-and-dance man to be on a show as a guest when you have twenty dancers who are on the show every week? They can entertain people equally as well."

As more and more variety programs figured it out for themselves, he tried going back to a comedy act—the kind he did when he started in showbusiness as a kid of sixteen, before he taught himself to dance in order to have a big finish on a night-club floor. He went out as one of a series of partners that Mickey Rooney worked with whenever the alimony bills got too high. And Bobby turned to writing, too, and sold an idea for a TV series to a production company. Some day, "next year," the company might make a pilot, with Bobby as producer and director, and the pilot might sell to a network, and the network might keep the series on for longer than thirteen weeks, and Writer-Producer-Director Bobby Van might be set for a long time.

Some day.

But he likes to sing and dance better than anything. "It's very hard to sing and dance all your life, and then all of a sudden do six or seven television appearances a year. It isn't enough to make your body work. I *need* to work. My body has to function; it's used to it. I don't get that from television."

In California, married for a second time—to young, pretty, blonde actress Elaine Joyce, who signed to play foil to comedian Don Knotts on a new TV series—Bobby eagerly took the call from Harry Rigby in New York.

"I'm dying to do a Broadway show," he says later. "I'm tired of television. There's not enough rehearsal. You do your dance right now and the next day it's forgotten. The only way to be successful in this business is to have constant exposure. That's what a Broadway show gives you. You're working every night, people are seeing you."

He is so eager to play the part of Billy Early, husband of Lucille and lawyer-friend of philandering Jimmy Smith, that he agrees to work at half-salary during the six weeks *Nanette* will be in rehearsal.

* * *

"When I thought of the part of Nanette, I said, 'Well, it's a Susan Watson role.' "

Buster Davis speaks softly and carefully in his roomy,

74

soundproof apartment on Manhattan's West 58th Street. The air is still, although the faint hum of an air conditioner can be felt more than heard. A small nervous dog, reddish as her master's thinning hair, moves fitfully about the room. The dog's name is Glinda, after the Good Witch that Billie Burke played in *The Wizard of Oz*.

As casting director on *Nanette,* as well as musical conductor and vocal arranger, Buster says the question was "whether we wanted Susan, or a new girl who maybe is younger than Susan."

"I wanted Susan from the beginning," says Harry Rigby. But Susan Watson has been a Broadway ingenue for a dozen years, and it was decided that the part of teen-age Nanette should be done by a new face—"someone delicious," in Cyma's words. Particularly in view of the "old" faces that would surround her in the show.

"I don't know of anybody that plays those kinds of parts as well as Susan," Buster said to his co-workers, "but maybe there *is* someone." He remembers auditioning "the usual amount of vapid little blonde girls with high soprano voices." They were, he says with a chuckle, "deadly."

In time, he thought of someone.

Carole Demas.

"She has a marvelous face, and a marvelous personality, and a voice with—you *know*. I thought the voice didn't mean as much to me as her *look*. I thought she had some of that Susan Watson *quality,* and she obviously must have because she often followed Susan in a show, playing the same part."

Although she is past her late teens by a decade or so, Carole Demas does not look it as she sits in a rehearsal studio. Her long dark hair is pulled back into two braids, and she wears a striped T-shirt and blue jeans. Her brown eyes are huge and sparkling.

"I had sung with Buster on some concert musicals," she says, "and he asked me to audition for Nanette. It was at Mrs. Rubin's house, that big cluttered lovely house with all that sculpture and art. I sang for her and Harry Rigby, and they told me they wanted a deeper, chest voice—but not a belter. Then Mrs. Rubin asked me to dance. Well, I'm not a dancer, but I've done a lot of work at Tom Jones and Harvey Schmidt's workshop, where you do stilt-walking and *everything*. So I kind of gave my impression of what a soft-shoe dancer looks like. They asked me if I could take some tap lessons over the summer, and I said yes. And they told me 'thank-you-we'll-let-you-know.'

"At midnight that night, Harry Rigby called me and said they didn't want to keep me in suspense any longer. I had the part."

Young Broadway "unknown" Carole Demas signed a contract at a salary approximately one-fifth the weekly wage paid to Louise Groody in the same part forty-five years earlier.

\* \* \*

The less important roles in the show were wrapped up quickly.

A handsome, tall juvenile, Roger Rathburn, was signed as Tom, Nanette's boyfriend. A former English teacher who decided late to go into showbusiness, he played several musical roles in stock and was to make his Broadway debut in *Nanette*.

Choosing at least one of the three gold diggers who get their hooks into meek-mannered Jimmy Smith was simple. Cyma Rubin's daughter, Loni Zoe Ackerman, had had a small role in *George M* on Broadway, and had played the "Ruby Keeler" part as a replacement in *Dames at Sea* Off-Broadway. She started her dancing lessons at the age of six, some fifteen years before auditions began for *No, No, Nanette,* and there was little doubt in anyone's mind—or, at least, in Harry Rigby's—that all those years of tap, ballet, jazz, singing, and acting instruction would go to waste.

Small and dark, her hair pulled into a severe style to match her mother's, and wearing the same kind of tailored 1930-ish clothes, Loni shrugs when asked if she thinks her mother's role as a producer has much to do with her own casting.

"I don't know, and I don't care," she says. "I've had experience and they've all seen me onstage, and I'm going to do the best I can with the part." She smiles youthfully. "I'm playing Betty from Boston, and I'll be good."

A chance meeting on the street between Loni and Cyma and singer-comedienne Pat Lysinger fills the part of Winnie from Washington. Pat worked with Loni in the chorus of a musical that tried out on the summer music-tent circuit, and also was in *Dames at Sea*.

Finally, Buster Davis taps a friend, K. C. Townsend, for the part of Flora from Frisco. Bosomy, blonde, tall and with a raucous giggle, K. C. scored heavily on Broadway a few seasons earlier in *Henry, Sweet Henry*. Her costume consisted of a small towel clutched around an ample figure.

"Buster lives down the block from me," K. C. recalls, "and he thought I had a job. But I was just doing some backers' auditions to raise money for other shows. When I walked into his auditions, he said, 'You're exactly what we've been looking for.' "

* * *

Finally, the all-important male lead is set.

"For Jimmy Smith, we wanted—well, Hiram Sherman *is* Jimmy Smith," Buster Davis says. Living monk-like in the coolness, with the shades pulled to keep the bright summer sun at bay, Buster presses his hands together, spreads his fingers, and tucks the joined forefingers under the point of his chin, musing. "There was no doubt about it. Hiram Sherman was the perfect casting."

An old friend agreed, long before *Nanette* went into rehearsal. When writer-director Burt Shevelove, who had worked with Buster and Harry on *Hallelujah, Baby*, passed through New York on a trip from his London home, he raved about having just seen Hiram Sherman in an English musical. Even without Shevelove's plug, "Chubby" Sherman seemed well suited to the role of the misunderstood and muddled Bible publisher.

The actor began his career in Chicago in the mid-1920s. Now in his sixties, he has appeared in hundreds of plays, musicals, and revues on Broadway, in London, and in stock.

77

A consummate performer, Chubby has one idiosyncrasy that some producers fret about. He has a habit of leaving productions suddenly and without notice. Recently, in fact, he had walked out of a musical at the end of the first day of rehearsal.

The lyricist of another show that suddenly found itself without the actor's services in mid-contract tells why: "He cannot stand to work with amateurs. He is such a perfectionist himself, and has been in the theater for so long, that he insists on professionalism."

But, adds the lyricist, "Chubby works all he wants to, because there is simply no one better at his kind of role."

Soft-spoken, portly, and fairly radiating warmth, like a kindly grandfather, Hiram Sherman met with Harry Rigby, Buster Davis, and "Charlie" Gaynor at Gaynor's apartment to talk over the show. They met again. And again.

"The third time," he remembers, "Cyma appeared."

**7** The business of raising money for a production is an element of show business that is least publicized, and probably the most important. Without money, nothing begins; without more money, nothing is completed.

A minimum investment for a Broadway musical, circa 1970, is half a million dollars. Many shows go several hundred thousand dollars over that figure. Several have been known to more than double it . . . and to lose it all.

Financing on such a heavy scale usually means that the producers, as General Partners in the production com-

> "Other investors? There are no other investors."
>
> SAM RUBIN

pany, must obtain funds from a number of investors, called Limited Partners. If the show is a hit, the investors get back their money and split the profits equally with the producers. If the show is not a hit, the investors may get nothing back —but the producers collect a small percentage of the weekly gross box-office receipts, and also get several hundred dollars a week as office expenses.

Some musicals appear to be such sure-fire hits that they readily attract important investors. CBS put up all of the money for *My Fair Lady*. RCA backed *How to Succeed in Business Without Really Trying*. Ampex was behind *Purlie*. More often than not, however, the producers must wearily conduct a series of "backers' auditions"—miniature performances of the show—before invited groups of potential investors. At these events, the show's plot is outlined, some of the music is played and sung, and the producers diligently try to sound as enthusiastic and positive as they can.

The backers' auditions may seem like the financial starting point of the production. But much that takes money has gone on before. In order to acquire a property, sign a star and director, print scripts, pay attorneys, and the like, the producers of a big Broadway musical may require some $25,000-$50,000 in "front money."

This money is entirely risk capital. If it is spent, and the show is not produced, the money is lost. (A Limited Partner's investment must be returned to him if the show is not produced.) To get front money, if he does not want to risk his own savings, a producer frequently will take on a coproducer or an associate producer. These individuals put up the cash needed to get things moving on the producer's idea.

Customarily, the associate producer has little to say about the artistic values of the production. He receives billing credit and a share of the profits, if any, that eventually go to the producer. If, in addition to furnishing front money, he brings in investment dollars, he gets a profit share as a Limited Partner as well.

"Sometimes," writes Attorney Donald Farber in *Producing on Broadway*, "a Co-Producer will contribute all of the front money in exchange for the other Producer furnishing the property. The facts should be set forth in the Co-Production Joint Venture Agreement as to who is responsible for the front money, and what the party receives for it."

Cyma Rubin knew she had the front money for *No, No, Nanette*. But could the Rubin bank account afford more? Probably not. She would have to look for the half-million dollars that it would take to get the show on Broadway. Cyma wasn't worried. Hadn't she been raising hundreds of thousands for the American Symphony year after year? And Harry had connections, too.

Or did he?

"I made it very clear to both Sam and Mrs. Rubin," Harry insists, "that I was not a money-raiser. I *never* raised money. Well, I raised the first show—I didn't *raise* it—it came from friends and things like that. I am *obviously* not a money-raiser. That's not my bag." He waves an expressive hand and sweeps it through the long gray hair, brushing back a lock that has fallen over his lined forehead.

"Harry was supposed to raise half the money," Cyma says with animation. She furrows her brow and bitterly bites off the words: "Not ... five ... cents!"

Confident that the necessary cash could be raised from a few close and wealthy friends, Cyma and her husband did not register an offering with the Securities and Exchange Commission. Similarly, if an offering is to be made to fewer than twenty-six persons, no registration is necessary with the New York attorney general, if each investor waives the right to receive information that would normally be contained in an offering circular. "If it is possible to avoid the use of a circular," advises Donald Farber, "I usually recommend it as it must contain some provisions likely to discourage investment."

Even without a circular, the money-raisers found discouragement.

"Did you say *Ruby Keeler?*" was often the incredulous response when the cast list was discussed. *"Ruby Keeler?* From those films? She must be in her *sixties*!"

The laughter was louder when Busby Berkeley's name was mentioned. "My god, isn't he—? Berkeley—*and* Keeler —and, wait, don't tell me, I'll bet you're going to get *Patsy Kelly* for the maid! Remember her? Patsy Kell— You *are?*"

There are ways, impressive and otherwise, of holding backers' auditions. Some producers hire several Broadway performers to sing the songs and back them with a small group of musicians. Free champagne and cocktails are poured liberally to loosen tongues and the checkbooks of prospective investors.

The *Nanette* producers felt that they could be less expansive—and less expensive.

"We were killing ourselves," says Cyma. "We did a three-way act, Buster and Loni and I. Buster at the piano. Loni singing the goddamned songs to save money on singers. And me doing my champagne bit, describing the set, and wearing a dress that I have from the twenties, and the whole thing. Harry dragged me all over, and everyone thanked me politely, and that was the last we heard from them.

"Two people Harry *did* produce turned out not to be investors, but came just to meet me and see the Rubins' house."

When time grew short—contracts had been signed with performers and others calling for the start of rehearsals in

**81**

September—Cyma Rubin went to her husband. Sam had talked about the show to friends, business acquaintances, and philanthropists such as Stewart R. Mott, Martin D. Fife, and Ralph E. Ablon, who support the American Symphony and serve as directors. They had turned Sam down. Now he must have been expecting Cyma.

"I tried to bewitch my husband," Cyma frankly told an interviewer. And then, even more frankly, she says, "Then I screamed and shrieked until he gave in."

Harry notes that initially Sam Rubin agreed to put up all but $100,000 required for the budget, and that he and Cyma were expected to raise $50,000 each. "I got some people together to do it," he says, "and then Sam got indignant and said, 'Oh, the hell with it, I'll do it myself.' "

"There was a point halfway along," Sam Rubin states, "where I had to make the decision to pour more money into the show or get out and let it die." He touches the tip of the full white mustache that covers his upper lip, and smiles: "I made the right decision."

With the money assured, the curtain was almost ready to rise on *No, No, Nanette's* final stages of production. Only a few details remained—such as the selection of a costumer who could clothe the performers in authentic 1925 style. The veteran designer, Raoul Pène du Bois, was tapped for the job, but only after a battle, according to Cyma.

Du Bois, a tall and imposing figure with the long nose, flowing shoulder-length hair, and mustache of a seventeenth-century French nobleman, began designing for the stage in 1925 when—at the age of sixteen—he did some costumes for Rodgers and Hart's *Garrick Gaieties.* Ziegfeld used him for his *Follies,* and he worked on dozens of musicals over the years, including *Jumbo, The Music Man,* and *Call Me Madam.* After *Gypsy,* he spent five years in the mid-1960s as a serious painter in Paris, but then he returned to New York, low on funds and ready to work. After designing a few ballets and a short-lived musical called *Darling of the Day,* Raoul Pène du Bois was available.

Harry Rigby, who says Raoul's sets and costumes were

the best thing about his ill-fated production of *Make a Wish*, and who had worked with the designer on *Almanac*, did not want to use him on *Nanette*—or so says Cyma Rubin.

"I had met Raoul socially," she says, "when Harry brought him to a Symphony concert months and months—oh, six months—before we started talking about costumes and scenery. Then, when Harry and I started discussing possibilities, he said, 'Why don't we get the designer who did *Applause?*'

"I said, '*Applause?* That is the tackiest, cheapest-looking *dreck* I've ever seen.' He says, 'Well, then, we can get Irene Sharaff.' " Her imitation of Harry's voice sounds like a tape recorder running backward.

" '*Irene Sharaff?*' I said. 'She's *had* it. She's not what I'm thinking of. I want Du Bois.' " She imitates the tape recorder, faster. "He said, 'I don't want him, he's very difficult to work with, and *naaa-naaa-naaa*. And, anyway, we're not talking.'

" 'I don't care if you're talking or not,' I said. We were in my kitchen having a *fight* like you cannot imagine! Then he said, 'Why don't we get the guy who did the movie, *The Damned?*'

" 'Are you crazy?' I said. 'I want Du Bois!' He said, '*Naanananana,*' " and the tape recorder screeches out of control. "I said, 'I will call Du Bois . . .'

" 'No, we don't want him, we'll never get anything out of him—'

"I said, 'Harry, I am calling Du Bois. There is *no one* better than Du Bois.'

"And he finally said, 'Well, all right, if you insist.' "

So Harry, who had dealt with Ruby and Busby and the other performers, called Raoul. The soft-voiced, childlike, trusting artist agreed to design three stage settings and 127 costumes, and to select clothes for the leading ladies from a couturier line.

In order to make sure that Raoul's costumes fitted her idea of the period, Cyma flew to Paris and spent several days going through old photographs and magazines. She

**83**

returned in the spring of 1970 to work with Harry on the final loose ends of the production. A general manager was hired to handle the business details of the production. An orchestrator was signed, along with a dance-music arranger. A lighting designer, a stage manager, and a publicist completed the production staff.

All that was needed now was to cast the chorus—sixteen beautiful girls and eight boys who could dance and sing—and begin rehearsals under the guidance of the great Busby Berkeley.

**8** When Busby Berkeley signed a contract on February 25, 1970, with Rubin and Rigby Productions, Ltd., to serve as director and choreographer for the proposed revival of *No, No, Nanette,* only Harry Rigby had met him face to face.

Too shy to make the initial contact with the famed, almost godlike director, Harry subsequently phoned him regularly and flew to California at least three times to make plans. Once, the two men discussed signing Ruby Keeler or, if she was not interested, either Charlotte Greenwood or Jane Withers for the part of "Sue Smith." Another time, they

> "There's something obscene about trotting out all those old people for others to laugh at."
>
> CLAY FELKER, editor, "New York"

talked about getting Patsy Kelly as the Smiths' maid. If anyone connected with *No, No, Nanette* can be said to have *known* "Buz," it was Harry.

But Harry did not know him. When he looked at Berkeley, he was blinded by adulation, and his eyes did not see a man who was seventy-five years old, whose mind held dim memories of alcoholism, hedonism, and self-destruction—not to mention what a psychiatrist might call an obvious Oedipus complex, and a charge of murdering three people.

What Harry saw when he looked at the big man slumped in an armchair like a sack of potatoes was only those shadowy dancers swirling in white evening gowns atop pianos, or *ratatat*-tapping briskly down tiers of mirrored steps. And when Berkeley spoke, growling in a voice reminiscent of Wallace Beery's, Harry heard only Dick Powell's youthful tenor on "I Only Have Eyes for You," or a chorus girls' rendition of "We're in the Money."

Before she met him for the first time a month after he had signed his contract, Cyma Rubin knew little about Berkeley, other than that he had directed many great musicals for the stage and screen in the past. Perhaps she had read a major article that appeared in *The New York Times Magazine,* on March 2, 1969, in which author William Murray heralded "The Return of Busby Berkeley." After discussing the surge of interest in the old Warner Bros. musicals, Murray wrote:

> Berkeley himself is gratified by all this attention, but he conveys the distinct impression that he'd much rather be back at work. He is a big man in his early seventies and the first adjective that comes to mind is "gray." Gray eyes, gray hair, a gray suit, gray skin. Much of the time, sitting or standing, he sags. . . . His stomach bulges, his lower lip is pendulous, and his nose seems squashed against his face. In other words, he looks his age. But when he talks about his work, an extraordinary transformation takes place. Everything seems to lift into place. His stomach moves up into his chest, his lower lip tucks in under his upper one, and his features seem to throb with suppressed energy. He speaks in a booming, husky baritone and emphasizes his points with heavy strokes in the air of big, thick-fingered hands. The realization comes abruptly that the man is a dynamo, ready to go into action instantly at the sight of a signed contract. 'Hell, I've had loads of real big propositions, but they never get all the money up,' he booms and the frustration of the long wait is evident on his face.
>
> There's something obscene about the sight of an energetic man in full possession of his faculties forced to remain idle. . . .

Encouraging words, those. And surely the man who had once been so full of ideas—ideas enough to create the dances for almost four dozen pictures and a dozen stage musicals —and who often boasted, "I never repeated myself," well, surely, that man would have no trouble directing a single two-hour revival of *No, No, Nanette,* and planning three or four dance numbers. Even if that man had been born in 1895, and had directed his last Broadway show in 1930, and had not worked professionally for the last eight years (and only once in the last seventeen) —he could still do it.

Couldn't he?

Somehow, he always had done it in the old days, although he boasted he never danced a step himself. He had gotten his experience as a dance director, the story goes, when he served as General John J. Pershing's entertainment officer in France during World War I and put the battalion through intricate marching maneuvers on the parade ground. Earlier he had learned the commands—*By the right flank, Harch!*—at a military academy outside New York City, but after graduation he spent three years working in a shoe factory. He enlisted in the army on the day the United States declared war in April, 1917, and later sought a discharge on the grounds that his mother needed him at home.

It appears that the talents of William Berkeley Enos, as he was christened, were suited more to a theatrical life than a military one. His father, Wilson Enos, was the director of a small stock company. His mother, Gertrude, was an actress who was never far from her son's side throughout his career.

Returning to New York, young Berkeley changed his name—taking his first name from Amy Busby, the leading lady in his father's stock company, and using his mother's maiden name as his last name. A family friend offered him a part as an actor in a touring play, and later he played the role of "Madame Lucy," a male dress designer, in a revival of the musical *Irene* by McCarthy and Tierney.

*New York Times* critic Alexander Woollcott said in his review of *Irene,* "If there is one thing the American theater can be counted on to play to the queen's taste, it is a male dressmaker. The one in *Irene* is a perfect scream."

After his brief fling at turning on the swish, Busby Berkeley found himself directing shows for a number of stock companies around New York. The producer of a Broadway revue admired his work on a musical in Boston and called him in to stage the dances. *Holka Polka* had only a short run, but Buz was off and winging.

He worked on several Rodgers and Hart shows, and then on a series of musicals for the Shuberts. Max Meth, musical director for such hits as *Finian's Rainbow* and *Gentlemen Prefer Blondes,* was a young man in the late 1920s and remembers working with Buz on several Shubert productions.

"We were on *Pleasure Bound, A Night in Venice,* and

*Street Singer* together," he says, "and on his last show, *Nina Rosa*, that Harbach and Caesar wrote with Romberg. He left that one in Montreal to go to Hollywood. He's known now for his film work, but he had great work in the theater first. His dances on stage would build . . . and *build* . . . for eight or ten minutes, and when they were over, the show would be stopped!" A gnarled elf of a man, Meth pounds the table vigorously. "He made his dances as important—as—anything—else—in—the—show!"

Berkeley's habit of working his dancers until they were breathless caught the attention of Samuel Goldwyn, who had negotiated to film Flo Ziegfeld's production of *Whoopee* with Eddie Cantor and the other Broadway stars. Buz and his mother headed for the coast.

When the Museum of Modern Art in Manhattan recently unearthed the only print of *Whoopee* still in existence, borrowing it from the Czechoslovakian Film Archives for a single showing, the "Berkeley touch" was only marginally in evidence. The dances are photographed head-on, directly from a stage set, and only once or twice does the camera tentatively shoot down from overhead to frame some poorly rehearsed floral patterns below. In one routine, twenty chorus girls dressed as cowboys pass their ten-gallon hats from one to another—behind their backs, between their legs, etc.—as they doggedly and raggedly time-step. One innovation, however, was the first use of close-ups of the dancers, which Berkeley accomplished by having the girls march toward the camera, one by one. He did it, he says, " 'cause I wanted to show the public those beautiful girls."

In a year or two, as he worked on several pictures at a time, the director began to move his camera more and more, in order to get away from the static "onstage" look. He also moved closer and closer to the girls, showing not only their pretty faces, but row upon row of thighs, breasts, and legs. The effect was to dehumanize and de-sex the dancers. Instead of individual women, there were only dancing dolls, kaleidoscopic patterns, and a thoroughly asexual feeling to his work.

Perhaps his attitude toward women in those early days had much to do with his personal involvement with them. Six times married, five times to a succession of chorus girls and actresses, Berkeley seems to have sought an unattainable goal. "He had the eye to pick beautiful women, and he always picked the most beautiful one for himself," recalls Max Meth. But he remembers too, one of the young brides coming to him as a friend when he and Buz were working on a show.

"She was in tears," says Meth, "and pleaded with me to help. 'Please,' she said, 'please help me. His mother—he talks about her all the time. Day and night. Such interference . . . she's always with us. She's all he thinks of. I'm going out of my mind. He'll drive me to suicide. Tell him, please. . . .' "

Blessed with almost total recall of events that took place some forty years ago, Meth adds, "It's very, very funny, but I don't remember that he ever mentioned his father. It was only his mother." He pounds the table again, three times in succession.

"Mother . . . mother . . . mother."

With his mother in Hollywood, Berkeley was on top of the world in 1934. At Warner Bros., *42nd Street, Gold Diggers of 1933, Footlight Parade,* and *Dames* had made his name as famous as some of the stars of the pictures—Ruby Keeler, James Cagney, Dick Powell, Joan Blondell. His credo, "Forget the dances, forget all the trick steps, and think *only* of the camera!" was fast becoming the watchword among his peers. The thirty-nine-year-old director was an imposing figure as he rode like a god high over the set of a waterfall or staircase on a specially designed monorail that he ordered built to let his camera "travel." To the women in the huge sound studios, he was a romantic figure as well. Thick black hair curled haphazardly over his high forehead, which was slashed across by a nearly solid line of heavy eyebrows. He accentuated the dark, brooding effect by dressing in an expensive white sweater, white slacks, and white shoes.

To add to his professional glory, Berkeley's personal life had taken an upturn. His first marriage to young actress

Esther Muir had ended in divorce in 1932, but on February 11, 1934, he married again. This time, the bride was Merna Kennedy, a dainty, dark-haired beauty who had been Charlie Chaplin's love interest in *The Circus*. Studio boss Jack Warner was the best man at the ceremony in Hollywood's Methodist Episcopal Church, and when the couple flew to San Francisco for a honeymoon, their pilot was noted speed flier Colonel Roscoe Turner.

And then, like a plane plummeting to earth, Busby Berkeley's career took a horrifying downturn.

It happened near Santa Monica, California, on the afternoon of September 8, 1934. The director was tooling along the Roosevelt Highway when a tire went flat on his expensive sports car. He pulled over to the side of the road, had the tire repaired, and continued on his way.

Suddenly, he saw two cars heading toward him. One drew alongside the other attempting to pass. Something went wrong with his left front wheel. There was a scream and a thunderous noise, a flash . . . and darkness.

Minutes later—he doesn't remember how long it was— Berkeley was found walking down the highway. He was dazed, his head was cut and bleeding, and he showed signs of a possible brain concussion.

A quarter of a mile behind him was the silent wreckage of his car and two others, the ones he had slammed into, head-on, at a speed of forty miles per hour or more.

In one car slumped two twenty-year-old college students, unconscious and bleeding from cuts and internal injuries.

In the other car, nineteen-year-old Laura von Briesen moaned softly from the pain. She had a fractured pelvis, four broken ribs, and a broken jaw. No sound came from her mother, her brother, and her cousin, who were crumpled around her. They were dead.

At first, it looked like an accident. Berkeley made a statement that his left front tire had blown, causing his car to swerve into the others. He was charged with manslaughter as a technicality, and released on $10,000 bail. He entered the hospital.

But when local authorities began investigating, they found a number of witnesses who indicated the accident was not such a simple matter at all. The odor of alcohol, they said, was strong on Berkeley's breath immediately after the crash. He had also been seen driving on the wrong side of the road, and at a high rate of speed.

Brought into Los Angeles Municipal Court on a stretcher, the director heard himself charged with three counts of second-degree murder. A judge, after hearing testimony of twenty-five witnesses, set aside the original lesser charge of manslaughter and said, "The evidence in this case has clearly shown that a probable greater crime . . . has been committed."

The director's studio jumped in quickly to aid him and avoid scandal. Famed Attorney Jerry Giesler framed his defense on the blown left front tire, and actually brought the car's front wheel into court to show the torn and battered rubber. The question was whether the tire had exploded before the crash, or was ripped open in the collision. A tire dealer who examined it testified that it was flat when the cars crashed.

With delays and adjournments, it was more than a year before the trial ended. On Christmas Day, 1935, a perspiring Berkeley heard the bad news. The jury was hopelessly deadlocked, ten for acquittal and two against. He would have to stand a second trial.

He turned to his mother, who had sat at his side all through the long hours of judicial proceedings, and smiled wanly.

During the months of preparation for the first trial, Berkeley had managed to keep working. *Gold Diggers of 1935* and *I Live for Love* were put into the can. But now, hating the thought of having to go through the whole thing again, he found it harder to come up with ideas. A new *Gold Diggers* picture—for release in 1937—benefited from his dance routines, but the spark was gone. Even after he settled $250,000 worth of seven lawsuits filed by the crash victims and their families against him, for $95,000, Berkeley was well aware of the three murder charges he still had to face.

The second trial began on April 6, 1936, and ended two weeks later—with the same result as the first. After more than twenty-five hours of deliberation, the jury reported that it was hopelessly deadlocked. But this time, the vote was seven for acquittal to five against. The walls of prison, the end of his career—and separation from his mother—all were looming nearer.

Berkeley, his mother at his side as before, told newspapermen that he was disappointed. "I had hoped for acquittal," he said softly.

A few days later, Attorney Giesler asked the court to dismiss the charges against his client. But the judge refused, despite Giesler's assertion that "we have fought prejudice . . . because there has been injected into this case the question of alcohol and because of the fact that the defendant happened to be engaged in the motion picture business, causing him to receive exceptional publicity." The end of Prohibition in 1933 and previous notorious scandals in the film capital, he implied, produced in the public mind an attitude of, "Well, what else can you expect from those drunken degenerates out there?"

Some five months later, a third jury deliberated for ninety minutes and took five ballots to decide the fate of the director.

The first count was eight to four for acquittal.

The second was nine to three.

The third was ten to two.

The fourth was eleven to one.

The fifth was a unanimous verdict. *Not guilty.*

On September 26, 1936, two years and eighteen days after the accident, Busby Berkeley found himself a free man.

He was free in more ways than one. A month after the trial, Merna Kennedy was granted a divorce when she testified that her husband cared more for his work than he did for his home.

The director returned to Warners with a vengeance, hoping to lose his personal problems on the gigantic stages.

But his work on such films as *Garden of the Moon* and *Gold Diggers in Paris* in 1938 was less innovative—perhaps because he could not free his mind of other things.

One of those things was shapely film actress Carole Landis, nineteen years old and married to actor Irving Wheeler. In May, Wheeler filed suit against Berkeley, charging that the director had carried on a relentless campaign for some months to win the affections of his wife. The effort, he added, had been successful, and Miss Landis had left their home. Berkeley had stolen her love after she had danced in a chorus line in one of his pictures, Wheeler charged, and he asked damages—$150,000 for the lost love and $100,000 more as punishment.

The suit was quietly settled, and no further romantic entanglements between the director and film star are recorded. The misalliance may—or may not—have played a part in the suicide of Carole Landis in 1948, a burned-out star at twenty-nine.

In 1939, Berkeley moved on a new long-term contract to MGM, where he was to work on dances for such pictures as *Babes in Arms*, with Mickey Rooney and Judy Garland, *For Me and My Gal*, which introduced Gene Kelly, and *Ziegfeld Girl*, with Lana Turner. But in that same year, he was hit with a lien by the government demanding $11,675 owed on his income tax.

Now forty-four years old, Berkeley again tried to solve his personal problems by following the same route he had taken unsuccessfully so many times before. He drank heavily, he played hard—and married a twenty-two-year-old actress, Claire James, in a ceremony before a justice of the peace in Las Vegas. Again the marriage cooled quickly, and again he threw himself into the film routine.

But the calls came less often. After *Girl Crazy* and *The Gang's All Here* (which he directed on loan to 20th Century-Fox) in 1943, the studios seemed to have no need of his talents.

And then, suddenly, he received a chance for a real "comeback."

Songwriters Jule Styne and Sammy Cahn, who had been

toiling in the Hollywood gold mines for years, had written a musical for comedian Phil Silvers that they wanted to take to Broadway. Silvers was unable to do the show, but the writers had other stars, a producer—David Wolper—and a musical director—Max Meth. And they wanted Busby Berkeley to take charge of the entire production.

Champing at the bit, raring to go, Berkeley agreed.

With Jane Withers, the child star of films now grown up into a brash comedienne, as leading lady, the cast and production crew of *Glad to See You* gathered in New York early in October, 1944, to begin rehearsals.

Along with Busby Berkeley from Hollywood came his mother.

"The Buz that came East was not the Buz that I had known in the late 1920s," says Max Meth. "The brilliant guy of those days was gone. Nothing functioned. And all due to liquor—and his mother."

Throughout his career, Berkeley always depended on assistants to furnish his dancers with the actual steps they needed to get through eight or ten minutes of dancing. He has said himself that he never knew when an idea would strike him—while driving down the street or sitting in an office or on a park bench—but once he had the idea, he told his assistants the effect he wanted to create. In Hollywood, the prop departments would scurry at his command to create lighted violins, mobile pianos, a taxicab with a roof that Ruby Keeler could dance on. It might take him hours, his co-workers knew as they waited outside his Warners office, and it might take days or weeks, but Buz would eventually burst through the door with a brilliant idea, an *inspiration.*

They *always* came.

But this time it was different.

On *Glad to See You,* Berkeley's assistant was a young ballerina, Valerie Bettis. Several years later she would explode on Broadway to do a show-stopping "Tiger Lily" dance in *Inside U.S.A.,* but at the time she was a very confused young choreographer. "I am not supposed to do *all* the dances," she complained. "Buz said I was only going to do part of them." Trained in ballet, she was now called upon to choreograph tap routines and other unfamiliar kinds of dances.

Putting a Broadway musical together requires speed and flexibility on the part of directors, writers, musicians, and performers. Lines that do not get laughs where there should be laughs have to be tossed aside, and new lines have to be written. A song that does not work in the first act may have to be moved to the second act, and the story line has to be altered to accommodate it. A dance routine that is disappointing might have to be scrapped and a substitute number worked up in its place. And it all has to be done—literally—overnight.

There is little room on Broadway for a genius who needs *time*.

In Hollywood, Berkeley planned his routines minutely, putting each camera angle on paper long before the dancers were called in. Then he would take a blackboard and diagram the dances for the chorines and principals, much as a football coach outlines a new play for the team. Now, pressed by the dictates of time, in a territory that had grown unfamiliar to him during his fifteen-year stint in movieland, he found himself unable to think.

A story, perhaps apocryphal, is told by one of the people who worked on the show: "It seems that we had waited for weeks for him to come up with an idea for a number. Everyone was worried and getting more and more impatient. We were sitting around, twiddling our thumbs, beginning to feel scared. Finally, one of the writers said, 'Buz, we've got to do *something*.' And he said, 'Okay, I want all the dancers to move 'way back . . . 'way back upstage, right against the back wall.' And the writer said, 'But if they do that, the audience won't be able to see them.'

"And Buz held up his hands in front of his face, peering through the opening framed by his fingers and thumbs, like a Hollywood director, and said, 'Well, we'll just dolly in on 'em—like this.' "

Max Meth does not recall that precise situation. But he says that when Berkeley worked on *Glad to See You*, there was "just no trace" of his old executive ability. "He tried some things in rehearsal in New York that were all right for film technique, but when we got out of town and had to make changes, he just couldn't work. I knew the man when he was *on top*, and when I first heard from the producer about the show, I was very excited. 'If Buz is right,' I said, 'after the accident and his other problems, it's a brilliant move.' But, when we opened in Philadelphia, it was like being hit over the head—but *good!* We had meetings night after night after night, and just didn't know what to do."

Meth quit the show to work on Sigmund Romberg's *Up in Central Park*, after advising the producer of *Glad to See You* to close in Philadelphia rather than continue the tryout in Boston and lose more money. "Before I left," he says, "Buz was out of it and had flown back to the Coast."

The director took a souvenir from the production along with him: beautiful young chorus girl Myra Steffens, who had become the fourth Mrs. Busby Berkeley in a quiet Philadelphia ceremony in late November.

The marriage, following the pattern, lasted only a short time, a matter of months. Later, Berkeley was to say, "I always was a little impulsive in my marriages. Sometimes I wonder where those dolls are now. I was payin' off three and four at a time." Another time, he will tell an interviewer that he can't remember the names of all of his wives.

If the name of his fifth—twenty-two-year-old starlet Marge Pemberton, who married him in 1945—escapes him, the director can plead extenuating circumstances. His mother became seriously ill shortly after the newlyweds returned to California from Philadelphia. The diagnosis: terminal cancer.

Berkeley hired three nurses to attend the dying woman. But he sat day after day and night after night for months on end by her bedside, to be there when and if she needed him. "I worshiped her," he says matter-of-factly. When his mother died on June 14th, he looked at what he had left and saw only emptiness. His latest wife, weary of the endless hospital vigil, had left him two and a half months earlier, on April Fools' Day. The old creative fires that had burned brightly on Broadway were cold ashes now, and the film studios were getting along without him. Money was in short supply.

Busby Berkeley brooded about his troubles for a month— and then slashed his throat and wrists.

Bleeding from razor cuts on his neck, hands, and arms, the fifty-year-old Wonder Boy of Broadway and Hollywood remembered something he had meant to do. He reached for the telephone and carefully, painfully dialed the number of the *Los Angeles Times*. It was eight o'clock in the morning. The July sun had already climbed high into the California sky. Berkeley drew a deep breath and stared into the brightness outside his window. He heard the buzzing of the phone at the other end of the wire.

"*Times*," answered a still-sleepy operator at the newspaper.

"Lemme speak to the city editor, please," Berkeley said slowly, staring in fascination at the rivulets of blood that trickled from the hand holding the receiver . . . down . . . down along the arm to the elbow. He waited, thinking, watching the crimson streams ripple over the white skin. Perhaps some day he might stage a dance . . . a hundred girls in flaming red dresses swirling on a river of white silk . . . in Technicol—

"Yeh?" said a male voice in his ear.

Berkeley began speaking quickly now, growling in the deep voice that had barked commands at so many women . . . commands that were instantly obeyed.

"This is Busby Berkeley. I jus' wanted to thank you people at all the papers. You wrote won'erful stories about my mother's dea—" He could not say the word. "About my mother las' month. You were all very kind. I 'preciate that."

The distant voice sounded confused. "Yeh, well—uh, well, thanks. She got a lot of space, I guess. We—"

The director nodded. His arm now was almost solid red.

His neck felt warm and sticky. "She *deserved* it," he said very soberly. "I jus' wanted to say thanks. An' for all the other favors in the past."

"Okay, pal." There was a long pause. "That it?"

"Oh, one more thing. If you come out here, you'll find what's left of me." Berkeley hung up the telephone. He lay down to wait.

Within minutes a police car slid to a stop near the house. An ambulance screamed up behind it. Two detective lieutenants from the homicide bureau raced up the sidewalk and pounded on the door. An excited Japanese houseboy let them in and pointed to the bedroom where he had found the director only moments before.

"Come on in," Berkeley growled. "Come on in and watch the has-been die . . . I'm a has-been, and I know it. Come on in . . ."

The officers grabbed towels and wrapped them around Berkeley's arms and neck. They dragged him from the damp, crimson sheets, shoved him out to the street, half-carried him into the ambulance. He was mumbling now, only partly conscious:

"There's no comeback trail for a has-been, fellas. I can't seem to get myself straighten' out. Y'know how many times I been married? Fi' times, and ev'ry time it turns out wrong. An' last month, my mother—Y' read about it? It was in all the papers. Did I thank the papers? Oh, yeh . . ."

The ambulance raced to the emergency room at the Georgia Street Receiving Hospital. A team of astonished doctors began working over the director's huge, slumping figure. Although the slashes were both numerous and messy, they were little more than skin-deep. No stitches were taken to close the wounds, and several hours later, Berkeley was permitted to leave the hospital on the arm of Marge Pemberton, whom newspapers described as "his latest ex-wife."

When reporters hounded him for an explanation of his headline-making suicide attempt, he gave a rambling story of a wild night on the town, during which he drank heavily and asked a doctor for a sleeping pill. The combination of alcohol and medicine heightened his despondency, and brought on a state of mind where he was unsure of what he was doing.

It took nearly three years—and a stay in a psychological ward—for Berkeley to shake off the effects of the breakdown. And just as he seemed about to snap out of it, the headline that was all too familiar to Los Angeles readers blazed once more in the papers:

BUSBY BERKELEY JAILED ON DRUNK-DRIVER CHARGE
*Dance Director, Reportedly on Comeback*
*Trail After 13 Years of Misfortune, Held*

This time, two officers had seen the fifty-two-year-old king of the high-kickers run a stop sign in Culver City at sixty miles an hour. They chased him, hitting seventy miles per hour before his car was forced to the curb a half-mile further down the highway.

A friendly judge listened to Berkeley's explanation: He had driven to the beach "to relax," and realized "too late" that he had gone through the sign on his return drive. "My studio," he said, with tears in his eyes, "has given me another chance, and I'm proud of my record since my comeback."

The judge, however, took note that when Berkeley had been fined $10 three years earlier on a charge of public drunkenness, he had been warned: "You've been getting into too much trouble on account of liquor and you'd better change your drinking habits." Now, noting that Berkeley had failed to pass a sobriety test at the scene, he fined him $250 and took away his driver's license. The director entered a guilty plea to a charge of misdemeanor drunk driving, and left the courtroom in obvious relief. It might have been worse, he knew. What if he had hit someone?

He renewed his determination to succeed. Once more he *would* be on top. MGM gave him a shot at the dance routines for Gene Kelly, Frank Sinatra, Jules Munshin, and Esther Williams in *Take Me Out to the Ball Game*—and the film took *Photoplay's* Blue Ribbon Award for 1949. In the early

1950s, he created water ballet sequences for Esther Williams in *Million Dollar Mermaid* and *Easy to Love,* once more moving his camera high overhead as graceful swimmers circled to produce the same floral patterns in the water that his dancers had created on a stage so many years before in *Whoopee.*

In 1953, he worked with Bobby Van and Jane Powell on a picture called *Small Town Girl.* Van remembers the way things went:

"Buz sat on a set for—a week, maybe—and stared at the scene we were supposed to do a number in. And finally, he said, 'This is what we're goin' to do,' and he described this number to me. Then he said, 'Okay, go put it on.' We had assistants—my father was a choreographer who was helping me at that time—and we put the number on exactly as he described it. He told us where he wanted us to go, and the number came out *terrific.*

"He's a remarkable man. A very quiet man. And the reason he's quiet is that he's always thinking. He never talked much. But his mind is going all the time. He's somewhere else, not listening to what you say, thinking about what he wants to do. Some people are confused by that, and think he's day-dreaming, but he is thinking. *You* are tuned out when he's working something out."

After *Small Town Girl,* Hollywood more or less tuned Busby Berkeley out.

He worked on one film, *Rose Marie,* in 1954—but at the end of that year, he again made the kind of headlines that led some of his strongest supporters at MGM to give up on him. In November, an aunt of film juvenile Freddie Bartholomew sued Berkeley for nearly $11,000 she said he owed her for property damage and back rent. A month later, after two policemen found him sitting in a doorway on Santa Monica Boulevard, he was given the choice of paying a $50 fine or serving twenty days in jail. Berkeley, who pleaded guilty to a charge of "plain drunk," paid the fine.

The legendary director, now fifty-nine years old, dropped from the Hollywood scene. In 1962, some eight years later, he reappeared briefly to work on MGM's super-circus musical, *Jumbo*. But he was a long, long way from calling the shots as he once had done. This time around, he was a second-unit director—filming background scenes and less important parts of the picture, while the director and choreographer handled the major scenes with Doris Day, Jimmy Durante, and the other stars. He worked in a similar fashion on a low-budget picture called *Moonwatch*.

When his final film-making assignment was over, he returned to the small, pink stucco house in Palm Desert, near Palm Springs, and sat silently while his sixth wife, Etta, bustled about, feeding stray cats and fixing her husband the large breakfasts that his mother had always insisted he should eat. He had married Etta Dunn, the divorced wife of a friend, and a woman near his age, in 1958. An animated, heavy lady with motherly warmth, the new Mrs. Berkeley had no showbusiness background—and so she clucked delightedly over the clippings in the scrapbooks that her husband's mother had kept for him over the years.

The clucking grew louder in the mid-1960s when the tide of interest in the old Berkeley films brought new clippings for her to paste into the books herself. And, when the phone calls and letters requesting interviews and personal appearances started to pour in, she was overjoyed. The trips to film festivals throughout the United States and overseas meant new adventure—no, an entire *new era* in the Busby Berkeley career. Mrs. Berkeley watched her husband's usually dour expression turn, over the months, into a broad smile. She heard the growl that passed for a conversational tone occasionally break into a laugh. She was joyous—not because the trips and the applause and the obvious adoration were important to her, but because they were important to Buz.

Her husband basked in the acclaim, but tried his best to shrug it off. *He deserved it, didn't he?* After all he had been through, he deserved it. What other director's dances would be cheered forty years after they were committed to film? *Nobody's.* Who else would be singled out—when everyone thought he was all washed up—as a leading figure in the

Golden Age of "Camp" (whatever that was)? *Nobody.*

And he might *still* get a chance to use those ideas that were never worked into films. The one about the Negro cleaning women and the copper cuspidors, for example. Maybe . . . perhaps . . . if only all the publicity and the personal appearances and the film festivals brought *one good, solid offer* . . .

Busby Berkeley would show that he still had it.

He *did*. He *really* did.

And then, from New York, came a call asking if he would be interested in talking to Harry Rigby about a Broadway musical.

**9** As do many people who have found their way into "Society" by acquiring money, rather than through bloodlines, Mrs. Sam Rubin often takes pains to associate with the "right kind of people." Aristocratic people. Wealthy people. Artistic people. People who have "style."

Now, it is conceivable that had Cyma known the chaotic background of Busby Berkeley—a background of alcohol, near-suicide, death in triplicate, and more—she might have thought twice before hiring him, since he appeared to lack any element of "class." (His "suicide" failed; his automobile accident was extremely messy; "intoxication" is one thing, public drunkenness is quite another, and so on.)

> "I knew that Mr. Rigby initiated the production of 'No, No, Nanette' and that it was he who suggested my employment in the production."
>
> DONALD SADDLER

But Berkeley appealed to her for an important reason. He was a *bargain*.

In wanting to put *No, No, Nanette* on Broadway, bargains were frantically sought by Cyma. It wasn't only that her husband had agreed to put up a specified sum, roughly $300,000. But she also had her eye on every producer's goal of bringing in a show *under* budget, of turning out a hit for the least amount of money.

And what better way to save than to hire a living legend who was anxious to make a comeback? Of *course* Berkeley would work for less than he did in his heyday. Considerably less.

Cyma learned, too, that by hiring him to serve as both director and choreographer, she could get the work of two men for a single salary.

Under the contractual regulations of the Society of Stage Directors and Choreographers, the minimum fee that a director can work for is $2,000, plus 1 percent of the gross weekly receipts. Few directors of musicals work for the minimum, however. Most are "names"—Gower Champion, Jerome Robbins, Bob Fosse—and their fees run $5,000, $8,-000, or higher, along with a weekly take of between 2½ and

**103**

4½ percent of the gross. The minimum fee for a choreographer is $1,500, and he must get at least one-third of 1 percent of the weekly gross receipts. Like the directors, few choreographers with any reputation at all will work for minimum.

Busby Berkeley, though, was a "name" of a different kind. And he could be had—as *both* director and choreographer—for a reasonably low price. The contract he signed in February, 1970, called for him to be paid $5,000 as a fee—$500 upon signing, and $900 weekly for five weeks beginning on the first day of rehearsal. He was to get 2 percent of the weekly gross receipts until the show's initial investment cost was repaid, and 3 percent thereafter. Additionally, he was to receive $40 a day for expenses—a "per diem"—during the out-of-town tryouts.

Since the union stipulates that a director and choreographer each must receive a per diem of $25 when they are working on a show out of town, Cyma figured on a saving of $10 a day on that item alone.

A month after he signed and sent back his contract, Busby Berkeley and his wife flew to New York to meet Harry, Cyma, and the publicity people who would promote his return to Broadway. Signed on as General Press Representative for *Nanette* was Merle Debuskey, a solidly built, soft-spoken man in his late forties, who had handled the publicity for *Hallelujah, Baby,* and so knew Harry. Cyma had hired him briefly to work for the American Symphony, after first hiring—and subsequently firing—Harry's public-relations-man friend. The antithesis of the Hollywood idea of a press agent, Debuskey is affable, serious, and successfully makes producers feel he is more of a "consultant" than a "flack." His ability to argue politically on any side of a question has helped him reign as president of the Association of Theatrical Press Agents and Managers since 1967.

The publicist set up several interviews with newspapermen for Berkeley. All that was needed now was the great director himself. And Harry Rigby went one spring afternoon to Kennedy Airport to meet the Berkeleys' arriving jet.

Almost beside himself with excitement, Harry watched the big 707 roll to a stop. The loading ramp stretched out with a *whoosh* of air, and the plane's door swung open. A few passengers squeezed out, chattering happily. Then the familiar gray figure bulked in the doorway. Harry smiled broadly as Buz, with Etta clucking behind him, walked forward slowly, hand outstretched.

As he neared Harry, Berkeley seemed to notice that the hand he had extended to shake Harry's held his briefcase. He shuffled to a stop, leaned forward to place the case on the ground, and then, in one continuous motion, like a giant gray walrus sliding off a rock into the water, Berkeley pitched slowly forward to the ground.

The sound of his heavy head hitting the tiled floor echoed up and down the corridor. Harry's mouth gasped open, but already Etta was at her husband's side, trying to lift his seemingly boneless body.

"He's all right," she said quickly. "He's all right. He has a spastic colon, and he took a painkiller on the plane. It just made him dizzy." She was tugging at Berkeley's arm, and he was trying to lift himself. Now Harry was on the other side, lifting, too. And Berkeley was up, waving an arm and muttering, "I'm all right, I'm all right," while a large blue bruise darkened on his forehead and a trickle of blood ran from a cut across the bridge of his nose.

An hour later, when Sam and Cyma arrived at the Algonquin Hotel to meet the famed director for the first time, they listened sympathetically to the story of his untimely fall. But there was a glint of suspicion in Cyma's eyes as she studied the bruised face. Hadn't she heard somewhere about a "drinking problem"?

When Berkeley and Debuskey met a *New York Times* reporter in the hotel lobby the following afternoon, the director appeared to be his old self again—that "ready to go" dynamo whom writer William Murray had seen just a year earlier. In his article the next day, the *Times* man wrote: "Exuding confidence that he would be able to knock 'em dead again, Mr. Berkeley settled deeply into a maroon sofa in the lobby. . . ."

Merle Debuskey remembers that the director settled so deeply into the cushions that he almost disappeared from sight, and when the interview ended the other two men had to pull him to his feet.

The readers of the *Times*, however, who gazed at a four-column photograph of Berkeley, hat perched jauntily on his head, smiling in a Times Square setting, read this: "Age doesn't mean anything to me. I claim that a person doesn't grow old by living a certain number of years; a person grows old by deserting his ideals. In my book, you're as young as your faith, and as old as your doubt. You're as young as your self confidence, and as old as your despair."

"By these non-linear tests," the reporter wrote, "Mr. Berkeley put his own age at 'about 35 or 40.' "

Although he was weary from a series of interviews, Berkeley obligingly trekked downtown the next afternoon to pose for pictures with Cyma's daughter, Loni, who was appearing in the Off-Broadway production of *Dames at Sea*. In the part of "Ruby," based on the understudy-turned-star character of all the Ruby Keeler pictures, youthful Loni—and the aged director—seemed a "natural" for publicity. Then, after a brief production meeting in which it was decided the show would go into rehearsal in mid-September, Buz and Etta rushed to Kennedy for a return trip to the warmth and peace of Palm Desert.

Behind them, in the chill of March in Manhattan, they left a worried Cyma Rubin.

"My reaction to meeting Berkeley," she said, "was *worse* than terror. And at that point I had not invested too much money."

The Berkeleys' California-bound jet was still taxiing down the runway, states Cyma, when she began talking hurriedly to Harry. "I told him, 'It's a mistake. Maybe we can use his *name*—and that's interesting at this time. But it's a total mistake. Harry, this is a sick man. He's too old, and—' "

Harry, who had signed Berkeley's contract as president of Rubin & Rigby Productions, is said to have lifted a reassuring hand. " 'Don't worry,' he told me," says Cyma. " 'I'll get it out of him. Etta promised—'

" 'Get it out of him? *She* promised? Why, she would put him on the *rack* if she thought she'd get five cents out of him! She's just using him to get what she can get.' I said, 'Harry, this man *can't* do a Broadway show!'

"Then he said, 'So we'll get a very good assistant director. We'll get a very good assistant choreographer.' "

Cyma claims that the confident tone in Harry's voice calmed her. It sounded good. After all, Harry had worked on a half-dozen shows. This was her *first*. Maybe this was the way things were done. And Berkeley's contract *did* specify that he could have two assistants—who would not share in the gross receipts, but would be on straight salary.

But several months later, after Harry and Raoul Pène du Bois had made a trip to Palm Desert to show Berkeley the models of the musical's three sets, Cyma asked about the assistant choreographer Harry had discovered on the Coast.

"He was someone that Buster recommended," says Harry, "and had staged a revival of a musical with Bobby Van and Helen Gallagher. He helped Buz and myself with the chorus auditions, showing the girls the steps and everything. But when I told him some of my ideas for dance numbers, and realized that he didn't have anything to add—well, I began to think we'd better get a *real* choreographer." Then, with a cackle of a laugh, he adds, "Heavens, I'm not one."

Cyma recalls it somewhat differently. " 'He's *great*,' Harry told me. 'He's done all kinds of television work and blah-blah-blah.' So I told Harry I wanted to hear some ideas of this guy's on the phone. 'Call him up,' I said, 'and tell him I want to know what he's going to do.' "

Shortly afterward, Cyma was on the long-distance line to California, listening to a man describe a dance routine under the apparent handicap of not being able to illustrate it with his body, hands, or feet. "It went something like this," Cyma says. "He said, 'This place in the show—well, what we'll do, instead of having Ruby do it in one, she comes out with Bobby—and they look at each other, and they each

**107**

do a little thing, and Bobby says, "Take it, Ruby," and that's it.'

"I said, 'Oh, mygawd, it's all over. Get that sonuvabitch out of here! It's all over.' And that's when I knew I had to get myself out, and I started looking for a choreographer."

As Cyma tells it, she consulted her daughter's library of theatrical books, and spent an entire night writing down the name of every musical that had been produced on Broadway since 1950. She listed them on a chart, along with the name of the choreographer on each show, and the period in which it took place.

"I figured that someone who had done a show in the last twenty years would still be alive and able to work," she says. When she finished the chart, she studied it, looking for the one man who would be most suited to direct a 1920s musical that starred a tap-dancer.

Her "logical" choice was Donald Saddler, a ballet-trained choreographer whose primary credits were: *Wonderful Town*, a show about 1930s Greenwich Village life; *Shangri-La*, a musical that took place in the Himalayan mountains; *Milk and Honey*, about life in an Israeli kibbutz; and *Wish You Were Here*, a 1950s story of young love in a Catskill resort.

"It all added up to one man," notes Cyma, shrugging to show just how simple it was. "Saddler."

Saddler, who does not tap-dance, also happened to have once worked with Harry Rigby as choreographer on *John Murray Anderson's Almanac*.

Nevertheless, says Cyma, when she mentioned to Raoul Pène du Bois that she thought Saddler would be right for *Nanette*, Raoul said that Harry would not want him. "*I've* been thinking about him for six months," Raoul is supposed to have answered, "but Harry won't like the idea." Cyma says that she met that possibility head-on.

"I called Harry up at eight o'clock in the morning, and I said, 'Harry, I want Donald Saddler.' And he said, 'Awwrrrnotdonaldsaddler' "—she makes the tape-recorder-racing-backward sound— "and I said, 'Harry, I don't give a

108

shit what you want at this point! It's *my* money, and I'm going to close the fucking checkbook, Harry! Because going the way you're going, we are going no place.' "

The problem, she points out, was that she did not want to call Donald Saddler herself. "I felt very strange. I was brand-new, and I felt like an interloper. I didn't feel like I had the courage—" She pauses, thinking it over, then hurries on, confidently. "Oh, I *could* have done it, but I didn't think it was becoming of a strange lady to call up and say, 'I want you, Donald Saddler.' " And so, says Cyma, Harry was delegated to make the call.

"Do you know," she asks in wide-eyed amazement, "until two months ago, Saddler thought *Harry* was responsible for bringing him into the show?"

There was another problem in hiring a *choreographer* to "assist" Berkeley, rather than two assistants agreed upon previously. Saddler had to be paid according to the union regulations. As a choreographer of some repute, he refused to work for minimum—and ended up getting more than double the lowest fee, plus 1 percent of the weekly gross, and the standard $25 per diem out of town. In addition, *he* needed assistants—a tap-dance specialist, and another dancer to work on the nontapping routines. At $200 and $300 a week apiece, and their own per diem, one thing was apparent:

The Berkeley "bargain" was shrinking all the time.

The search for a choreographer consumed several frantic weeks in the sizzling heat of August in New York, but at last it looked as if things were really moving. Cyma and Harry could look at the growing stack of contracts that had been signed, and realize that the show would go on. In addition to the principals, other people—understudies, orchestrators, music copyists, a lighting director—were signed and waiting to be called. Harry Rigby flew to the Coast, and with Berkeley and the choreographer whom Cyma subsequently vetoed, auditioned dozens of West Coast beauties for chorus jobs. Five girls, who evidently met Berkeley's criterion that they must be "gorgeous, not just beautiful," were signed and furnished with plane tickets to New York. Meanwhile, Cyma and a friend in the fashion world began laying an elaborate promotional scheme to reap profits from apparel lines based on "the *Nanette* look."

The days were busy, and so were the nights. The "three-way act" continued giving auditions—but not for prospective backers. This time, the producers were trying to persuade theater owners to give them a home for *Nanette* on Broadway. Buster at the piano, Loni belting out the songs, and Cyma and Harry and Raoul talking up the miracle that would soon be onstage—all were selling, but the theater owners were not buying.

Theater owners generally are as tough and hard-headed as heavyweight champion Joe Frazier. They control a piece of real estate that costs them roughly $100,000 a year in taxes alone, just sitting empty. At the same time, they know they can make around $30,000 a week in rent if their house contains a big musical hit. The problem is to pick the hits from the flops. If an owner, forced to choose between two prospective tenants, accepts a show that opens and closes the same night, he is doubly reminded of his mistake for the rest of the season: Each evening around 7:15, just a few minutes before "magic time" on Broadway, he has only to look up at the darkened marquee of his own house, and the empty sidewalk beneath it, to realize he is losing money. Then, he can glance down the street where a competitive owner has crowds before his open doors, and a marquee that flashes in brilliant lights the name of the "other" show, the one that hit big.

For the producers of a musical, finding the "right" house is important. Some places are too big for an intimate musical. Some are too small. Some, like the Billy Rose Theater on West 41st Street or the Martin Beck on the "wrong" side of Eighth Avenue, are out of the main theater district and might be considered less attractive.

When the Rubin-Rigby project was unfolded before the half-closed eyes of a number of theater owners, the reactions were much the same as when it was presented to potential backers:

"Did you say *Ruby Keeler?*" . . . "Hey, Sol, guess what I had in my office today? These people came in and actually *auditioned*—you won't believe this—they actually auditioned 'Tea for Two'! Yeh, 'Tea for Two.' No, not a new one—the same old song." . . . "*Busby Berkeley?* Is he still around? Is he still *alive?*"

Perhaps a dozen Broadway houses can accommodate a musical, which requires a large stage, an orchestra pit, and sufficient mechanical equipment and backstage space to handle the scenery. Everywhere, owners of such houses listened to the producers plead that *Nanette* should be given room at the inn, and then they checked their computerlike memories on what other shows would need space come fall.

There would be Danny Kaye in Richard Rodgers' new one, *Two by Two*. That one could not miss, and would be paying rent for years.

There would be *Ari*, a musical version of *Exodus*. What with New York's Jewish theatergoers (look what they did for *Fiddler* and *Milk and Honey!*), it was a sure thing.

There would be *The Rothschilds*, by the guys that wrote *Fiddler*, and it would get the Jewish crowd, too.

And *Lovely Ladies, Kind Gentlemen,* a musical version of *Teahouse of the August Moon*, with Kenneth Nelson, who was raved over in *Boys in the Band*. It looked good.

And there were others: *Follies;* a new show by Alan Jay Lerner called *Lolita, My Love*, from the famed Nabokov story; and Gower Champion's *Prettybelle* with Angela Lansbury.

Looking up from their lists, the theater owners put it bluntly. Almost *anything*, they said, had a chance of running longer (and paying more rent) than the revival of a 1924 musical with its creaking stars and septuagenarian director. Sure, there was interest in nostalgia, and there had been recent revivals on Broadway of *Three Men on a Horse, Room Service*, and *Harvey*, but only a limited audience turned out for them. The widely quoted odds on a successful revival of an old show are a thousand to one—and few theater owners thought *Nanette* could beat them.

Eventually, Cyma and Harry were offered a musty old

house just off the Main Stem, whose owner figured he would have trouble selling it to more experienced, knowledgeable producers. Another promised the use of a house that was too large for the "intimate" show. Other owners, however, turned *Nanette* down cold, preferring to wait until other showmen came shopping. "Now, of course," they said, "if I book *Ari* or *The Rothschilds* or *Lovely Ladies* and it closes quickly, then you might bring your show in next . . ."

*Nanette* could not find a suitable Broadway home. It would have to wait until one of the musicals running in New York—shows like *Hello, Dolly, Man of La Mancha* or *Fiddler*, for example—closed and vacated a theater, or it would have to hope and pray that one of the new musicals coming into town was a quick bomb. Meanwhile, the cast and crew would cool its heels out of town, performing for whatever audiences they might find. As Farber writes with considerable understatement in *Producing on Broadway:* "It is possible for a show to wait around for one or two months for a theater to open up. This could be expensive."

The lack of confidence expressed by New York theater owners was echoed by counterparts in other cities. When General Manager Jack Yorke began lining up the tryout tour for *No, No, Nanette*, he reported back to Cyma and Harry with depressing news. Owners in Boston, Toronto, and Baltimore would give *Nanette* only two weeks in their theaters. A friendlier owner in Philadelphia would agree to a three-week deal, and, if more out-of-town time was needed while the show waited for a New York house to open up, several weeks could be spent in Washington, D.C.

Moving *Nanette* five times—at a cost of perhaps $40,000 each time—was obviously not the most economical way to spend Sam Rubin's money. Still, contracts had to be signed. The schedule called for an opening in Boston on Monday, November 1st. Two weeks later, Toronto would see the show. Two weeks more, and Philadelphians would get their chance. Three weeks, and on to Baltimore. Two weeks, and Washington. And then . . . *maybe* . . . New York . . . somewhere . . . sometime.

The producers checked their calendar. The November 1st opening meant that if six weeks were allowed for rehearsals —standard for a musical—they should get things under way around September 15th. The date seemed logical. After all, the director, choreographer, and cast were ready to go; costume and set designs were in the works; the theatrical advertising agency of Blaine-Thompson Company, Inc., was working on a campaign to sell tickets.

Importantly, too, the publicity mill was grinding. Merle Debuskey himself had marginal—if any—faith in the production, and preferred to concentrate his attention on such other shows in his office as Philip Rose's musical, *Purlie,* and a new John Guare play, *House of Blue Leaves,* produced by the son of columnist Leonard Lyons. Add to that a series of disputes that he had with Cyma Rubin over publicity for the American Symphony, and Debuskey decided to assign the day-by-day chores on *Nanette* to a new member of the press agents' union. M. J. Boyer, an attractive and enthusiastic blonde in her late twenties, was named press representative on the show—her first Broadway-bound musical—and she began cranking out news releases.

Each week throughout the summer, readers of the *Times,* the *Daily News,* and other papers learned that Ruby Keeler was set for a comeback in *No, No, Nanette* . . . that Helen Gallagher would dance again in *No, No, Nanette* . . . that a new young star, Carole Demas, would play Nanette in *No, No, Nanette* . . . that Hiram Sherman would be back on Broadway in *No, No, Nanette* . . . that Patsy Kelly was coming in from Hollywood to do *No, No, Nanette* . . . that Bobby Van would return to the New York stage after seventeen years for *No, No, Nanette* . . . that Busby Berkeley would hold auditions shortly for chorus girls "who are gorgeous, not just beautiful" for *No, No, Nanette* . . . and on, and on, and on.

Then, with the start of rehearsals only a month away, Cyma and Harry came to a frightening realization.

They had no script of *No, No, Nanette.*

Or, rather, they had *two*—both useless.

**10** The souvenir booklet for *No, No, Nanette* at the 46th Street Theater in New York— which sells, by dictate of Cyma Rubin, for the unusually high price of $2—includes some skillfully written notes by theatrical historian Miles Kreuger on "the year *No, No, Nanette* was born." He points out that 1925, when the show reached Broadway, "was one of those in-between years." The Roaring Twenties were only beginning to growl. One major war was far behind, another far in the future.

"It was a world of comfortable moderation," writes Kreuger, "with a thriving economy and a thoroughly tedious administration by Calvin Coolidge." And, in such a time, the audiences who could easily afford the $2 and $3 tickets for *Nanette* at the Globe Theater were content to sit in comfortable tedium for more than three hours while the convoluted script meandered on its way.

> "Without Bert Shevelove, there is no 'No, No, Nanette'—and I want to say that for all tape recorders."
>
> **BUSTER DAVIS**

Take the opening scene, for example. As written by Otto Harbach and Frank Mandel, it went like this. Pauline, the maid, is discovered using a vacuum to gather sheets of newspaper off the floor of the Smith mansion. The doorbell rings. Pauline, muttering, "Darn that bell," goes off to answer it and admits two girls who ask if "Miss Nanette" is home. Befuddled, the maid bumbles around the stage before going off to answer the door a second time. As she leaves, she warns the visitors to watch out for a chair with a broken leg and complains that she spends "so much time picking up the *Daily News*, I never get to read it." Shaking their heads, the two chorus girls discuss the "funny maid" and the fact that Mrs. Smith won't pay for a good one.

And at this point, another half-dozen young flappers enter and break into the show's opening number. It is called "Flappers Are We," and it tells the audience that the girls are—in case no one has guessed—flappers.

The world of 1925 *had* to be much slower, much more

lethargic than the world of 1970. Otherwise, audiences would have grown restless at such a scene—a scene that contributes absolutely nothing toward moving the show along. What did the first dozen lines of the original script tell anyone? They revealed the totally unimportant character names—"Miss Mays" and "Miss Webb"—of two chorus girls. They showed that Pauline, who resents answering the bell, "thinks" Miss Nanette is at home and, in the space of two lines, forgets whom the callers want to see. The one thing theatergoers did learn is that Mrs. Smith is so miserly she will not pay for efficient household help.

Perhaps Pauline's antics drew a laugh or two, but the entire little scene seems to have been written only to allow latecomers to get settled in their seats before the opening chorus. That song, by the way, serves much the same purpose, and similarly has nothing to do with the characters or the plot line of *No, No, Nanette*. Only *after* the song did the 1925 audiences meet the philandering husband, the suspicious wife, the gold diggers, the obstreperous young ward and her strait-laced boyfriend, and the several other principals in the story.

With very few exceptions, the lackadaisical and repetitious musical comedy "book" was the accepted thing for the first forty-two years of the twentieth century. Then, in 1943, Rodgers and Hammerstein shattered the mold with *Oklahoma!* Virtually overnight, audiences became attuned to literate, intelligent books, in which the songs helped to move the story along, because the tight script called for each song to be a continuation of it rather than an interruption.

The original script of *No, No, Nanette* runs to 120 pages, while most recent Broadway musicals have typescripts of well under 100 pages, and 80 can make for a long evening in the theater. But Cyma and Harry knew the problem, and had taken steps to solve it. In March, Harry's friend Charles Gaynor had begun rewriting the original script—cutting it—and adding new lyrics to the unpublished Youmans melodies. His contract called for payment of $1,000 monthly for four months against 1 percent of the gross, and the producers licked their lips in anticipation as the months wore on, the money went out, and the script came in.

Eagerly, they turned to page one, Act One. Again, Pauline, the maid, was busy with the vacuum. And the opening of *No, No, Nanette*, with "book revisions and additional lyrics by Charles Gaynor," read almost exactly like the original, right up to the point where, once again, the girls break into song—a different song this time, but with the same idea. It informs the audience that the girls are up-to-date young ladies whose role in life is to be "gay, gay, gay." At the end of the number, Pauline returns to ram the point home. "Darn little flappers," she says.

Obviously something was wrong somewhere. The new, *tighter* book had a longer and no more informative opening scene than the one in the forty-five-year-old original script.

True, there were new lyrics in place of old ones. And the new script *was* a dozen or so pages shorter than the original —but it had been typed on a machine that had a smaller typeface. In the 1925 version, the chorus girl had commented, "What a funny maid." In the new version, she said, "What a peculiar maid." At one point in the original, the maid had drawn a laugh by introducing herself with a haughty, "I'm Pauline—from Peoria," and the line had probably tickled H. H. Frazee, who hailed from the Illinois town. In Gaynor's rewrite, the line read, "I'm Pauline—from Punxitawney."

Harry Rigby has an explanation for what happened. "Charlie is such a purist," he says, "and such a *historrrian* that he just couldn't bring himself to cut the script enough. Now, who knows? Maybe his approach was right. But I was worried about it. It seemed to me that the show wasn't properly routined, and the scenes didn't go *fast* enough."

Author Gaynor, reluctant to comment on any dissension over his work, says only, "There was a difference of opinion over the approach to be used." But he appears to have labored under a handicap common to numerous adapters: an overwhelming admiration for the original material. Such passion frequently leads to an effort to preserve as much of the original as possible, so that present-day audiences will appreciate it for what it *was*, not what it has become. At times, the traditionalists become adamant in their views. Miles Kreuger, for example, who wrote the record album liner notes and the souvenir booklet for *Nanette*, had not seen the new production some six months after it opened for fear that it might run counter to his impressions of earlier versions. ("There is also the fact that Mrs. Rubin would not pay $150 for extra work I did," he adds, "and I wouldn't give her the satisfaction of attending the show.")

Harry Rigby was reluctant to press his friend Gaynor for an extensive rewrite. Cyma, puzzling whether "a peculiar maid" was better than "a funny maid," and whether Punxitawney was funnier than Peoria, was unsure of what to do, other than ask for the return of her $4,000 advance. (Her lawyers subsequently did. Gaynor's advised him to ignore the request.) Buster Davis, however, decided to seek help elsewhere.

He turned to an old friend, Burt Shevelove.

Although Shevelove lives in London, he is a frequent visitor to the United States, where he works regularly in television and on Broadway. He directed *Hallelujah, Baby,* on which he worked with Buster and Harry, but he is perhaps best known in the theater as the originator and co-author of the 1962 musical comedy hit, *A Funny Thing Happened on the Way to the Forum*. Composer-lyricist Stephen Sondheim, who wrote the score for *Forum* (and later for *Company* and *Follies*), considers Shevelove an excellent lyricist in addition to his book-writing and directing talents.

When Buster Davis sought him out, the burly, bearded Shevelove was recuperating in a New York hospital after having his blood "thinned out" to correct a medical condition. Lying in bed or pacing the hospital corridors, the fifty-five-year-old writer-director had been tinkering with ideas for a musical version of a 1928 play, Philip Barry's *Holiday*, that would use unpublished Cole Porter melodies. "The show never came off," he says, "but I was steeped in nostalgia when Buster came in to see me."

Perched on an antique sofa in his Algonquin Hotel suite, Shevelove recalls the meeting. (But first he pushes back the floppy sleeves of his dressing gown and washes down a Vitamin C tablet with orange juice. "I've been taking these for three years," he says offhandedly, "and I haven't had a cold since.") He begins speaking slowly, choosing his words with uncharacteristic care:

"Buster told me that he had been working on this project with Cyma and Harry, and he had thought at one time it had a good chance. Now it looked as if it had no chance at all. He asked me to read the script, which I did. It was interminable.

"Then he showed me the original 1925 script, which *also* was interminable—but a little shorter than the one they planned to go into rehearsal with. The new script had some added songs, and lead-ins to the songs, that just made it longer."

He finished his glass of juice, nodding thoughtfully. "I told Buster that I thought there was the book of a modern musical lurking within the ponderous original script, but that it would take a lot of work to get it out."

Buster Davis saw that his friend—"We have a lot of mutual respect for each other," notes Shevelove—was bored with the invalid routine and anxious to get to work again. He told Harry, who hurried to the hospital to talk over some ideas of what might be done. Then, Cyma came calling with Buster for an exploratory meeting. At this point, Shevelove says that his business agent stepped into the picture. He set a price for his client's services as a script adapter. The price was not low.

"Negotiations broke down," Shevelove says matter-of-factly, "and I thought no more about it." There could have been a feeling on the part of the producers, he notes, "that since most musical books in 1925 were bad anyway, why spend money to get a good one?" He smiles, recalling the time he directed a show that had a particularly bad opening number. "I complained to the producer, who said, 'But *Bells Are Ringing* has a bad opening number—and look what a hit it is!'"

Cyma and Harry and Buster were not so positive that *No, No, Nanette* would succeed in spite of its book. But time was getting short. It was already August, and in a few weeks Berkeley and Keeler and the rest of the company would arrive to begin rehearsals. Even if a new writer was hired, was there time for him to come up with a script? Perhaps Gaynor's version could be worked with, trimmed and improved during the six weeks of rehearsal. Was there any guarantee that a new adaptation by Shevelove might be better, Cyma wanted to know. *Nanette* already was shaping up as the laugh of Broadway, with its doddering director, its tap-dancing grandmother as star, and its inability to find a theater to play in. Could it take the chance of producing total hysteria by calling in a "script doctor" *who worked from a hospital bed?*

And the money. The money. How much had to go out before any started to come in? Sam Rubin had always been a businessman, not a spendthrift. In the museumlike townhouse off Central Park, the family dog—a huge, nervous animal called Philippe—began to sense tremors of panic. Morning after morning, the wary hound watched as Cyma rose before seven, dressed in her complete riding habit, and sped out the front door. Around the park's bridle paths she raced her saddle horse, Dondi, slashing him angrily with her crop if he showed the least sign of independence.

The decision was made. Gaynor was ordered to rewrite the script, and quickly. The author, who "saw the original *Nanette* many times in 1925, when I was a kid in high school—and loved it," went back to the typewriter. He produced a second version. Harry reported to him that Cyma thought it was "a million times better" than the first one. But was it good enough?

"Look," Cyma says today, bitterly, "we have Ruby Keeler coming back to Broadway after forty years, and the entrance he wrote for her has her coming onstage hidden behind two huge bags of groceries. They take the groceries away, and there's Ruby. That's the *star's* entrance? I said, 'Is he out of his mind?'"

In actuality, a reading of Gaynor's script shows that it

calls for Pauline, the maid, to carry on the bags of groceries, with Sue—played by Ruby Keeler—coming on a moment later, empty-handed and smiling at the group of flappers waiting expectantly to meet her. But it wasn't only Ruby's initial appearance that made Cyma unhappy. "I made Gaynor sit through a reading—Buster played all the parts— and he agreed that it would run until 2:16 in the morning," she says with just a hint of hyperbole.

Time, time was running out.

Designer Raoul Pène du Bois had been working up costume sketches for months, going only on the general outline of the original *Nanette* book. Buster Davis and the orchestrators were sketching musical arrangements, without knowing for certain which songs would be in the final script and which would be "cut." Choreographer Donald Saddler was dreaming up ideas for dances, mindful of the possibility that the show might not have a place for them.

The book of the musical, everyone timorously agreed, could be adjusted as rehearsals went on. After all, most new shows get entire rewrites—whole new acts, sometimes—during their out-of-town tryouts. "Don't worry," Harry Rigby told his co-workers, smiling and seeming to exude confidence from every pore of his lanky frame. "When Buz gets here, he'll straighten everything out."

The legendary Berkeley was due in New York late in August, to choose the final members of the *Nanette* chorus. Before he arrived, much of the work was to have been done for him. Saddler, Davis, Cyma, and Harry had already sat through a series of "cattle calls"—chorus auditions—and had selected a number of performers.

"Trying out" for a Broadway musical can seem a degrading thing for performers—particularly those who have long lists of professional credits in other shows, TV, and films. Still, a call for chorus boys or girls brings out dozens, perhaps hundreds, of applicants who are eager to compete for a job that is strenuous, routine, and unglamorous. The pay is about $175 for a six-day week, four hours a night on Monday through Saturday, an extra four hours for each matinée on Wednesday and Saturday afternoon. If auditions are grueling for performers, they are not much easier on producers who, under Actors Equity rules, must see and hear any and all people who want to show their talents—which frequently are limited. The producers must rent a theater or studio for the auditions. They must pay for a pianist. And they must at least *appear* to be paying attention.

To prevent mob scenes, as well as an eternity in the gloom of an empty theater, producers spread the wearisome audition chores over several days. They call Equity members first, looking for professional dancing boys at one time, dancing girls at another, and for singing boys and singing girls at other times. Then, in the faint hope that a fresh new face will be uncovered, "open calls" are scheduled, at which non-Equity people may appear. At these calls, a cherubic singer-dancer barely out of high school might be followed by an over-age, overweight soprano from a "little theater" group in Brooklyn. In a bare rehearsal hall or semi-dark theater, the production people who are impatient to get their show on the road sit for hours as the parade of willing, eager, and all-too-often-untalented performers passes by.

Late in July, Harry had joined Berkeley in Hollywood to choose a half-dozen girls from some forty who tapped their toes and waved their hips to the accompaniment of "That's Entertainment" on a cheap upright. Now, in New York, at the Equity calls, the process was to be repeated. Out of the hot summer sun would come the "gypsies"—dancers who move from show to show, working year after year in the choruses behind the stars—in blue jeans and leotards, in dirty sneakers and ballet slippers. Crowded into the cramped backstage area of an unused theater, the singers and dancers would wait . . . and wait . . . and wait while the audition procedure followed a familiar pattern.

A tall young baritone's name is called by a disinterested man with a clipboard. The singer nervously walks to the front of the stage and peers into the dark rows of seats. Halfway back, some shadowy figures are indifferently carrying on a whispered conversation. He launches into his song, hoping that he will not hear a shouted "Thank you" before he has finished eight bars. He does. He smiles feebly into the darkness and stumbles offstage, outside, blinking in the sunlight. At the newstand on the corner he buys a copy of *Show Business* to see which other musicals are auditioning soon.

Dancers get even less opportunity. They are trotted out in groups of eight girls or boys at a time. A sweating director demonstrates a few steps. The group attempts to duplicate the brief routine. "The girl in the blue," says a voice from the rear of the empty theater. "The others—thank you." And the girl in the blue moves to join a small, waiting group at the side of the stage, while the rejects shrug their shoulders, slip on their street shoes, and move out silently past the next group waiting to be called onstage.

Everyone knows that directors have "favorites," and that "It's-who-you-know" is terribly, terribly important. In the highly homosexual world of the theater, male singers and dancers who have pleased a producer or director in a past show can count on working with him in future shows. Unless, of course, the producer and director are the kind who are always on the lookout for fresh, young faces. And, of course, they always are.

Where chorus girls are concerned, experience and appearance are primary assets, much more so than sexual prowess. It is not that the tales of the "casting couch" are myths—but the large number of homosexuals in the theatrical world works against too many females being desired for their horizontal talents. And, where a "straight" producer or director *is* interested in feminine companionship, the sheer length of the chorus line often precludes him from getting around to all of its members. A smart girl, however, knows that it does not hurt to be friendly toward each member of the production team—if only in a professional sense. The competition on Broadway for a job is fierce, the odds against getting one are astronomical, and it sometimes takes a lot more than talent to emerge as a winner.

One of the early winners who landed a job in the chorus of *No, No, Nanette* was a wide-mouthed, dark-eyed redhead named Joanne Lotsko. A native of New Jersey, she had sung and danced in three companies of *Mame,* and had first auditioned for Buster Davis in midsummer when he was looking for girls to play the three gold diggers. When she did not get a principal role, she returned for a chorus call. "Buster kept me," she says excitedly, "and then I danced for Cyma and Harry. And they just *flipped.* I could sing and dance, and I had the look and the figure and *everything.* They decided on me right away."

She pauses, remembering how wonderful it all was at first, and then smiles tight-lipped as she shakes her head. "I was perfect." By signing her contract the first week in July, Joanne became the first of twenty-one girls to be hired for the chorus of *No, No, Nanette.*

One of the first of thirteen men hired was a tall, ramrod-straight singer whose trained voice booms loudly in a chorus, but who speaks in soft, modulated tones offstage. "I was ill when they had the Equity call for male singers," says John Roach, "and so I went to the open call later. Buster Davis had done the vocal arrangements for *Half a Sixpence,* and I had gone out with the bus-and-truck touring company of the show, so he had heard me sing before. When he saw me, he said, 'Oh, I *hoped* that you would come.' He didn't remember my name, but he remembered me. So, a large group of people sang, and I sang, and he said he would call me back. And I was delighted.

"A week or two later, I was called back. This time, there was no singing. It was to see my tap dancing. I had never studied tap, and I told them that, but they said I could manage it—and they hired me."

So far as Busby Berkeley was concerned, there was only one category of chorus people to worry about: "Gorgeous girls." In his heyday he had never been concerned with a girl's dancing ability. Valerie Bettis recalls that when she was frantically trying to dream up a dozen different dance routines for *Glad to See You* in 1944, Berkeley gave her this advice: "Just have the girls do one step over and over until they applaud."

In March, on his first production meeting trip to New

York, the director had told the *Times* that there are millions of pretty girls in the world, and a plentiful supply of beautiful girls, but gorgeous ones are rare. He boasted of once having to audition 723 girls for a picture before settling on three who stood out. In late July, he told a *Newsweek* reporter at the Hollywood auditions his criterion for finding the type of girl he needs for a show: "Beautiful eyes. I can picture a girl through her eyes. They mirror the soul."

When the ponderous figure of Busby Berkeley stepped slowly off a Los Angeles-to-New York flight at the end of August to begin searching for "24 girls who are not just beautiful, but gorgeous"—in the words of M. J. Boyer's press release, which had been sped to newspapers, magazines, TV and radio stations—Buster Davis, Donald Saddler, and Cyma and Harry already had decided on a number of performers. Saddler, for example, had contacted a dancing school in Miami, where he once served as a guest instructor, and asked any interested students there to come to New York for auditions. Three girls, who were members of the June Taylor dancers on Jackie Gleason's television show, took up the offer. All three—one is Duke Ellington's granddaughter, Mercedes Ellington—were signed for *Nanette*. Berkeley might want gorgeous girls, but Saddler wanted dancers, and Davis wanted singers.

The Ambassador Theater on Tuesday, September 1st, was more of an audition riot scene than ever when *Nanette* held its heavily publicized open call for girl dancers. Because Busby Berkeley was back now, *really* back on Broadway for the first time in forty years, the news media came out in force. Backstage, some two hundred-odd girls laced the ribbons on their tap shoes and limbered up tensely as they waited to be called. Many had seen the old Ruby Keeler-Dick Powell films on television and at local movie houses. They knew the name, Busby Berkeley. But what was he like?

\* \* \*

In the front row, dead center, in the darkened theater, Busby Berkeley sits slouched in the dark blue suit that perpetually folds limply around his bulky body. The blue hat worn indoors and out seems a weight on the heavily lined face, and the bulging nose only half conceals the glowering eyes and thick lips set in a rigid, unsmiling line. Two radio interviewers have been carefully allotted a few precious minutes with "Buz" by Miss Boyer, who consults a turquoise note pad to see who gets to talk to him next. The interviewers sit, one on each side of the aged man, as if they are afraid he might jump up and escape. To make doubly sure he does not, they have draped wires around his neck, leading to microphones and tape recorders.

In groups of two dozen girls at a time, the would-be chorus members are lined up on stage. An energetic, balding little man with a towel over one shoulder to wipe his perspiring face puts each group through a few basic tap steps. Berkeley half-looks at the dancers, and the voice that growls answers to his interviewers sounds both bored and tired.

A young woman from Associated Press gets a nod from the publicity girl; her turn has come, as if she had waited with a numbered ticket at a bakery counter. Pencil in hand, she leans over Berkeley and asks a question. He mumbles a reply. Then his voice barks out toward the back of the dark theater: "Harry! Who were some of the other stars I discovered? Lucille Ball . . . Betty Grable . . ."

Rigby's high-pitched voice promptly suggests "Paulette Goddard?"

Berkeley grunts. "Yeh. Paulette Goddard. And Ginger Rogers." The girl is busy making notes. "And Ann Dvorak."

"Who?" says the young reporter. "Ann—?"

"Dvorak," snarls Berkeley. "Ann Dvor—oh, never mind."

His plump wife, Etta, is sitting well away from him, isolated at the rear of the theater, like a curious tourist who has wandered onto a Hollywood set and fears she may be pushed out at any moment by a studio guard. "He has been asked the same questions so many times," she explains to no one in particular. "And the trip tired him out." A few weeks before, she adds, Buz had attended a film festival in Michigan against his doctor's orders. "And then he threw his back out at home."

Suddenly there is a commotion onstage. One girl has been

waved aside to the group of rejected applicants. But now she has rushed back out from the wings to the center of the stage, and she is standing squarely in front of Berkeley, looking down at him as her fingers fumble hurriedly with the buttons on the front of the white blouse tucked into the black tights. "Mr. Berkeley," she says very fast, "you didn't look at my body. I want to show you my body." She strips the blouse off swiftly, and stands there.

The silence falls over the theater like an asbestos curtain sealing off the make-believe stage world from the real one out front. The girl stands there, blinking, the nipples of her small breasts pointing directly down at Berkeley. His face is immobile, registering nothing at all.

After a moment, May Muth, the production manager, steps forward. She is a forceful female whose lined face has the hardness of an aging Bette Davis—and who once actually understudied Bette Davis in a short-lived 1950 Broadway revue. Before May can reach the girl's side, the half-nude dancer has dispiritedly slipped into the blouse. She turns, glassy-eyed, and heads for the stage door. May hustles along behind her, wary of trouble. The crowd parts silently to let them through. Several boy dancers, who have shown up in the hope that there might be time for them to audition, glare at the girl's partly covered breasts with open disgust.

Berkeley sits, saying nothing, seeing nothing. The auditions resume, as the wizened dance director onstage says, "Okay, let's try this, now. One-ta-*dum*, ta-*da*, ta-*dum*." And the twenty-four girls behind him try it.

Hours later, a line of eighteen girls has been chosen— mostly by Donald Saddler, Cyma, and Harry, who have been whispering throughout the afternoon. Occasionally, Harry has scurried down the aisle to indicate to Buz a particular face or figure or dancing style that impresses the other members of the production team. Whether Berkeley's grunt of acknowledgment is acquiescence or negation evidently does not matter. These girls are only semi-finalists, or less. The selection of the real *Nanette* chorus is yet to be made.

The television camera crews, impatiently waiting their

turn, move in. Banks of floodlights blink on. The eighteen girls kept behind are lined up across the stage. Berkeley is asked to walk up and down the line, to chat briefly with each dancer. He rises slowly from his front-row seat and starts toward the small flight of steps leading to the stage. Suddenly he is caught on something, and bats his hands through the air as if at invisible gnats. Bob Schear, a middle-aged chorus boy lately turned stage manager, hurries to Berkeley and unhooks the microphone wires still strung around his neck. Schear tries to help the director up the steps, but Berkeley waves him aside and makes the slow climb unaided.

The cameras whirr. "What's your name?" Berkeley asks the first girl in line. She tells him, smiling. "Where are you from?" he asks her. She tells him, smiling. He moves to the next girl. "What's your name?" he asks. "How long you been in the business?" He moves again. And again. Finally, he is at the end of the line. "How was that?" he asks the TV cameraman. "Was it all right?"

"It was beautiful," is the reply.

"I don't care if it was beautiful," Berkeley growls. "Was it all right?" The line gets a laugh from the chorus girls, who are standing docilely, like cattle at sundown. Finally, May Muth tells them it is all right to leave, that they will be notified of further auditions. As the TV crews begin wrapping up their equipment, publicist Boyer checks which newscasts will show the film that night, and which will hold it over until the following day.

Berkeley starts blindly down the steps. Harry calls out quickly, "Bobby, help Mr. Berkeley," and the stage manager hurries to catch the septuagenarian in the semidarkness. "Sit in the front row, Mr. Berkeley," says Schear. The director nods an okay and heads into the third row. "That's two rows down," Schear points out firmly, and Berkeley returns to his seat.

Far in the rear, Donald Saddler, whispering as always, discusses with Cyma and Harry the girls who have been chosen. Everyone is tired, everyone wants to get out of the dust-choked theater into the sunlight. Berkeley almost appears to be nodding, dozing, in his seat.

Suddenly, down the left aisle, moving swiftly from seats in the shadows beneath the balcony, come four female figures. They are tall, broad-shouldered, walking with swift, mincing steps. Seemingly, they are early discards from the chorus tryouts. They sweep past Etta Berkeley, their high heels clomping noisily, and a tiny gasp escapes from her throat as she sees them.

The quartet are dressed in faded, midi-length gowns that have obviously come from attic trunks and rummage sales. One member trails a feather boa fully nine feet long. All of their faces are heavy with lipstick, eye shadow, and rouge, but the yellow pancake make-up cannot cover the trace of beard. As they reach the row behind Berkeley, their rumbling voices climb upward into shrill whispers and giggles. Three of the figures crowd into the seats directly behind the slumping showman. The fourth moves ahead, quickly, casually, and then turns and points an Instamatic.

The pop of the flashcube freezes Berkeley with the three drag queens draped around his shoulders. They change positions and the cube fires again. Berkeley sits blinking from the brilliant explosions. "We're just thrilled, so *thrillllled* to meet you, Mr. Berkeley," one of the queens screeches, holding out a hand that the director ignores.

With a trace of panic in her voice, Etta Berkeley half-turns in her seat and calls out to no one, *anyone*, pleading: "Don't let them do *that*. Please—"

And suddenly, Harry is sliding into a seat alongside her, patting her shoulder, his voice soothing her. "It's all right. It's all right. They just want a picture. They admire him *so* much."

The queens are being shooed away from Berkeley now. Their high-heeled, old-fashioned size 11 pumps carry them awkwardly up the steps to the stage. One is still blowing kisses at Berkeley as he is led—*rushed*—offstage. Then they are gone. The silence falls over the house again. The scent of embarrassment is heavy.

Berkeley rises slowly and moves to the aisle. He climbs toward his wife. "I'm a little tired," he says. "Let's go back to the hotel."

Suddenly, Harry is talking swiftly, cackling and giggling. "You *should* be tired, Buz. We've been here all day. There were at least two hundred girls, at *least*. And all those interviews!"

On the stage, the house manager begins snapping off switches. In seconds, only a single safety light is left glowing. Harry helps Berkeley find his way up the dark aisle, while Etta trails a step or two behind and clucks softly, "Watch that step, now."

Across the darkened theater, Cyma Rubin stares at the trio moving carefully out into the daylight. She bites her lip thoughtfully, then looks at Donald Saddler, who whispers something to her. Cyma nods.

In the sunlight as Berkeley waits with his wife and Harry for a cab, a young dancer—one of the girls who was held back for the TV cameras—strolls by.

"Hello, Mr. Berkeley," she calls out cheerfully.

Berkeley says to Harry, "Did I pick that one? I don't remember her." A cab slides over in answer to Harry's anxious wave, "Oh, well—let it go, let it go," Berkeley says, meaning nothing in particular, as he climbs into the front of the cab alongside the driver.

"It's easier for him to get in and out there than in the back," Etta explains, getting into the rear seat alone. Harry nods, understandingly, and watches the cab pull away. He half yawns, a little tired but still tingling with excitement.

Cyma and Saddler come out of the theater behind him.

"Did you ever see so many *dogs?*" asks Cyma. "I don't think we can use *any* of them."

"I know," says Harry. "Buz says all the pretty girls are working in Vegas."

Cyma nods. "Except for the publicity, the whole thing was a waste. We'll have to see some more girls. These were dogs—all of them. Dogs."

That evening, and the next day, however, the "dogs" played their part toward the eventual success of *No, No Nanette*. Virtually every New York television station showed films of the chorus hopefuls tapping away while Berkeley looked on approvingly. Photographs and feature stories ran in local papers, and the young Associated Press interviewer filed an article that went out to newspapers all across the country:

"Preparing for a comeback on Broadway, Berkeley auditioned 350 starry-eyed dancers. . . . 'I look at the personality, the looks, the face, and the figure. . . . I talk to them. I can feel pretty quickly if they've got that verve,' said the white-haired director who launched the careers of stars such as Betty Grable, Lucille Ball and Ginger Rogers. . . ."

And Ann Dvorak.

Not to mention Ruby Keeler.

**11** Ethel Hilda Keeler did not want to be a Broadway star.

In 1920, when she was ten years old and appearing in her first public performance in a school-sponsored minstrel show, or in 1929, when she was nineteen and starring in Flo Ziegfeld's *Show Girl* on Broadway, the winsome little dancer the world knew as Ruby Keeler did *not* want to be a Broadway star.

As a matter of fact, it is highly possible that she never wanted to be in showbusiness at all. And, if she could have made $45 a week at it in the 1920s, Ruby Keeler might have become a secretary, a waitress, or a nun.

> "If I wrote a book, it would be about the last twenty-seven years of my life as Mrs. John Lowe— and nobody would want to read it."
>
> **RUBY KEELER**

Born August 25th, in 1909, Ruby Keeler was three years old when her family moved from her birthplace of Halifax, Nova Scotia, to the Yorkville section on the Upper East Side of New York. At the time, the area was not the locale of the "swinging singles" bars and apartments rented by the airline stewardesses and bachelor advertising copywriters who inhabit it today. It was filled with a homogeneous mixture of impoverished Irish Catholics, Italian laborers, and Jewish immigrants.

It was the perfect neighborhood for Ruby's father to land a job as foreman of the Knickerbocker Ice Company, and for her mother to settle down to the business of raising six children. There were Ruby's older brother, Bill, and four younger sisters—Gertrude, Helen, Anna May, and Margie. The family was close-knit, attending Mass on Sunday in warm togetherness, and "making do" happily on Ralph Keeler's salary at the ice plant.

At St. Catherine of Sienna Grammar School (the only school Ruby ever attended), she took part in the usual amateurish productions, bounding about as an Easter Bunny in a pageant or appearing as a member of "The Eastside Sextette" in an annual fund-raising show. Like other neighborhood kids—Jimmy Cagney lived not far away—she attended dancing school at the cost of a hard-earned nickel a week. A friendly instructor at St. Catherine's arranged a brief course of ballet lessons at the old Metropolitan Opera House at Broadway and 41st Street, and Ruby walked more than thirty blocks in each direction to save the Third Avenue El fare.

The amount of dancing that Ruby learned by the time she reached her teens—a smattering of tap, very basic ballet, and folk dancing—probably was not as much as a student today gains from watching Fred Astaire and Gene Kelly in old films on television. Still, her mother noticed that what steps the young girl did, she did with enthusiasm and a smile. Mrs. Keeler soon took her daughter by the hand and enrolled her in a school for dancers run by Jack Blue, one of several instructors of the day who freely boasted of the stars they had helped to the top of the showbusiness ladder. ("Fred and Adele Astaire, Marx Brothers, Marilyn Miller, Eddie Cantor, Gilda Gray and Al Jolson," suggested one ad, which promised that, upon graduation, a dance student would "possess credentials that lead to prompt and remunerative engagements.")

At Jack Blue's studio, thirteen-year-old Ruby taught elementary steps to a class of youngsters in exchange for her own lessons. Money was in short supply now because her father had become ill and required a serious throat operation. He was working on a part-time schedule. The medical bills were mounting. After three months of Blue's tap lessons, Ruby Keeler figured she had learned enough; she would try to make a few dollars to help out at home.

Legend has it that she went with a girlfriend to the chorus auditions of a new show written, produced, and directed by George M. Cohan. It was *The Rise of Rosie O'Reilly*, and its score contained a Cohan song called "There's a Ring to the Name of Rosie." Looking for fresh young faces to play along with such old-timers as Margaret Dumont (the perennial foil for Groucho Marx in many later shows and pictures) and comedian Bobby Watson, Director Cohan gave thirteen-year-old Ruby Keeler her first professional contract.

She quit school in the sixth grade and, chaperoned by her

mother, who brought along baby sister Margie, Ruby went to Boston for the tryout of *Rosie O'Reilly*. It was 1923, and the young girl was paid the near-unbelievable sum of $45 a week—$10 more than the chorus minimum.

"I had never been in a real theater," Ruby later told a *Chicago Tribune* interviewer. "My parents didn't know anything about showbusiness, but it meant $45 a week and we were poor—not struggling, however. I don't go for that bit about a struggling childhood. Kids aren't unhappy about finances because they don't know any better."

The show came into New York and opened on Christmas night. Ruby and her family had attended Midnight Mass, and had prayed things would go well. The prayers—and the show—were not strong enough. After ten weeks, *Rosie* put up its closing notice, and the tiny, ninety-five-pound dancer with the sparkling blue eyes and auburn hair saw that the end of her paycheck was in view. Fast on her feet, she jumped out of the show and into rehearsals of a night-club revue at New York's Claridge Hotel. *Rosie O'Reilly* was to be the first of many musicals that Ruby Keeler left before the show's final curtain.

The Claridge revue fell apart after eight weeks of rehearsal, when the producers ran out of money. Young Ruby Keeler took her single pair of tap shoes and started making the rounds of "talent shows" and "amateur nights." Every night club had one evening set aside when young and old performers could get up and let the crowd laugh at their antics as they vied for a prize of five or ten dollars. When the amateurs were through, the management usually brought on a "ringer"—an attractive, skilled professional—who would easily walk off with the prize, and return it later.

One of the biggest amateur shows in town was conducted at the Moulin Rouge club by famed vaudeville producer, radio celebrity, and nightclub impresario Nils T. Granlund. According to a fan magazine of the day, the stable of professionals hired by "NTG" to hang onto his prize money included beauteous Claire Luce and Frances Upton, who went on to star in the *Follies*. But on one particular night, according to the magazine, this is what happened:

"Among a number of unknown girls, one had entered who was not yet thirteen. She was skinny and poorly dressed and looked underfed. She handed in her music, a lead-sheet of a fast tap. She had no orchestrations and had to work with the pianist alone. She had no costume and came on in her shabby street attire, with clumsy, cheap, muddy shoes. She 'went into her dance.' And she stopped the show. The crowd wouldn't let her off. She knew only a few steps, but these she had to repeat again and again."

The magazine writer might have dramatized a few points —Ruby was fourteen, and why should an "amateur" have full orchestrations?—but he was right about the crowd liking her dance. The report continues: "When all the contestants were lined up, the house voted for the little ragamuffin, and NTG had to give the prize to the intruder who said her name was Ruby Keeler." Granlund had his own eye for talent. He latched onto Ruby and got her an audition with the choreographer of the revues at the Strand Roof. This was a cheap, second-class cabaret that paid the young performer $50 a week to do her "fast rhythm tap" on its dime-sized dance floor.

But Ruby's dance only took about ten minutes to perform twice nightly. And customers made thirsty by Prohibition were jamming dozens of nightspots all up and down Broadway. Why couldn't Ruby do her dance in another club—or several—each night? Granlund showed his dancing doll to Larry Fay, an underworld figure who had parlayed a taxicab business into one million dollars and a piece of several night clubs around the city. Fay's partner—ostensibly a silent one—was notorious racketeer Owney "The Killer" Madden, whom police claimed had masterminded many killings of the era. He also was the undercover backer of virtually every Manhattan night club during Prohibition.

Madden and Fay shared the profits from a nightspot known as the El Fey Club, hosted by the irrepressible Texas Guinan. Texas' practice of overcharging well-heeled patrons for their drinks and her genial cry of "Hello, suckers!" made her club one of the more popular in town. Larry

Fay thought her customers would get a kick out of Ruby Keeler's dance, and promptly booked the youngster to appear twice nightly at El Fey between her stints at the Strand. Granlund also put her on as a professional in his shows at the Moulin Rouge—and young Ruby found herself making upwards of $150 a week, although she practically had to ride a bicycle to do it.

Her personal life during the three years she worked as one of "Texas Guinan's girls" was shrouded in secrecy and rumor. "Texas was very good to her girls, very protective," Ruby told the *Chicago Tribune* interviewer. "We weren't allowed to go downstairs and mingle." On *The Dick Cavett Show* recently, she told the host that she "guesses" that the places she worked in were illegal speakeasies, but that she didn't drink in those days and really did not pay much attention to what the customers were imbibing.

One thing is certain. Ruby's mother was much on hand to keep a watchful eye on her daughter. The officers of the Gerry Society insisted that the young girl had to continue school, and a private instructor managed to squeeze in a few hours of lessons a day. For a brief time, Ruby was enrolled in the Professional Children's School—where Patsy Kelly was a classmate.

But her world really began after nightfall, when Texas Guinan stepped out on the tiny floor of the shoebox-shaped club at the top of a rickety flight of stairs and called on the customers to "give this little girl a great big hand." Perhaps it was the fact that her *rapataptapping* feet could be heard above the din in the low-ceilinged club. Perhaps it was the fact that this blue-eyed, auburn-haired youngster looked like she belonged in a church choir rather than a smoke-filled clip joint. Or, perhaps it was her smile which said, "I'm out here to please you all because I have to help out my sick father and a big family in Yorkville, and I hope you like me."

Whatever it was, Ruby Keeler always got a great big hand.

She also got offers of more work. The Strand Roof choreographer got a chance to do a Broadway show, and Ruby went into it. On the Sunday after *Bye, Bye, Bonnie* opened in January, 1927, Ruby Keeler's mother turned eagerly to the front page of the drama section of the *New York Times*. Smiling, she read:

"Ruby Keeler, a name well known to the devotees of night clubs, did a tap dance the other evening about 10 o'clock and completely stopped *Bye, Bye, Bonnie*. This young girl, so young that the law requires her mother to sign her contracts, seems to possess that pearl of great price, personality."

The article noted also that, after the curtain came down on *Bonnie* at the Ritz Theater nightly, Ruby Keeler entertained night-club patrons at a place known as the Silver Slipper.

The Silver Slipper was only one of a dozen clubs with a polished hardwood floor on which young Ruby's taps drummed furiously. She also appeared at the Deauville, the Mimic, and the Frivolity, and later—when Texas Guinan opened her own spot—at Tex's 300 Club. But it was at the Silver Slipper that Ruby Keeler became romantically—and seriously—involved for the first time.

The object of her admiring teen-age glances was described as "a young, square-shouldered, square-shooting, hard-hitting remarkably handsome playboy of Broadway and its tributary streams."

His name was John Costello, but in the netherworld of hoodlums and night-club habitués, he was known as Johnny Irish.

He was one of the operators of the Silver Slipper, which lured patrons with a sensational comedy-and-music trio made up of Jimmy Durante, Lou Clayton, and Eddie Jackson. The U.S. marshals eventually padlocked the Silver Slipper (Texas Guinan satirized the government action in a revue, *Padlocks of 1927*), and Johnny Irish and his partners opened a new club for Durante—The Rendezvous, in Broadway's Winter Garden Theater Building.

Now, Johnny was a cut above the usual run of mobsters,

according to the old-timers who knew him. Was he a boot-legger? "Hell," says long-time restaurant owner Toots Shor, "in those days everybody was a bootlegger. If you ran a club, you had to sell liquor, and that meant you were a boot-legger." Former Broadway columnist Louis Sobol remem-bers Johnny Irish as "a nice, articulate guy," and several other newsmen who covered the night-club beat similarly swear to the young man's legitimate character.

However, two things seem reasonable assumptions. Top underworld figure Owney Madden—who had his hand in New York's laundry business, West Side dock operations, the prize fight racket, and other industries—had money in the Silver Slipper, as well as in most of the other clubs that Ruby Keeler played in, and Madden was a "friend" of Johnny Irish. Additionally, the support of Johnny and the mob probably went a long way toward making Ruby Keeler the toast of New York night life.

It is difficult to explain it otherwise. After all, the young girl was pretty—but there were many pretty girls around. And she could tap-dance—but there were many tap-dancers around. In interviews of the day, Ruby freely admits that she never could sing onstage—and there were many pretty tap-dancers who could.

But Ruby had the "push" behind her that only a real insider could provide. And she also had his protection.

"Let it not be intimated," wrote a biographer of the period, "that less than many a pass was made at this bud-ding youngster, for many an amorous drunk, many a jaded chaser, many an aggressive roughneck took one look at the dimpled, auburn-haired, adolescent dancing-doll and said, 'Well, here's where I move in.' "

But they all moved out, the writer continued—as Ruby fended them off with the tactful notice that she was inter-ested in other things, or, if that didn't work, with a display of tough Irish temper. She seldom had trouble with rowdy patrons, however. "She was so clean, so frankly unspoiled, without being mincingly hoydenish, that she appealed to the decency of men who had any decency left." And, if nothing else worked, an angry glance from Johnny Irish was all it took to scare off a pest.

The young star's Model T would park outside the clubs where friendly policemen and doormen watched it for her. Newspapermen and fellow show-people took turns entertaining her—"I remember taking her to Roseland 'cause she liked dancing," says Joe Moore, an Olympic champion ice-skater employed to dig up material for columnists. Ruby was a good companion at movies, or sharing a sandwich and cup of coffee after the clubs had closed just before dawn.

But everyone on Broadway knew that Johnny Irish was closest to Ruby Keeler. He had first met her when she was fifteen, and the story was that when she "grew up" he would marry her.

Perhaps he would have—except that he already had a wife.

Though the "romance" of Ruby and Johnny lasted for some three years, its ending had been foreshadowed when the young dancer first stepped out to do her specialty at the El Fey Club. And was seen by the most formidable entertainer of the era.

Al Jolson.

It is almost impossible for young people today to realize how big, how important, Al Jolson was for more than two decades. A combination of Frank Sinatra, John Lennon, and Elvis Presley, perhaps. The highest paid entertainer of the day—$17,000 for a single week in 1927, $23,000 in 1929. The first man to sell a million records, and to go on selling a million copies of six records in a row. The term "Mr. Show Business" was created for him. He called himself "The World's Greatest Entertainer"—and no one laughed. The Shuberts named their new theater on 59th Street after him. His Broadway shows—he starred in eleven, one every two years—consistently set box-office records.

And his personal wealth was placed at $3 million to $5 million.

The incredible thing about Jolson's career is that he reached the highest rung of the showbusiness ladder without benefit of the mass media that today can catapult a performer to success. There was no radio or television in 1909 when "Jolie" got his first review in *Variety* ("Haven't seen a demonstration for a single act, or any act for that matter, as was given Al Jolson."). In 1913, when the Shuberts paid him a bonus of $10,000 to sign a new contract, moving him from $250 a week to $1,000 and escalating over seven years to $2,000, radio was still in experimental stages.

No, except for records, Jolson did not use electronics. He got where he was—on top—by coming out on stage, on Broadway and on tour across the country, and overwhelming the audience with the force of his personality. He had to.

For, on the first day that eleven-year-old Asa Yoelson, son of a rabbi who had emigrated to America from the Russian village of Srednicka, found that he could earn pennies by singing on the streets of New York, a desire burned inside him.

Al Jolson wanted to be a star.

At any cost.

At any sacrifice.

Over the bodies of his enemies, if need be.

Over the bodies of his friends and his relatives, if need be —and the need arose. At one point, Jolson double-crossed his own brother, Harry Jolson, an older, experienced vaudeville singer in his own right. To make sure that audiences got only the World's Greatest Entertainer when they saw a Jolson, Al promised his brother $150 a week for life if he would stop performing and become his agent. Harry agreed. And Al fired him shortly after "because I need a bigger agent lookin' out for me." His brother sued. But a lot of people—agents, producers, musicians, other entertainers—sued Jolson. Al Jolson did not care.

In *The Brothers Shubert*, biographer Jerry Stagg notes that the Shuberts, who employed Jolson for more than a decade as he ascended to showbusiness heights, were vicious in their dealings—but that Jolson was more than their match. "Jolson," he writes, "was undeniably one of the great entertainers of all time, but as a human being—Hollywood biographies to the contrary—he was an unpleasant, arrogant man."

It is unlikely that fifteen-year-old Ruby Keeler knew anything of Jolson's offstage behavior when he dropped into the El Fey Club around two o'clock one morning in 1926 just in time to catch her introduction. She knew him, though, as the star of *Bombo* and *Big Boy* and the Sunday night Winter Garden variety shows that were attended by showbusiness people and political celebrities.

"Hey, Al Jolson," called Texas Guinan in a voice that blared over the band's loud sound, "give this l'il girl a hand! Make some noise!"

And she tossed a wooden noisemaker, the shakeable kind that makes a clacking sound, across the room toward the rear table where Jolson sat. The flying missile caught Jolson on the forehead, and the King of Broadway let out a yelping curse of pain.

Texas ran over, consternation on her face. Jolson's handkerchief was in his hand, dabbing at the blood trickling over his eyebrow. "It's all right," he said. "Just a little cut." But Texas, apologizing, insisted he go downstairs and relax. Nodding, Jolson moved out of the club, hardly looking back at the tiny figure tap dancing so furiously in the center of the small stage. Ruby Keeler was paid to dance, and no matter what happened in El Fey, she would dance.

But when she finished the number, Ruby went to the famous room beneath the club. It was a room closed to outsiders, and its bar was stocked with a better grade of liquor than the patrons drank upstairs. Here, the young beauties that were the Guinan girls rested between shows and met their intimate friends. Millionaires, reporters, mobsters, and politicians mingled on a single level of camaraderie in the tiny club room. When Ruby entered, Jolson was chatting amiably with some friends and appeared to have forgotten the incident upstairs. The cut on his forehead was scarcely visible.

Still, Ruby felt she had to apologize. After all, Texas had

asked the star to applaud *her,* and if she hadn't been dancing—

Al Jolson looked at the teen-ager who seemed so upset about a scratch. She had a vitality, a freshness about her that was appealing. Especially to a man who was nearly twenty-five years her senior. "It's nothing," he said. "Forget it. Sit down. Have a drink with me, and we'll talk about something else."

According to one report of the couple's first meeting, Ruby sat and drank a glass of orange juice. Then she excused herself to go upstairs and put her tap shoes on for another show.

More importantly, other reports have it that Jolson turned to the club hostess and asked a few questions about the little dancer. "She doesn't look old enough to be dancing here," he said.

"She's old enough," answered Texas Guinan. "But forget her. She's Johnny Irish's girl."

Jolson laughed, shrugged. "I just forgot it," he said.

But it was hard for him to forget Ruby Keeler. For one thing, she kept getting favorable reviews in a series of Broadway musicals. Shortly after Larry Fay closed her old haunt, the El Fey Club, on January 1, 1927, Ruby opened in *Bye, Bye, Bonnie,* and Jolson, looking for reports of his own activity, chanced to note in *Variety* that "in a conventional musical, Miss Keeler's dancing was a sensation which carried with it a touch of the sentimental as she fixed most of her attention on Texas Guinan in an upper stage box." A few months later she appeared in *Sidewalks of New York* with comic Ray Dooley and a new young comedian named Robert Hope. And then she went into *Lucky* with Skeets Gallagher and bandleader Paul Whiteman. The shows were not always successful—*Lucky* ran only seventy-one performances—but the little dancer usually got kindly notices from the columnists and reviewers. Many of them, of course, had followed her career for the last few years.

She continued dancing at several clubs each night, and no

one was surprised when Jolson began appearing regularly wherever she played. In late 1927 and the early months of 1928, no club owner—not even Johnny Irish—was big enough to keep "Jolie" out of his place, even if he thought the entertainer was interested in his girl. Almost single-handedly, Jolson had revolutionized the motion picture business. Although Director D. W. Griffith had sued him for $500,000 after Jolson quit work on a silent film, *Black and White* (and later was awarded $2,267), Jolson's decision to wait for sound films proved to be a brilliant one. Warner Bros. had bought the rights to a stage play, *The Jazz Singer*, about a cantor's son who became a popular singer and brought sorrow to his father. The play, which was loosely based on Jolson's career, was a huge success on Broadway with George Jessel as its star. But when Jessel was asked to do the movie—and sing on the screen—he refused. He did not trust the new medium of sound film, and did not want to be anybody's guinea pig.

The Warners, on the edge of bankruptcy, went next to Jolson. A born gambler who delighted in risking $2,000 or more on the turn of a card, a prize fight, or a horse race, Jolson bet that if anyone could make a successful talking-and-singing picture, it was the King of Broadway himself. The studio did not have enough money to pay the salary he demanded, so he took his payment in stock. When the film was released, with a half-dozen songs by Jolson and a couple of lines of dialogue almost accidentally recorded during the musical introductions, audiences were entranced. The film earned more than $3 million for Warner Bros. The stock that Jolson held eventually was worth almost as much.

And now the King of Broadway was the King of every Terre Haute and Butte and Topeka. His image was playing in every hamlet and village, in every capital around the world. His friends were everywhere.

They even were in the underworld, Johnny Irish knew. One story had it that Al Capone himself once had kidnapped the entertainer and ordered him to sing at a private party, and then had promised to see to it that Jolson had no trouble with anyone whenever he was in Chicago.

Something more: Johnny knew Ruby was sincerely interested in the older man. Perhaps the pretty young dancer saw the loneliness and fear beneath Jolson's bravado. Everyone on Broadway knew that the King was a chronic hypochondriac. That he worried endlessly that he would lose his voice and be unable to sing. That the audiences would suddenly turn against him. "On opening night," recalls Patsy Kelly, who played opposite Jolson in *Wonder Bar* in 1931, "the man was a raving maniac who actually had to be pushed out onstage. He was deathly afraid on opening nights—and we played seventy-nine one-night stands on tour, so every town was an opening night to him."

Something else worried Jolson—although he seldom spoke of it to anyone. Twice, women had walked out of marriage to "The World's Greatest Entertainer."

In 1906, when he was twenty, the young vaudeville singer calling himself Al Jolson had married a chorus girl named Henrietta Keller, who briefly danced in a San Francisco nightspot. The marriage—to a girl described as "pretty, but quiet and reserved"—lasted thirteen years, was childless, and ended in divorce after a lengthy separation.

It almost had to: Jolson was on the road much of the time, endlessly entertaining, leaving his wife sitting alone in hotel rooms while he sang his heart out atop a piano in a local club—or, after the clubs all had closed, in a whorehouse. One woman at a time was not audience enough for Jolson. He could not spend hours cooped up in a hotel or an apartment or even a huge California home. He had to be out where there were crowds. And he could not understand why the wife of Al Jolson was not content to wait at home for him.

For a few months after the divorce, as Henrietta prepared to marry a San Francisco businessman, he led a life of "almost monastic loneliness," as one reporter put it. For Jolson, "almost monastic loneliness" meant that he was seldom seen at more than one party a night, or with more than one girl at a time on his arm. At a party in New York, where his latest show, *Sinbad*, was playing to capacity audiences, the star met Ethel Delmar, a beautiful brunette who had changed her name from Alma Osborne when she took a chorus job in George White's *Scandals of 1920*.

It took Jolson two years to win the showgirl, two years to convince her that he really intended to settle down and raise a family—to convince her that he would do a new musical just often enough to remain in the public eye. A doubtful Ethel married him, finally, and quickly learned that it was all lies, that Jolson could not be other than he was. He opened a new show, *Bombo*, and packed the theater that bore his name. He bought race horses, sponsored prize fighters, tried to buy a baseball team. He toured with *Bombo*, quit the show to fight off a cold in the Florida sunshine, and promised again that he would retire—then reopened *Bombo* on Broadway to give the Shuberts time to get *Big Boy*, his next musical, ready for him. Jolson opened it, closed it to flee to Florida once more when the wintry winds threatened his precious vocal cords, and promised that soon—very soon—he would settle down with Ethel and, maybe, a baby boy.

Through the tours and the openings and the promises, Ethel Delmar cried.

And drank.

In 1926, weary of her husband's evanescent assurances—now he was saying he would quit just as soon as he finished a "talking picture" that Warner Bros. had begged him to make—Ethel tossed in the towel. She sailed for Europe and won a divorce decree in Paris.

Jolson hinted at a reunion. "Ethel is the only woman in the world for me," he told newsmen. And over the long weeks the reporters wrote story after story that said, perhaps, maybe, possibly, Ethel Delmar once more would become Mrs. Al Jolson.

But the *Scandals* beauty, her mind blurred by alcohol, was in no condition to carry that burden again.

Ruby Keeler was.

\* \* \*

It was 1927, and Jolson was forty-one, Ruby seventeen, when they met in California where the King of Broadway was preparing to become the King of Hollywood with his second picture, *The Singing Fool*. A friend from New York, comedienne Fanny Brice, was due in from the East and Jolson went down to the station to meet her train. On the same train were Ruby Keeler and a girlfriend who worked with her at Texas Guinan's new spot, the 300 Club.

"Al," shouted Fanny Brice, "s' great to see ya." She wrapped her arms about him warmly, then noticed him eyeing the two young girls at her side. "Hey," she said, "I met these two hoofers on the train. They're out here on a vacation, right, kids? Their names are—"

"This one I know," said Jolson, nodding, smiling. "Ruby Keeler. Right?"

Ruby smiled. She extended her hand, and Jolson gripped it warmly. She introduced her friend Mary Lucas—but Jolson seemed interested only in her. Suddenly, the middle-aged superstar with the deep brown eyes and the receding hairline above the high forehead was asking if she would like to see the Hollywood premiere of Gary Cooper and Colleen Moore in *Lilac Time*.

"That would be very nice," Ruby said.

When Jolson showed up at the picture with the teen-ager from New York, the gossip columnists reached for their note pads and raced for their typewriters. It had been well over a year since Ethel Delmar had dropped from sight, and Al Jolson, growing older every day, had little time left to prove himself. Was this youngster, this tiny dancer with the well-curved legs, his latest—his next?

Ruby herself did not know. And evidently did not care. Back in Manhattan, in the world of speakeasies and dance halls that crowded the area between Fifth and Ninth Avenues, 38th to 59th Streets, she had plenty of friends. Close friends. Her family, the people who really counted, were all in New York, too. Whatever happened in Hollywood was only a lark, something to do on the spur of the moment. It was not meant to last.

But Jolson talked to her agent at the William Morris office, and a local club came out of nowhere with an offer to

Ruby Keeler of $350 a week to do her tap-dance. So she stayed on in movieland longer than she planned to. A poor little dancer with a real chance to help take care of some family bills doesn't pass up that kind of money.

And nightly, when the flowers and cards arrived from Al Jolson, Ruby Keeler accepted them with a nonchalant smile of gratitude. *Why, he must be really interested in me,* she thought, *to waste all this time and money sending flowers. Maybe he really is lonely, like everyone says.*

It is unlikely that Ruby Keeler was awed by Jolson's wealth or even his lofty showbusiness position. In the clubs she worked, there were millionaire playboys and stars by the dozens. Some of the youthful entertainers she appeared with —such as Charleston dancer George Raft at El Fey and showgirl Ruby Stevens (who later became Barbara Stanwyck) at the Silver Slipper—were well on their own way to stardom. No, Jolson's fame and power were not all that impressive. Not to a devout Catholic teen-ager, whose primary interests were her parents and her brothers and sisters, and making enough money to permit them to live comfortably. Not luxuriously, but comfortably.

No, there was something else that intrigued the ill-educated and relatively innocent young dancer. Jolson had a way of letting his thinning hair down when he wanted to impress a new girl, particularly one who was not impressed by his stature in the entertainment world. He would tell her, frankly and sincerely, about his disappointments in his previous marriages; about his fears of inadequacy and eventual desertion by his audiences; about his concern that most women were interested only in his wealth; about his nightmares of fading health; and, on rare occasions, he would even speak of the specter that loomed nearer each year—the death that he knew must come, *had* to come, and which he fought against so bitterly.

More cynical girls might have called it a "line." Ruby did not. And, in truth, there was no reason to. Every word of it was true. But it was not a speech that the bragging, swaggering Jolson trotted out for newspaper reporters or biographers. It was something that he kept in reserve—sometimes he held it so far back in his mind that the words sounded strange even as he heard them come hesitatingly from his lips. It took certain women, in certain situations, to bring the truth from him.

Ruby Keeler—vibrantly youthful, naïve, with daisy-fresh beauty—was one of those women.

When she headed for New York, she wore a new five-carat diamond, and when she got off the train, the papers at the newsstand in the terminal bloomed with column items about the biggest romance in years. Skeptics hinted that it was all for publicity purposes. It would not be the first time that Jolson had lent his name to an "affair" that would help a little lady's career. Besides, back in California, he certainly was not pining for his Ruby, who was three thousand miles away. Well publicized were his dalliances with starlets and film queens such as Lupe Velez, the nineteen-year-old "Mexican spitfire" (whose suicide in 1944 at thirty-six created sensational headlines).

Perhaps Ruby needed some publicity. The nightspot business was beginning to fall on hard times. There was an overabundance of clubs, the Treasury agents kept raiding many of them, and the costs of running a club (with payoffs to the right people) were soaring. Even by selling champagne that cost $80 a case at $25 a quart, and $50-a-case Scotch at $20 a bottle, many clubs were losing money. Owners who were paying as much as $5,000 a week to performers found that customers were staying home to listen to big stars on the growing medium of radio. Texas Guinan's "Hello, suckers!" became such a popular catch-phrase that tourists began to wonder if she meant it, and stayed away from her new 300 Club in droves. Singer Ethel Waters took over the bankrupt nightspot, and promptly busted. A third owner, who reopened it as the Club Hitchy, posted a "Closed" notice five days later.

Ruby Keeler still had her friends in New York. She kept working, doing her tap-dance routines at, among other places, the Pavillion Royale, a remote Long Island roadhouse that was popular during the summer season. Her old mentor, Nils T. Granlund, was the master of ceremonies at the Royale, and emcee of a Sunday night radio program that featured the dance band. Sunday was also "Celebrity Night," and NTG was not surprised when he received a call that told him Al Jolson would be on hand one evening.

When the star was introduced and called to the microphone, Jolson gave a couple of quick plugs for his new picture, *The Singing Fool*, that he was working on at Warners. And he gave out with a few bars of the new song that had been written especially for the picture. It was "Sonny Boy."

Then he added hurriedly, in his best Jolson tremolo: "Friends, I hope some day to have a 'Sonny Boy' of my own —of our own—for Ruby Keeler has promised to be my wife."

The announcement caught most of the nation—and Ruby —by surprise. Jolson was hazy about when or where the marriage was to take place. And a few weeks later, when the papers carried the announcement that Ruby Keeler would have a prominent role in the new Ziegfeld show, *Whoopee*, starring Eddie Cantor, it was obvious that Jolson once more had been giving the kid's career a push. The Sunday *Herald Tribune* carried a quarter-page picture of the new Ziegfeld beauty, twice the size of a photo of Claudette Colbert on the same page, as if to prove the motive was publicity.

Besides, whispered Broadwayites, what about Johnny Irish?

It is showbusiness legend that Johnny Irish talked seriously to Ruby, and Ruby talked tenderly to Johnny. Then she told Jolson that Johnny wanted to talk to him. The singing star, who was bouncing from coast to coast like a tennis ball, wrapped up his new film and came east. Ostensibly, he was in New York to attend the premiere of the picture. But a meeting was arranged between the two men.

Probably no one—not even Ruby Keeler—knows precisely what words passed between the night club operator and the superstar, alone in a hotel room. According to one reporter's version, Johnny Irish warned Jolson that if he was trifling with Ruby's affections, "There's gonna be a singer wearin' a cement overcoat at the bottom of the Hudson." It made good copy, but friends and people who knew Johnny in those days insist he never made that kind of threat. Another writer claimed that Johnny merely asked Jolson if he loved Ruby and, assured that the feeling was mutual, he told the singer, "Get married as fast as you can. And don't pay any attention to what anybody says."

Some old-time newsmen who tell the story say that whatever Johnny's exact words were, they added up to a warning: "Marry her—or else." But it is unlikely that Jolson took them for that. He carried a thousand little formless fears about with him, but he was not a physical coward. Johnny Irish, even with "connections," would not have frightened him. Still, Jolson knew that the club owner had less intelligent, less restrained pals who might resent someone's stealing a friend's girl. He agreed to marry Ruby just as soon as he got a few odds and ends straightened up.

*Variety's* front page on September 12, 1928, shows how open the secret was:

> There is an inside report that Al Jolson will essay a third marriage during his current visit to New York. Before leaving the city, Jolson will witness the premiere of *The Singing Fool* at the Winter Garden Sept. 19. After that he may go to London for the premiere of *The Jazz Singer*. Inside Broadway gossip has it that an ex-Tenth Avenue girl who herself has made a name along Mazda Lane, Ruby Keeler, will be the next Mrs. Al Jolson, marrying the millionaire comedian whose personal fortune is placed beyond the $3-million mark. Miss Keeler, still in her teens, is regarded as one of the greatest tap dancers.

A week later, Jolson and Ruby attended the premiere of *The Singing Fool* together. Sitting in the darkness of the Winter Garden, which charged a record $3 a ticket for a motion picture for the first time, the couple witnessed a scene that in part was prophetic. In the picture, which eventually outgrossed *The Jazz Singer*, Jolson played a singing waiter who is infatuated with a shoe-leather-tough chorus singer. When he writes a song that is snapped up by a

Broadway producer for a big revue, Jolson insists only the chorus girl can introduce it—and she is on her way to stardom. They marry, and have a child, "Sonny Boy." Jolson continues as a successful songwriter, introducing his new numbers in the night club he now owns, but his wife is two-timing him. Finally, she says she is leaving to get a divorce and is taking the baby with her. In a tearful telephone scene, Jolson pleads:

"Wait, wait . . . you can't take Sonny Boy. You can't. He's all I got. He's my whole life . . . You can't take him . . . No, no . . . please . . . please . . . not Sonny Boy."

Almost exactly a dozen years later, those lines which were scripted so carefully to choke unsophisticated audiences with emotion would come back to haunt Al Jolson.

But he and Ruby had no time then to worry about the future. Things were moving too fast. The night *The Singing Fool* opened, racketeer-club owner Larry Fay announced he was through running "speaks" and had bought his way back into the taxi fleet business. (He was gunned down in a fight with a night club doorman a year afterward.) A day later, Johnny Irish organized a party for his underworld friends and took them all to Atlantic City for a long weekend.

And Al Jolson and Ruby Keeler drove to Port Chester, New York, near the Connecticut line, where they were hurriedly and quietly married by a local judicial official. They raced back the next morning to the Manhattan docks and boarded the White Star liner *Olympic,* where they took over the Prince of Wales suite for the honeymoon cruise to Europe. Only when the ship was at sea did the newlyweds appear in the main salon and announce their marriage.

The date was September 21, 1928. Jolson was forty-two. Ruby was one month past her nineteenth birthday.

And, according to legend, she was now a millionaire in her own right.

Overjoyed at the fortune that had befallen her daughter, Mrs. Ralph Keeler told newsmen that Jolson had been afraid people would say that Ruby had married him for his money. So, she explained, before the wedding, the star had given Ruby $1-million of her own, to do with as she pleased.

So what if Jolson was not a Catholic, and her daughter had been married outside the church? What did it matter? In a magazine article that carried Mrs. Keeler's by-line, she said she had advised Ruby: "Marry the man you love, Ruby. Real love, true love, is all that matters. If you find you have made a mistake, that'll be all right, too. Other people have made them."

It is possible that Ruby began to think she might have made a mistake on the day the newlyweds sailed for Cherbourg.

Mark Hellinger, the Broadway columnist and close friend of Jolson who was ghostwriting the singer's life story for the papers, sailed along with them at Al's invitation. *Three* on a honeymoon? Jolson had warned his bride that he hated to be alone, that he loved crowds and being the center of attention, but still—?

\* \* \*

After a wild whirl of parties and sightseeing in Europe—a whirl that lasted for only a few weeks—the Jolsons returned to New York. And immediately had to go separate ways. Jolson had picture commitments waiting on the West Coast, and a month without work was about as much as he could stand. Ruby had signed for Ziegfeld's *Whoopee* before she was married, and she had to join the company that was already rehearsing in New York.

At the train station, the pert little brunette with the bobbed hair peeking out from under the tiny ribbon-trimmed hat kissed the short man with the receding hairline. He warned her again that he wouldn't write much— "too busy for that, y'know"—but he promised to be on the long-distance lines day and night.

In New York, Ruby took off the new frocks her husband had purchased for her in London and Paris. She put on the inexpensive and unadorned practice clothes that she wore to rehearsals. Once more she was plain, tap-dancing Ruby Keeler, just another girl in another show. That other woman —Mrs. Al Jolson, wife of a multimillionaire—did not exist any longer. Indeed, she had only existed for a very short while. Was this the way her marriage was going to be? With her in one place, her husband in another? Her parents' marriage had not been that way. No real marriage was that way.

And Jolson's phone calls—sometimes two and three a night—did not help matters. He was lonely, he said. He needed her at his side. He didn't feel well. A cold was coming on. The picture's first scenes were not going well.

But Ruby had signed a contract. And this was *Ziegfeld*. A performer could go no higher. She didn't *want* to be a Broadway star—one star in the family was enough, she said, laughing, but meaning it—but she *had* been asked by *Ziegfeld* himself.

Jolson fretted. At least on the phone. But rumors came back to New York that he was making his usual rounds, at the track, at the clubs. One improbable report reached Ruby's ears that her husband was seen frequently with his former wife, Ethel Delmar. Ruby closed her ears to the stories, stopped reading the papers, and kept on dancing.

*Whoopee* opened in Pittsburgh early in November. "The chorus almost stopped the show with its stepping, and Ruby Keeler's tapping won her second- or third-place honors," noted *Variety*. The local papers' reviews were also favorable. Ruby was on her way to being a Broadway star, after all.

But when Conductor Max Meth assembled his musicians for the Saturday matinée, a grim stage manager called him aside.

"Hold it up, Max. We can't find Ruby."

After twenty minutes' delay, an understudy was shooed onstage in Ruby's role, and the show began. By that time, Mrs. Al Jolson was on board a train that was roaring along the tracks toward Hollywood.

She *had* to go, she later explained to Ziegfeld. Al was sick. He needed her desperately. The problems with the picture were making him a nervous wreck.

Still, when she got off the train, the Jolson who greeted her was the picture of health. Just knowing that she was on her way had made him feel better, he said.

Within a day or two after Ruby's arrival, Jolson was feeling so good that he slugged a fellow patron in the Coconut Grove. The man, he said, had made offensive remarks about the Jewish religion and had used language that was offensive to Mrs. Jolson.

In no time, the cycle of clubs and race tracks and prize fights began to pall on Ruby. Yes, she loved the excitement of watching the horses pounding toward the finish line. Dining in a fine restaurant was fun, too. But night after night after night? Jolson's boundless vitality put demands even on her youthful energy. He could work all day at the studio and be ready to go out at night, staying up until the next morning.

"Al," she asked one day, "do you think we could get off somewhere, just the two of us, by ourselves?"

Her husband, wearing a muffler loosely around his neck to ward off any stray California breeze, looked at her. "Whaddaya mean, honey? We're by ourselves now."

"No, we're not. There's always a gang of people around you."

"Yeh, I guess you're right. You know how I am 'bout that."

Ruby nodded. "I'm not complaining, Al. It's just that I haven't seen much of you at all since we got married."

Jolson cocked his head to one side. He thought it over. "Yeh, you're right," he said. "Tell you what, let's go to Hawaii—kind of a second honeymoon."

Ruby had never been to Hawaii, and she agreed enthusiastically. But she was not sure her husband understood what she was talking about.

When the couple returned early in January, the usual mob of reporters was at the docks to greet them. The newsmen got more than they bargained for. Ruby jumped into a car and went one way. Jolson, with his attorney, got into another car and went in the opposite direction. The typewriters were clacking before Jolson could explain that he and his attorney had important business to discuss while the lawyer rushed for a train. "Ruby and I are very happy," he said later. "She simply has no faults."

But two weeks later, Ruby sat alone in the new rambling ranch house that Jolson had bought. She swam alone in the tile pool. Her husband, the Singing Fool himself, was on his way to New York to do some radio broadcasts. On the air, he caused an early sensation by gagging about Clara Bow "sleeping cater-cornered in bed," and the eyebrows of listeners—and censors—shot up around the nation. Listening in California, Ruby, too, wondered how her husband knew the sleeping habits of the "It" girl.

The singer returned to his home in California—he had also kept one he bought for Ethel Delmar in Scarsdale, N.Y.—and started working on the final numbers for his next film, *Say It with Songs*. The marriage was beginning to fall into a familiar pattern. Jolson wanted his young, attractive wife isolated at home, where she would be unlikely to fall for a younger man (not that any sane girl would *ever* leave Al Jolson!). Ruby wanted her busy, wandering husband at home—but knew that he had to have his audience. Tensions mounted until springtime, when Ruby got a strange offer from Flo Ziegfeld.

A popular magazine series and novel, *Show Girl*, had already been made into a film. Now Ziegfeld wanted to turn the adventures of "Dixie Dugan," a small-town girl trying to make it on Broadway, into a musical. He had already signed Clayton, Jackson, and Durante to handle the comedy. George Gershwin was writing the score. Was Ruby interested in coming back to Broadway in the starring role?

It is not likely that the imperious Ziegfeld would have offered a starring part to a girl who had walked out on him without notice in *Whoopee*, if he had not been in trouble. His last several *Follies* had been poorly received—partly because of competition from George White's *Scandals* and other revues that siphoned off top talent—and he was well on the way to running up the debt of more than $1-million that would be his legacy upon his death in 1932. Now, an extremely popular story that starred Ruby Keeler JOLSON might just turn his fortunes around.

Ruby was grateful that Ziegfeld thought enough of her talents to give her a second chance. She did not even consider the possibility that her husband had told the producer she "might be available," just to keep her busy. She got out her tap shoes and began rehearsals.

Much had changed in the few months she had been away from New York. Many of the clubs she once danced in had closed. Johnny Irish had moved to Boston and was running a hotel there. No longer did she have to live in a crowded Manhattan apartment; now she was in the Ritz Towers. And when she went to visit her family, as she did frequently, she rode in a chauffeur-driven Rolls to the new home that she and Al had bought for them in Jackson Heights.

But Broadway was ready to welcome Ruby back. *Variety* announced her signing by calling her simply "one of the fastest tappers in New York." Gershwin had written a song called "Liza" that she would dance to, and the whole show looked good in rehearsal. Comedian Eddie Foy, Jr., would be on hand with his eccentric dances, and character actor Frank McHugh would help get laughs.

On long distance, Ruby told Al how smoothly things were going. The singer had promised her that he would be all right, alone, in Hollywood for a few weeks. He seemed to be living up to his promise. The weeks of rehearsal flew by, and suddenly it was June. Opening night in Boston.

Before the show, Al Jolson came backstage. He kissed Ruby warmly, checked to make sure the floral display he had ordered was the largest one in the dressing room, and went out front to his third-row seat. He smiled to himself: It was incredible that Ruby had not been nervous back there.

The overture, which included a sampling of the show's big ballet, "An American in Paris," blared from the pit. The show was on. Durante's clowning . . . Foy's dancing . . . Harriet Hoctor's classical arabesques. They flew by in a blur.

Now the melody was the rhythmic song, "Liza." And Ruby was a machine gun onstage, her toes and heels ticking off multiple beats to every note.

And, all at once, Al Jolson—"The World's Greatest Entertainer"—was standing up, in the aisle, his arms stretched out toward the stage, and his strong, distinctive voice giving out the lyrics for all he was worth. Startled, Ruby kept dancing, and the applause for the pair of performers was thunderous.

(More than fifteen years later, when Columbia Pictures filmed *The Jolson Story*, the incident was dramatized so that it seemed as if Mrs. Jolson, suffering from first-night jitters, almost fell as she danced down a high, curving staircase. In the audience, the film's Jolson sensed her panic and stood up, singing to give her confidence. On a recent *Dick Cavett* program, Ruby denied that she was ever nervous in *Show Girl*. "Then why did he sing?" asked the host. "I don't know," replied Ruby. "I was just as surprised as anyone. I guess he just liked to sing. But I don't *know* why he did it. I'm not very bright, you know.")

Broadway insiders knew well why Jolson sang at the Boston opening. And why he sang at the New York opening on July 2nd, and why he sang occasionally throughout his wife's brief run in the show. *Show Girl* was not a strong property, and it needed all the help it could get to attract audiences. If people thought they might hear Jolson singing for free in the audience, they might buy tickets—and both Ziegfeld and Jolson were showmen enough to know it.

Ruby's notices were kind, considering that she herself admits that she was never an actress or a singer. In the *Daily News*, critic Burns Mantle said, "Ruby Keeler is a nice child and agreeably modest. She speaks her pieces with a good understanding of their meaning, presents a picture of youth and good looks that few eighteen-year-olds command, and goes periodically into tap dancing at which she excels."

*Show Girl* did not do well at the box office, even with ads that trumpeted "Ruby Keeler JOLSON and Clayton, Jackson, and Durante." At the end of the first week, a gossip column carried the news that "Ruby Keeler might leave *Show Girl*, with Pert Kelton replacing her. Word is that a little Al Jolson is expected."

Nearly three weeks went by, and then on a Saturday night, after the curtain had come down on the first act of the show, Ruby collapsed in her dressing room.

**156**

The *New York Herald Tribune* reported the incident a day or two later, and said, "Although she is seriously ill and needs an operation, Miss Keeler will continue in her role, according to her physician, until Dorothy Stone arrives from California to replace her." Miss Stone arrived soon after, and Ruby checked into Lenox Hill Hospital, where she was operated on at ten o'clock on August 1st. The newspapers of the day did not mention what the surgery was for, but "acute appendicitis" later was listed as a possibility.

Jolson himself once cryptically remarked to a newsman that Ruby wanted so desperately to be by his side, "she deliberately fell down a flight of stairs so she could get out of a Ziegfeld show and be with me." But he gave no details.

Whatever the cause of the operation, Ruby was well enough six days later to attend the premiere of *Say It with Songs*. As usual, Jolson made his own news at the film showing. He was going to make more films and settle down with his wife in California, he announced. And, perhaps, with a little Jolson or two. First, though, he was taking Ruby to Florida to recuperate in the sun.

Behind them, they left *Show Girl* limping along. It closed six weeks later, losing a lot of money for Ziegfeld. It did not make much difference. A month afterward, in an event that *Variety* chronicled as *Wall St. Lays an Egg*, the stock-market crash wiped out the showman completely.

Jolson is figured to have lost more than $700,000, but he was not in the market as heavily as other showbusiness millionaires. He had put his money in real estate, buying heavily into Catalina Island, hotels, and utilities.

In Hollywood, Jolson seemed to settle down a bit. The film work kept him busy. In March, 1930, his latest, *Mammy*, opened to big business, and he started shooting on *Big Boy*, a remake of his stage hit. That one opened in September and Jolson flew to New York with Ruby to catch the premiere. While there, he decided to pick up a quick $20,000 for appearing in person at the Capitol Theater on Broadway for one week, so that he could just get a taste of live applause again. He had signed a new picture contract with United

Artists and was collecting a weekly salary on that, so he didn't need the money.

"Ruby Keeler will return with her husband to the coast at the end of his Capitol engagement," said a newspaper. "She has refused all offers of New York stage musicals."

Had she? Or had her husband refused them for her?

There were plenty of indications that Jolson considered himself the star in the family, and one star to a family was enough. When *Variety* put out its twenty-fifth anniversary issue in 1930 at Christmas, it carried congratulatory ads from everyone of importance in showbusiness.

"Congratulations," said a full-page ad in the paper. "Congratulations from Al Jolson . . . Ruby Keeler."

There was a picture in the ad, too. Of Jolson.

Two years had gone by, and the Ruby who had hoped to be a homemaker and mother was nowhere in sight. Servants ran the household. There was no child, no pregnancy. Jolson's moods, his flashes of hostility and arrogance, his sudden changes of mind all began to get his young wife down.

When Ruby's Irish temper flared and she complained about being left alone all day, Al arranged screen tests for her at Fox and United Artists. The Fox test, in which she did a tap-dance, showed that she was attractive and could tap-dance. So did the United Artists test. A third test—for Paramount—was canceled when Jolson decided to take her on a sudden Catalina Island holiday. No film offers came in. But Ruby did not want to be a film star anyway.

Soon, she knew, any day now, Al would make good on his promise to take it easy. They could start raising a family.

And then, almost casually, one evening Al announced that he was going to do another Broadway show. The Shuberts, who had sued him for $60,000 that they lost when he walked out of *Big Boy* six years earlier, had promised to drop the suit if he came back. He liked the script of *Wonder Bar*, and had already bought 50 percent of the production.

"But—" Ruby began.

"I know what you're thinkin'," Jolson snapped. "I promised to quit. But I told you, a long time ago, how I am."

"Yes," Ruby said half under her breath. "Yes, you did." The resentment showed in her tiny voice.

"Aw, come on, don't give me that crap. Did you hear 'em at the Capitol a couple months ago? Did you see those lines? I did nearly $80,000 for that joint in a week. Who else can draw crowds like that?"

Ruby bit her lip, hard. "Nobody, Al," she finally said. "Nobody but you."

He nodded, smiling now. "So I just gotta do it. Hell, we won't run it long. We'll open and then maybe tour, and then we'll come back here and make a film of the whole thing."

Ruby looked at him. "And then?"

"Then, that'll be it, baby. We won't step out of this place at all. We'll grow some oranges out there in back, and I'll be a farmer. Okay?"

The enthusiasm in his voice, that distinctive emotion-filled voice, made her smile, too. "I hope so. I hope it will be okay," she said, resignedly.

Because Jolson would be working in New York, the couple decided that Ruby might find something to do there, too. She signed for the *Vanderbilt Revue*, a series of songs and sketches with comic Joe Penner, but quit the cast before the show flopped in Wilmington and flopped in New York a week later. Unfortunately, she stayed with *The Gang's All Here*, a revue that opened in Philadelphia and, after getting unkind notices, closed there.

Said *Variety*: "Ruby Keeler Jolson looked great and had plenty of charm and assurance, but her tap dancing was many notches below what it used to be. In fact, it fell flat."

When Jolson read the reviews, he was enraged. The wife of the world's greatest entertainer should not—*could not*—get such notices. Ruby was out of the show even before the producers decided to close it.

Her stage career was officially at an end, by mutual consent. From here on out, she would be Mrs. Al Jolson, housewife.

*Wonder Bar*, the first stage show in which Jolson did not play in blackface, met an enthusiastic reception. After a successful Broadway run, Jolson and his co-star Patsy Kelly, took the musical on tour. "He loved to play practical jokes," remembers Patsy. "I did this 'dance of the dying flamingo' in one scene, and he was supposed to shoot me with a shotgun loaded with blanks. One night he put real buckshot in the gun. I did leaps that Nijinsky never saw! Jolson apologized and sent me flowers afterwards."

Meanwhile, Ruby returned home to California. The loneliness crept in again. Her husband tried to solve the problem. He bought homes near his for Ruby's mother and her sisters. Two of the sisters, Gertrude and Helen, went onto the Warner Bros. roster of stock players and got bit parts in films. Ruby's brother, Bill, did not want to go to the Coast, so Jolson set him up in business as a Wall Street broker. Now, with her family around her again, and their financial worries settled, Ruby would have nothing to complain about, the singer hoped.

But she had plenty. Jolson was—well, he was Al Jolson. He finished his tour with *Wonder Bar* and started a weekly NBC radio series for Chevrolet from New York. He managed to work a concert or two at Carnegie Hall into the schedule. He talked of a concert tour of the world, of turning *The Jazz Singer* into a grand opera, of playing the role of "De Lawd" in the film version of *The Green Pastures*. He flew from New York to Hollywood and back again, continually planning new deals. He made another picture, *Hallelujah, I'm a Bum*, which did badly at the box office—and he was sure that his career was over. But his agent and manager assured him that his radio fans adored him, and more films were scheduled.

If there was one thing Al Jolson did not have time for, it was a melancholy wife questioning him when he was at home. He talked to Darryl Zanuck, head of production at Warner Bros., and then told Ruby that he had a special present for her birthday. Something to occupy her time while he was away.

"What is it?" asked the little girl from Broadway's hot spots, who had been showered with cars and jewelry and clothes before she was twenty.

Jolson pulled a thick sheaf of papers from his pocket. "It's a contract," he said. "From Warner's. For $2,000 a week. They need a dancer for a new picture, and I told 'em I had the best little dancer in the business tied up here, but I'd be willing to let her go if they really need her. If they're payin' $2,000 a week, they must need you."

Ruby could no more turn down that kind of request than she could refuse Ziegfeld earlier. The talk of Al's retirement, of having children, of settling down and raising a family—once more, it all was to be put off. At least, until she made this one silly picture.

The film was *42nd Street*.

The chances are that Jolson had no more idea of how successful the picture would be than Warner Bros. had when the studio decided to make a "different" kind of musical film and perhaps revive that fading form of entertainment. To Jolson, Ruby's part was a small one—that of an understudy who goes on when the star breaks her leg. There were bigger names in the picture—Warner Baxter, Bebe Daniels, Guy Kibbee—and Ruby only had to do a couple of musical numbers with some young crooner named Dick Powell.

But *42nd Street* was a new kind of musical. It was tough, with real-life wisecracks—"I gotta run," says a chorus girl inspecting her stocking. "First door to your left," snaps her sidekick. And it was an old-fashioned Cinderella story at the same time. The major innovation was the style that Busby Berkeley brought to the musical numbers. Although the routines were supposedly taking place on a theater stage, they were designed for the silver screen for the first time. Depression-depressed moviegoers, searching for romanticism and poetry to offset the grim reality around them, opened their hearts to the lyricism of the Berkeley dances.

And they fell in love with Ruby Keeler.

This time the notices were more like the ones Ruby had received in her Broadway night club days. Said the *Times*: "Ruby Keeler (Mrs. Al Jolson) makes her motion picture debut. Her ingratiating personality, coupled with her dancing and songs, add to the zest of this offering." The *Herald*

*Tribune* added: "Miss Keeler, one of the best of all possible tap dancers, performs her dancing specialty eloquently."

Warner Bros. sent a special show train, with Bette Davis and other stars, racing across the country as a "*42nd Street Express*" to promote the movie at every whistle stop. Everything worked. The picture eventually took in $2,250,000 at the box office.

Publicly, Al Jolson was delighted to find all America at the flying feet of Ruby Keeler. But inwardly—simply because he was Al Jolson—he had to feel resentment and anger. What he had feared all his life, that a girl would use him to further her own career, seemed to have happened.

And he wasn't even sure how she had done it.

\* \* \*

After *42nd Street*'s overwhelming reception, Ruby and Dick Powell were rushed into picture after picture. *Gold Diggers of 1933. Footlight Parade. Dames. Flirtation Walk. Shipmates Forever.* She was too busy now to notice much that was going on around her. Sometimes she did not know the plot of the film she was working on, running from sound stage to rehearsal hall without bothering to read the script the other actors were following.

"There are sagas told about this girl, Ruby Keeler," wrote one fan magazine reporter. "A Ruby Keeler who works eighteen hours a day without complaint. A Ruby Keeler who apologizes when she is unable to fill the requests of the publicity department for pictures and interviews because she is dead on her feet. A girl who never demands more consideration than the humblest player in the cast."

Although she was busy on two—sometimes three—films a year, Ruby sensed that her husband was working less. He signed at $5,000 a week to do the *Kraft Music Hall* series on radio for forty weeks, and he filmed *Wonder Bar*, antagonizing Dick Powell and others by "hogging" the picture. But some of the old drive was missing. Perhaps he was tiring. Perhaps he really was serious now about settling down.

Jolson still liked the track. And he and Ruby both took up golf with much devotion. They played cards a lot. And they went to the fights regularly—or did, until one night when Jolson spotted columnist Walter Winchell strolling down the aisle toward Ruby and him at ringside. The singer made an angry comment to Winchell, and then swung a punch that hit him on the back of the neck, staggering the newspaperman. It was the old Jolson again, and newsmen came clamoring to learn the reason for the fray.

The explanation came promptly. Jolson had learned that his old friend Darryl Zanuck had bought a movie script, *Broadway Through a Keyhole*, from Winchell. The script's romantic triangle involved a chorus girl, a popular male singer, and the chorine's boyfriend, a gangster. The characters could have been based on Ruby Keeler, Al Jolson, and Johnny Irish Costello. Winchell said they were not. Apologies were later issued all around, and the public concluded that everyone involved had obtained publicity from the incident. Ruby, however, lost enthusiasm for the fights—by professional boxers as well as by her husband.

Jolson's habit of rushing to the defense of womanhood— "Winchell's story made a nervous wreck out of Ruby," he said—was less in evidence afterwards. He issued statements to the press that both he and Ruby would soon end their film careers. Soon.

Just after the next one, maybe.

Or the one after that. His own film offers were coming less and less frequently. Audiences had grown tired of his brassy, rolling-eyes, hyperactive style. They preferred the crooners—Russ Columbo, Bing Crosby, Dick Powell.

Ruby's career, too, seemed to have passed its zenith. She was getting $4,000 a week now on her film contract, but film-goers had discovered a new, sophisticated dancing style. Fred Astaire and Ginger Rogers were turning out film after film in which they actually *danced* . . . *floated* . . . *moved* all over the screen. Ruby's technique, in which she stood in one place and pounded her feet as fast as she could, appeared graceless and old-fashioned. The Berkeley numbers, in which mass motion and kaleidoscopic designs concealed the fact that the hundreds of chorus girls and boys really could not *dance*, also lost their effectiveness.

When Astaire and Rogers broke up to prevent audience apathy after six films together, Warners had already split up the Keeler-Powell combination for the same reason. There was some talk of Astaire teaming with Ruby for his next film, *Damsel in Distress*, but his studio decided that the picture called for someone with more acting ability than Ruby had evidenced. Joan Fontaine got the part.

A decision was made that Jolson and Ruby would star together in a single blockbusting film, and they made *Go into Your Dance*, with Patsy Kelly called in to supply the laughs. The picture followed the pattern that audiences knew too well: The big broadway star who is "all washed up" wants to put together one last show to prove he's still on top; the little unknown chorus girl gets her chance to work with him, and so on. It was far from original, and Jolson felt sure that the studio—First National—had only offered him the role in order to get Ruby into one of its pictures. The couple's onscreen styles did not mesh well, either. Ruby's shy sweetness, her flat acting style, and her nonchalant way of dropping out of character whenever the camera was not directly on her clashed with Jolson's powerhouse vocals and his habit of mugging through everyone else's scenes.

Ruby and her husband looked at the cool reception the fans gave *Go into Your Dance*. It was summer 1935, and all at once Jolson began talking about really slowing down. They had been married six years now, and perhaps it *was* time for Mr. and Mrs. Al Jolson to do something about raising a family.

Al gave instructions to plant ten acres of orange and lemon and grapefruit trees on the ranch in San Fernando Valley.

And Ruby went off to The Cradle, a famed adoption home in Evanston, Illinois. She returned with a seven-week-old son. The child was christened—what else?—Al Jolson, Jr.

But he was never referred to by his father as anything other than "Sonny Boy."

The reporters could not believe it. Jolson, the one-man dynamo, was actually going to take it easy? He was going to become a gentleman farmer? He was going to admit that he was nearly fifty years old?

It was true—for a while. Fretting over the inactivity—he was working only in a weekly radio series—Jolson began planning to produce pictures. Then he decided that, if he was going to raise citrus fruits, he might as well do it as a business and make money from it. Ruby's new picture, *Colleen*, was only a mild success, but Jolson worried that he was not even getting bids from the studios so that he could turn them down. It was at this point that he fired his brother, whom he had hired as his agent, and asked the big William Morris Agency to get him a job. When his brother sued, Jolson tried to make amends by presenting him with one of his cars.

The Morris Agency got him two small parts—supporting roles in *Rose of Washington Square* and *Swanee River*—and Jolson, for the first time in his life, accepted less than top billing. His mood of frustration and hopelessness did not improve.

He began insulting the young friends whom his wife occasionally invited to the house. He wanted her home, alone, when he was there. Except for her family, she should be there, alone, when he was not there. The baby, whom he professed to love so dearly, seemed to be a disappointment to him. The kid was not turning out to be a "man's man," interested in sports and constant activity. "Sonny Boy" was sensitive in his nature, artistic, a real "mama's boy."

In an interview after nine years of marriage, Jolson said: "The main secret of our happy marriage is this: Even though we live in the heart of Hollywood, we have never been a part of it. We seldom go out with the Hollywood crowd and we've both had our fill of night clubs, from years of working in them. . . . Giving parties in Hollywood is too difficult. You've got to invite everyone. . . . We manage to get to the Trocadero once every few weeks, but we go mostly to see the Sunday night shows. Otherwise, our night life is confined to the card table, or reading."

This was a new Jolson, everyone agreed. A whole new Jolson.

And Al Jolson didn't like him.

He craved action. It was nearly six years since he had heard the roar of a Broadway theater audience begging him to sing . . . and sing . . . and sing. Radio and films, where the applause came only from a small studio audience or a handful of technicians, did not thrill him. He began talks with youthful producer Mike Todd, about a show that would satirize the old Ziegfeld days. Oscar Hammerstein II agreed to think about a script. But days and weeks went by, and nothing materialized. Jolson was forced to spend more and more time at home.

Ruby was there with him. Her own film offers had dwindled to one a year, and it took her only a few months to complete a picture. In *Ready, Willing and Able* she danced on a giant typewriter and publicly admitted onscreen that she could not sing. ("We've been waiting a long time for that," said one film critic.) Then RKO offered her a straight dramatic role—already turned down by Katharine Hepburn and several other stars—in *Mother Carey's Chickens*, and she managed to act her way through the part.

But she was at home a lot now. And she wanted a larger family. She tried to catch Jolson between his endless sequence of business trips and discuss it with him.

"For some time Ruby and I have been thinking about adopting a girl," Jolson told New York newsmen late in 1938. "I told her long distance the other night that I'd stop in Chicago on the way back next weekend and pick out a baby."

He did nothing of the kind, of course.

If he had, the events of the next year might have been different.

But probably not. For Jolson was Jolson.

In the summer of 1939, the girl who once was said to "have a loyalty to Al Jolson which minimizes her own concerns to his needs," thought of her own happiness. With Al, Jr., she went to Honolulu for a temporary separation. She wanted time to think things over.

When she returned, Jolson was contrite. The couple embraced, kissed, cried, promised, swore, rejoiced.

And two months later, after Jolson had taken her to a prize fight on the evening of October 25th, Ruby took her four-year-old son, some toys, and some clothes, and moved out of the big house at Encino into her mother's home at nearby Toluca Lake. Jolson's tearful plea—"Don't take him, don't take Sonny Boy"—brought back a sudden sharp memory of that scene, so long ago, in *The Singing Fool*. But Ruby was determined, and she would not let his sentimental tears stop her.

She filed for divorce within the week.

The shock of his wife's leaving him—after eleven years and forty-nine days of a marriage that, as it was, had lasted eleven years and forty-eight days longer than the Broadway wise guys thought it would—hit Jolson like a thunderbolt. Even the public, which saw Jolson only as a human dynamo, knew it. He told newsmen that he was unsure of whether Ruby wanted out permanently . . . that it was all a mistake . . . that he did not know what had happened . . . that it already looked like a reconciliation would take place . . .

"It's just family trouble," he said. "Nothing important enough in my opinion to bring divorce." But he admitted that he and Ruby had talked about a settlement.

He offered her $400 a week in alimony, and a lump sum of $50,000 if she married again. He also said he would set up a $100,000 trust fund for Al, Jr., which "Sonny Boy" could collect on his eighteenth birthday.

Ruby rejected the terms. Reconsidered. And accepted them. Her divorce petition said simply: "Since the marriage, defendant has treated plaintiff with extreme cruelty and has caused plaintiff grievous mental and physical suffering thereby."

Called to provide additional testimony in court, Ruby said that Jolson had called her "stupid" and had kept her up all night calling her names. "He would sit at the table and refuse to talk and make me keep up the conversation. Then he would go upstairs to bed and leave me to entertain our friends," she told the judge in a Los Angeles court.

"He would never agree with me on anything; when I said anything he would fly into a rage."

In New York at the time, Jolson told reporters that he was "sorry" if his actions had given Ruby an inferiority complex. "She's a wonderful girl," he said, noting that the financial settlement should take care of her nicely. "I fixed it so nobody else can touch the money," he added. "Poor Ruby. She doesn't know the value of a dollar."

The Jolson-Keeler fans around the world were stunned by the breakup. Even the sophisticated *New Yorker* magazine said it never should have happened:

> There was a kind of pathetic elegance about Miss Keeler's testimony [wrote *The Talk of the Town* columnist]. "He would sneer at me whenever I opened my mouth," she said. "When I gave an opinion on any subject, he would say, 'Oh, so you know all about that, too!'" In reply to these charges, the comedian merely remarked that he still considers Miss Keeler the most wonderful girl in the world, though dumb. Seldom, we think, has the essential history of a marriage been put down so clearly or convincingly. We can hear Miss Keeler producing her considered opinions on various subjects at the breakfast table; we can imagine Mr. Jolson tossing in his bed, trying to figure out how so much beauty could harbor so much misinformation. We have always done our best to keep out of other people's emotional difficulties, but it hurts us to see one of the perfect romances of our time ruined. . . . There is no real occasion, Mr. Jolson, to be disturbed by the cultured conversation of your wife. You can be quite sure she's thinking of something else all the time. If you could look inside her head, you might easily be scared to death, but we'll bet anything you like you wouldn't be bored.

Jolson was not bored. He was desperate to get busy, to prove himself all over again, to win Ruby back in the year it would take before the divorce became final.

Or, perhaps, to get revenge on the woman who had taken his "Sonny Boy" away from him.

An old friend, George Hale, had done well on Wall Street and wanted to produce a Broadway show. And he wanted Jolson to play the part of a radio singing-cowboy who goes out West and captures some real-life rustlers.

It would be Jolson's triumphant return to Broadway. His first appearance in nine years. He could stand them in the aisles with new songs like "There's a Great Day Comin' Mañana" and, at the end of the show, there was a spot where the radio singer does a fake broadcast and he could work in all his old hits—"Swanee," "Rockabye," "It All Depends on You," "April Showers," all of them! He would be sensational. Then, *then*, Ruby would be sorry.

If he could only—

Wait a minute. There was a part in the show for a dancer. For Ruby.

Jolson got on the phone.

"Ruby, baby, it's me. Listen, I got a sensational idea."

"Yes, Al, but—"

"No, don't talk, lemme tell ya. I'm goin' to do this Broadway show. It's called *Hold onto Your Hats*. I may have to co-produce it myself. Who's goin' to take a chance on an old man like me?"

"Al, you're only fifty-three. But—"

"Naw, in this business that's ancient, baby, and you know it. That's why I need ya. I really do."

"You mean—in your show? But—"

"Sure, in the show. I'm gonna need all the help I can get. And, baby, with you there on the same stage with me, I know those box office phones would ring all day long. How about it baby? Will ya do it with me?"

"But, Al, don't you realize what I've just gone through? I mean—"

"I know what you mean. But, hell, Ruby, we're still friends, aren't we?"

"Yes, Al, but—"

"Then I'm askin' ya like a friend. Will ya do it?"

"I don't know. I—"

"It'll be a small part, baby. Just a dance or two. A few lines."

"But the baby—?"

"Bring him along. He's gonna see his ole dad plenty, anyway. Come on, baby, say yes."

"I just—"

"Ruby?"

"Yes?"

"I need you. Honest. It will be strictly friends. I swear."

"Well—"

"You don't have any picture deals or anything. Come on, baby. Please."

"Well—I guess—Oh, all right, Al, but—"

"Oh, baby, I knew you wouldn't let me down. I just knew it. I'll send the script right out to ya. We'll start rehearsing in March or April. Oh, gosh, thanks, Ruby. Oh, great, great, great!"

Ruby hung up the phone slowly. She did not want to do a Broadway show. She did not want to appear in a show with her ex-husband-to-be. She did *not* want to. *She did not.*

*   *   *

Even before rehearsals started, Jolson made the fourteen-hour flight to Los Angeles each weekend to see Ruby and "Sonny Boy," and then flew back to work on the production. At times, he was a changed man—a balding, pouching, aging man who sat on a bench in Central Park with a young girl, a worshipping seventeen-year-old fan from New Rochelle, a constant companion who listened to stories of his past glory while "Sonny Boy"—his for a New York weekend —whirled happily for hours on the carousel. At other times, he was the old Jolson, squiring warm-blooded, Chile-born Jinx Falkenburg, his latest flame, to clubs and shows all over town. He personally selected the chorus line for *Hold onto Your Hats,* picking out the beauties with a practiced eye.

Rehearsals got under way. Ruby came to New York, to work along with the other performers: Miss Falkenburg, Martha Raye, Jack Whiting, and Lionel Stander. The prolific and youthful Raoul Pène du Bois designed the costumes. Burton Lane and E. Y. Harburg worked on the score.

Al kept his promise. He treated Ruby like a friend. He proved he really did not think of her any longer as more than that—*if that*—by making sure she saw how happy he was with Jinx Falkenburg.

170

Ruby began to feel uneasy.

But she had *promised* him she'd do the show. He *needed* her.

The company left for Detroit. The first night audience was cool to the premiere until shortly before the finale, when Jolson went into the reprise of all his old hits. Then the roof fell in.

And with the thunder of thousands of hands clapping, the old Al Jolson returned. The Al Jolson who was born a star, had always been a star, and would always be a star.

The Al Jolson who didn't need anyone but himself and a crowd.

The Al Jolson who did not need Jinx Falkenburg.

Or "Sonny Boy."

Or Ruby Keeler.

Ruby was disturbed about some of the lines in the script that Jolson addressed to her. At one point, the dialogue called for him to tell her, "I'm old enough to be your father and I can give you lessons in carrying the torch." At another point, as the cowboy prepared to sing a song into the fake microphone, he said, "This one's for my kid who's listening on the Coast. He's four years old."

The lines, voiced with all the familiar Jolson sentimentality, hit too close to home for comfort. And then Jolson began to ad-lib. At one performance, when Ruby had nervously fluffed a line, the star turned to the audience with a grin. "Maybe y' saw in the papers," he said, "that I'm supposed to have called somebody stupid. Well"—and he tossed in a broad wink—"I think I was right."

As the audience chuckled in embarrassment, Ruby bit her lip. It was not the first time that she had been made ill at ease onstage. Eddie Cantor offended her with a joke about her marriage to Jolson in *Whoopee,* and she was said to have walked out of the *Vanderbilt Revue* in disgust at a near-pornographic sketch. She was not the kind of quick-witted performer who could fight back with a cutting ad-lib, even if she wanted to. Indeed, *Variety* reported that during

**171**

the Detroit run of *Hold onto Your Hats*, fellow actor Lionel Stander missed a cue one night, "leaving Ruby Keeler all alone and helpless in the middle of the stage. Conductor Al Goodman, however, saved the situation by striking up Miss Keeler's dance music just before she collapsed from fright."

She only knew one thing to do. She told Jolson she wanted out of her contract. He refused. He apologized. It was just nerves, he said. He was uncertain about the whole show, and was looking for easy laughs. If she would stay until they got to Chicago, she'd see that things would be better.

Ruby listened. She agreed to stick it out.

A week later, in Chicago, the show had to compete with the Democratic Convention for headlines, but the Keeler-Jolson situation won out easily. Newsmen, hoping for the reconciliation that Jolson hinted might take place on stage any night, haunted the theater. But the presence of Jinx Falkenburg on his arm puzzled them.

Again the show was a hit. Ruby's notices were kindly. "Miss Keeler is very sweet," said one reviewer, "although she is not yet possessed of enough wind to do justice to the tap dances she essays. Toward her, Jolson is considerate, almost tender."

A week later, Ruby was obviously seeing things that the reviewer had not caught on opening night. She refused to come out of her hotel room to do the show, and another dancer had to go on in her part. Jolson told the press that she had asked for a release from her contract, but that she would go on, "happy or not." If she broke the contract, said a news story, Actors Equity rules would bar her from the stage for life.

Ruby remained adamant. Finally, Jolson realized that he had obtained enough publicity out of the affair, and tore up the $1,000-a-week contract. Ruby gave a final interview to newsmen before she boarded a plane for California.

"Perhaps I shouldn't say this," she said, "but I know Al hoped our working together would bring about a reconciliation between us. That is, and always has been, impossible. And I haven't been able to understand his strange attitude."

If Ruby Keeler, who had lived with one of the world's

great megalomaniacs for more than eleven years, could not understand him, perhaps no one ever would.

\* \* \*

Jolson took *Hold onto Your Hats* to Broadway, played in it to disappointing business for five months, and then faded from public view. Except for a radio guest appearance now and then, he seemed through. When World War II broke out, he volunteered at once for USO tours and began traveling throughout the world wherever GIs, hungry for entertainment and any touch of home, would cheer him as Broadway once had done.

In California, soon after her divorce became final, Ruby Keeler met a young and handsome bachelor at a golf tournament. His name was John H. Lowe. They dated regularly for nearly a year, and then at the end of October in 1941, they applied for a marriage license. Ruby gave her age as thirty-one. Lowe gave his as twenty-nine.

Before the wedding could take place, each had to fulfill a pressing obligation. Ruby had signed with Columbia to make a picture, and naturally, she honored the commitment. The film was *Sweetheart of the Campus,* with Ozzie Nelson and Harriet Hilliard, and one reviewer wrote simply: "It's too bad for the diminutive tap-dancing star that Columbia did not give her a better deal for her comeback film."

As if Ruby was interested in a comeback.

John Lowe, a stolid businessman who worked for the California Cotton Oil Corporation, prepared for his future with Ruby Keeler by converting to Catholicism.

When the Catholic ceremony took place, the Church carefully announced that it had not recognized the validity of the Keeler-Jolson marriage, which had been performed without the services of a duly authorized priest and the necessary two witnesses. "Presupposing general sorrow and penance," said an official proclamation, "her former marriage has been declared non-existent by ecclesiastic authorities."

And now Ruby Keeler had what she had wanted for so long.

A Catholic husband with a sensible profession—he soon

began his own business of purchasing property, constructing office buildings, and leasing the space through his company, Lowe & Myers Properties.

A ranch house, with a few horses, some chickens, and five acres of land.

A young son—

Wait, the child brought harsh memories. She cut some of them off by calling him "Sonny" rather than "Sonny Boy." Later, when Jolson's career soared again with the making of *The Jolson Story*, and the restored star began traveling all over the world, John Lowe legally adopted Al, Jr. "It was a hard decision for the boy to make," Ruby later told newsmen, "but he had to make it himself. He chose to change his own name to Albert Peter Lowe, and we can only pray he will never regret it."

Now, almost every vestige of Al Jolson was gone from her life.

When her husband returned after World War II and packed away his navy lieutenant's uniform, Ruby began one of the truly meaningful activities of a Catholic wife. She had a child of her own—a daughter, Theresa. Two short years later, another daughter, Christine, was born. A son, John, came along a year afterward. And then, two years later, a third daughter, Kathleen.

In 1945, when she was busily occupied with her first babies, and trying to manage the comfortable home the family owned between Santa Ana and Costa Mesa, she was contacted by Columbia Pictures.

No, the studio was not asking her to make another film— *Sweetheart of the Campus* was quite enough. It wanted her consent to portray her marriage to Al Jolson in a film about his career. A young actor, Larry Parks, would play the singer and synchronize his lip movements to Jolson's singing voice on the sound track. A lovely actress, Evelyn Keyes, would play the show girl who marries Jolson—and then leaves him when she discovers that he prefers a showbusiness life to a married one.

Ruby refused.

"I wasn't for it," she said. "It seemed silly to me because

the script really had nothing to do with our lives together. But there was nothing I could do to stop it."

The studio paid her $25,000 to act as "technical adviser" on the film, which meant that she waived any objections to the way Jolson's only screen wife was portrayed. Instead of "Ruby Keeler," the dancer that the film's Jolson sang "Liza" to as she stumbled on the staircase was named "Julie Benson."

The film biography, of course, became one of Hollywood's all-time great moneymakers. Columbia promptly had to make a sequel—the first time a screen biography ever had a follow-up—and *Jolson Sings Again* was a smash hit in 1947.

To this day, Ruby Keeler Lowe has not seen either picture.

After the release of *Jolson Sings Again*, she told an interviewer: "I think the pictures were wonderful for Al. Knowing him as I do, I would say that he almost has to have fame to be happy." On top once more, this time to a whole new generation of fans, Jolson sought to increase his happiness. He married a beautiful X-ray technician he met in a hospital where he was recuperating after a lung operation. At the time, he was fifty-nine. She was twenty-one. They adopted a boy and then a girl.

But Jolson did not settle down. He kept on, as he always had, racing across the nation and the world to sing. When the Korean War broke out, he set off again to entertain the troops. He made personal appearance tours with his films. He did guest shots on all the big radio programs. He began to plan a film in which he would appear as himself.

And then, suddenly, in 1950, while he was playing a game of cards with some friends in a San Francisco hotel room, a few hundred miles from his wife and children and their home in Los Angeles, Al Jolson had a heart attack and died before he could be taken to a hospital.

In his will, he divided his $4-million estate equally between Jewish, Protestant, and Catholic charities, after setting up scholarships for needy undergraduates, a $1-million trust fund for his widow, and $500,000 trusts for his two adopted children.

At her home in the San Fernando Valley, Ruby Keeler Lowe's regret was mixed with a twinge of relief. The last shred of her former life was gone. Irreversibly, completely, finally gone.

In the Lowe household, for twenty-seven years, the name Jolson was never mentioned.

Neither was the fact that there once had been a dancing darling of Broadway and films named Ruby Keeler.

The scrapbooks that had belonged to the little girl who tapped nimbly on dime-sized dance floors in cheap Roaring Twenties clubs were hidden away, given away to Ruby's sisters.

And, as Terry and Chris and John and Kathy Lowe attended Catholic grade school and boarding school and college, they knew only that their mother was a wonderful woman who might occasionally do a quick little tap-dance step in the kitchen. Twice a week, or more often as the children grew older, she would be up before eight o'clock and out on the golf course. On rare occasions, perhaps three times a year, she might go to the race track with one of the older kids. But mostly, she and her husband and the youngsters stayed home, attended church regularly, watched television, swam in the pool, and had the aunts and uncles and numerous relatives in for long, relaxed evenings and weekends.

Ruby's eldest daughter, Theresa, who presented her with the first two grandchildren in recent years, recalls that she knew nothing of her mother's previous marriage until she was about nine years old. "I guess I found out like many children do," says the youthful and attractive Mrs. "Terry" Hall, as she sits barefoot on a sofa in her mother's New York apartment and keeps a watchful eye on her two boys, three and two years old, playing noisily on the floor. "I asked mom one day how she and dad could only be celebrating their twelfth wedding anniversary, if my brother, Sonny, was eighteen. She told me she had been married before. There was no big deal made about it."

John Lowe III heard from several schoolmates in the

fourth grade that his mother once had been a tap dancer in the movies. The daughters made similar discoveries as they grew up, but the level-headed Lowe kids did not want details. "I'm really happy that showbusiness was not part of our growing up," says Terry. "I knew a girl at school whose mother was a big star, and I used to hear her say she was proud of her mom. Well, she had been married several times and had all kinds of scandals during her career, and I remember thinking that it must be hard to say you're proud of someone with a background like that. Our mom says that her life began when she married dad—and she made it easy for us to be proud of her."

When the first tremors of the Nostalgia craze began, when the Camp followers began applauding the old Berkeley films, Ruby Keeler Lowe felt a moment of anguish. Suddenly, she realized that the old Ruby, the young Ruby, the dancing-doll Ruby was back, thirty feet high on hundreds of college movie screens, ten inches high on millions of television screens. But the image was almost that of a stranger to her. She hardly recognized the little girl in the bib-top and shorts, who talked her way through songs in a tiny little voice and made her feet fly with such energetic, awkward grace.

Occasionally, a newsman with a good memory would seek her out and ask her if she ever missed showbusiness.

"I'd love to do a guest spot on television," she told one in 1963, "but I wouldn't want to go back to the regular grind of showbusiness. I'm really a lazy person."

Her mild-mannered, thoughtful husband smiled knowingly and said, "I'm always running into men of sixty-five who tell me their mothers took them to see my wife's movies. But then, she started at such an early age." Ruby grinned at him. She told the interviewer, "I haven't seen a movie for years. Some of the ads make them sound so dirty. Some of the older ones were so delightful. I watched *An Affair to Remember* on television the other night, and it was wonderful."

Then, the interviews became more frequent. And the TV

calls from Jerry Lewis and Mike Douglas and others increased. And people were requesting that Ruby Keeler appear with Busby Berkeley at a "film festival"—whatever *that* was.

And John H. Lowe became seriously ill.

And, when he died on February 11, 1969, at his home in Costa Mesa, Ruby Keeler's second life had ended after twenty-seven years. Beautiful years.

Then, all at once, Busby Berkeley called, and an absolute stranger, someone named Rigby, Harry Rigby, was on the telephone, talking to her, pleading with her, saying he needed her, desperately.

Just as someone else had done so many times—that other man, that singer who used to get down on one knee and clasp his hands together.

And, as she had done so many times in that other life, Ruby Keeler bit her lip and thought it over.

And said, yes, she would do whatever they asked. If they really needed her, she would do it.

She would do a Broadway show.

If that's what they wanted from her, she would do a Broadway show.

But she did not *want* to.

**12** When the star of a Broadway musical comedy is paid $2,000 a week, plus 2½ percent of the weekly gross ("but not less than $2,500"), the least that might be expected is that she look and act like a Broadway star.

To Cyma Rubin, the aging woman with the graying hair who got off the jet from California at Kennedy Airport in early September was not a star. *She might be Ruby Keeler,* Cyma thought. *But she is not a star.*

Stars do not wear clothes that can be called, at best, "California resort"—simple blouses, and straight-line skirts that end just above the knee. Stars do not have long-sleeved white sweaters draped over their shoulders, casually, as if they were perpetually coming in from the golf course.

Stars talk about how excited they are to be back in New York ready to go into rehearsal for a new show, and how thrilling showbusiness is. They do not talk about how unhappy they are to have left California, and they do not wonder continually if their grandchildren miss them.

And stars are impressed by a producer's Rolls-Royce and chic clothes and all the money and trouble that is being expended to pave the way for their return—no one *else's*—to Broadway.

No, Ruby Keeler was not a star.

"The first reaction I had when I talked on the telephone to Ruby? Well, it was like the reaction I had last Saturday when I saw Joan Crawford in the *Nanette* audience," says Cyma Rubin. "I was a kid who used to sit in the movies from twelve o'clock in the afternoon until eight o'clock at night, and my mother would have to pull me out by the hair. I was movie crazy in the thirties—in 1933 I was seven years old—and I couldn't wait, I used to collect deposit bottles to get the ten cents to see the shows.

"And then to suddenly find myself in the position where I was going to say yes or no to someone like that, who had

> "The Busby Berkeley I saw in New York was not the same Busby Berkeley I had seen in Hollywood."
>
> HARRY RIGBY

179

been in those pictures, well, when I talked to her on the phone, I *screeched*, I really did. I was so excited. And I wrote her the most *beautiful* letter. But actually beautiful!

"And then, when I met her at the airport with Harry, I came away very disappointed because I found her very—cold." She pauses, and then repeats it for emphasis. "Very . . . cold."

It was not only that Ruby Keeler quickly revealed herself to be a down-to-earth, no-nonsense Republican follower of California Governor Ronald Reagan, while Cyma Rubin is a "Fun City" admirer of New York Mayor John Lindsay.

It was not only that Ruby Keeler could mispronounce the name of famed French designer Givenchy, so it came out "Ga-venk-y," in mock Italian, rather than "Gee-vahn-she." Or that having mispronounced it, she could laugh about her problems with foreign words. And it was not the fact that, if she saw one of several gowns by the designer in Cyma's wardrobe, she would not recognize it for what it was. Nor would she know which ones were the Diors, and the Mainbochers, and the other couturier fashions. Nor would she care.

It was not even the fact that Ruby Keeler disembarked from the plane with her younger sister, Gertrude, and her youngest daughter, Kathleen, and so gave every indication of being the leader of a midwestern Canasta Club on its way to see the Empire State Building, rather than being a star of a half-million-dollar musical comedy. Where were the agents, the publicity men, the photographers that are part of a real star's retinue?

No, it was none of these, and yet it was all of them. But, mostly, it was Ruby's obvious lack of enthusiasm that put Cyma off. Where were the stories, all those wonderful and funny and touching stories that stars tell when they're with a producer, or when they go on the air with Johnny Carson, David Frost, Dick Cavett?

Why wasn't Ruby prattling on about the funny thing that happened that day on the set with Dick Powell? And the time that Ginger Rogers made that wisecrack to the director, whatsisname, Lloyd Bacon, when they worked on *42nd Street?* And how about those years with Jolson? They must have been something . . .

It took little time to discover that Ruby *had* no funny stories to tell about Ginger Rogers, or Lloyd Bacon, or the other people she worked with. She knew Dick Powell so slightly that she usually referred to him—when she was *asked* about him—as "Powell," as if she did not even remember his first name. As for Busby Berkeley, who had directed her in a half-dozen films, she remembered that he was a hard-driving taskmaster—but she didn't really see too much of him or *any* of those people once the shooting day was done. The studio rushed her from set to set, from picture to picture. And she *seldom* brought anyone from "work" home with her. And it was all *so* long ago.

As for her life with Mr. Jolson, Miss Keeler wanted the press people notified in advance that it was one subject she would not discuss.

Now, if they wanted to ask about her *husband*, the late John Lowe, and her children, and her grandchildren, she would be delighted.

*This?* thought Cyma Rubin. *This is my star?*

Ruby Keeler had made arrangements to arrive in New York one week ahead of the rest of the company, so she could begin rehearsals early. After three decades away from the business on a full-time basis, she was uncertain about how quickly she could learn her dance routines, and about how long it would take to memorize her lines. She asked to see the script.

"Oh, don't worry about that," said Harry Rigby. "It's being worked on right now and we'll have it for you in just a day or two. But your part will be *eeeeeeasy.*" Harry was beside himself with excitement. She was here, actually here in New York. Smiling. Talking. Walking. Looking as if she could dance up and down the escalators at the airport, or on the wing of a giant plane. Ruby Keeler was in New York, and Busby Berkeley was in New York, and in a few days, they would all be working to make his dream come true.

Cyma's voice woke him.

"Harry, I'm telling you point-blank that I am not going to pay for any entertainment bills you run up taking her around town. I'll take her out the first two nights, and we'll have a dinner at home, and that's that. She's *working*, baby, and if you want to show her off to your friends, *you* pay for it. Don't come to me for it. Don't try to put any chits in."

Cyma, who always thought of money, had reason to be concerned. The bills were mounting daily now, and she was working to cut corners. Little things began to add up to big expenses. It had been recently decided, for example, that Raoul Pène du Bois would have to design the costumes for the principal women in the cast, rather than select them from a designer's line. A letter from Raoul's agent pointed out that the original fee agreed upon did not include his client's designing six costumes for Ruby Keeler, four for Helen Gallagher, five for Carole Demas, and five for Patsy Kelly. The twenty additional designs would cost $125 each, or a total of $2,500.

Money, however, could be had. What began to terrify Cyma—and to worry Harry—was the lack of a usable script.

And the physical condition of Busby Berkeley.

The event that might have precipitated a move to solve both problems was a taping of *The David Frost Show* just a day or two after Ruby Keeler arrived in New York. The show's "talent-bookers" thought viewers would want to see Ruby and Berkeley reminiscing together about old times, so arrangements were made to get them both to the studio.

The backstage area at the old theater where the Frost program originates resembles one of those amusement park fun houses that are all slanting floors and narrow corridors. The dressing rooms are beneath the stage, and guests must wend their way carefully down steep flights of steps. Maneuvering the slow-moving Berkeley downstairs before the telecast seemed to take as long as it would take to squeeze a Cadillac into a Volkswagen-size parking space. Etta Berkeley led the way with a steady flow of conversation:

"The hotel we're in is rather rundown, you know. When we

were here before, we always stayed at the Wyndham, right behind—*watch the steps, now, dear*—the Plaza. We're in this one, though, because we can cook on the little hot plate, but I thought there would be a stove. *Turn right, dear, and through the door.* Mr. Berkeley likes a big breakfast. I hope we get to see this television program. So many people—*now turn left, dear*—call for interviews and stories, and we never hear if they run or not. They say they will send tear sheets and reprints, but only the young people do. *That's fine, dear, I think you can sit down there.*"

Moments later, David Frost strode out onstage and the process was reversed. Like a proud but very old lion, Berkeley shook off the hands that reached to guide him, pulled his blue fedora with the narrow brim to a jaunty angle, and tromped upstairs. Slowly.

"Don't let him walk out onstage on camera," Cyma Rubin had begged the show's production staff. They had arranged that Ruby would appear first, to comment on some film clips from her old pictures (she told Frost she missed her grandchildren), and that the director's appearance would be announced as "coming up right after this commercial break." Two minutes later, when the cameras winked on to show a smiling David Frost, Berkeley was seated—almost miraculously—by his side. Only the studio audience, not the millions of TV viewers, saw him laboriously walk the few steps from the wings of the stage to the chair.

After a few introductory remarks, the irrepressible host turned to Berkeley and said, "Well, Mr. Berkeley, *do* tell us how you evah got all those great ideahs. Those one hundred girls dancing on pianos, f'rinstance. Where did that ideah come from?"

Berkeley put his head back and smiled broadly. "Well, David," he said, "ideas don't come easy, you know." He paused, as if to build expectations. "But one day I was out driving, and I got this idea to have a hundred girls dancing on pianos."

Frost hesitated just long enough to make sure that the famed director was through, and then smiled. "Fantastic! Just fantastic," he said. "And tell us, how did you evah get

183

that effect of the man dancing, with the camera underneath, so it looks like he's tap-dancing on a piece of glass?"

Berkeley smiled benignly. "Well, that was interesting," he drawled, sounding like Wallace Beery about to make Margaret O'Brien's eyes pop with a whopper of a fib. "I had the studio get me a piece of glass, oh, about this thick. And I put the camera underneath and had the man dance on it."

"Just fantastic!" said David Frost.

"We *have* to get somebody to direct the show," said Cyma Rubin when she saw the telecast. *"He can't do it!"*

Harry, struggling to keep the dream from becoming a nightmare, protested weakly, but eventually had to admit it. "He's ill. He's ill. When I first met him, he wasn't. It's like the difference between night and day. It's like before and after."

"We're going to have to get rid of him," Cyma said. "I'm not going to have him around."

Harry's pale face went white. "We can't, we *can't*. It will kill him. He wants to do the show. He's been looking forward to it for years. Let me talk to him. Let me work something out."

Cyma nodded. "There isn't much time," she said. "Harry, there isn't much time. We go into rehearsal next week."

The following afternoon, after a discussion with Harry and Buster Davis and Donald Saddler, Cyma made a phone call. There was one person whom the quartet knew might be available to direct *No, No, Nanette* on short notice. As she dialed the phone, her fingers were crossed.

"I wanted to do something with Donald and Harry and Buster—all of whom are old friends," says Burt Shevelove. "It seemed the best way to get back to work after having been lying in bed for so long. When Cyma called to tell me they had all decided to face the facts, that Busby was too old to direct the play, and that they hoped I would take over, it looked like just the right thing for me."

Shevelove had a few questions, however. "Who's going to work on the script?" he asked.

"Charlie Gaynor will do whatever you say," he was promised. "If not, we'll get you somebody else."

"What is Berkeley's position going to be?"

"We're working on that. Any suggestions?"

"Just one. Keep him out of my way. There is not going to be time for politics, for worrying about hurt feelings."

"It's all right, Burt," Harry said. "I'll work with him. I promise."

The director asked for one thing—complete authority, the final say on every decision that had to be made. He was promised that he would have it.

He asked for one thing more. Money.

The terms hammered out by Shevelove's agent, who knew that Rubin & Rigby Productions desperately needed his client, were far from minimal. They called for something like five times the least amount that a director can work for under the rules of his union. Additionally, he was to receive 1½ percent of the weekly gross, and 2 percent after the initial costs of the musical were recouped by the investors. His per diem of $50 was also the highest of any member of the company.

Shevelove did not know it at the time, but he was to earn every penny of it.

Cyma took stock of what had happened to her "bargain."

Berkeley was to get 2 percent of the weekly gross.

Shevelove would get 1½ percent.

Saddler would get 1 percent.

Gaynor would get 1 percent.

Ruby would get 2½ percent.

And then the designers, musical arrangers, and several others would get royalties of various amounts.

And once the show paid off its investment, the percentages would be higher.

Something had to give.

Harry went to Berkeley and explained the situation. It was painful, and unfortunate, but there was no other way. Would Berkeley accept new terms, a whole new contract?

Or was he prepared to fight Mrs. Rubin's battery of lawyers—at considerable expense—to get her to honor his present agreement?

Or did he want to withdraw from the production and

retire gracefully, as Mrs. Rubin undoubtedly would prefer?

Nodding, glowering, his heavy head sinking deeply onto his chest, Berkeley considered the alternatives. Yes, he admitted, he was old. And he was ill. And he was tired.

But he would not quit.

A day or so later, he read the letter that detailed his new contractual arrangement. The previous agreement, it said, "is hereby cancelled, terminated, and of no further force and effect."

Instead of continuing as *Nanette*'s director and choreographer, he would be "consultant and advisor to the producers."

Instead of 2 percent of the gross weekly receipts, he would receive 1 percent.

Instead of a fee of $5,000, he would receive $500 weekly for five weeks as an advance against his royalties.

Instead of choosing his own assistants, he would give the producers "sole and absolute control of all personnel to be engaged—cast, director, and choreographer."

Instead of a program credit that read "Entire Production Staged by Busby Berkeley," it would read "Production Supervised by Busby Berkeley." (He had asked for "Entire Production Supervised. . . .")

About the only item that was not changed under the new agreement was the $40-per-day granted the Berkeleys for living expenses out of town.

"Mrs. Rubin wanted to send him home to save the per diem," Harry says bitterly. "And I wouldn't let her do it. I went to Merle Debuskey, and I said. 'She can't do it. It'll be such a *scannnndal!*' " The publicity office was convinced that Berkeley was worth $40 a day in news value alone. Berkeley's name, along with Ruby's, was magic when it came to setting up broadcast interviews and articles in the press. A clause went into the new contract with Berkeley:

"You agree to cooperate in attending press conferences, publicity interviews, and so forth."

Harry Rigby put his name at the bottom of the single page, and Berkeley signed carefully and slowly after him.

Harry smiled as he folded the paper and prepared to take it to Cyma. *It will be all right,* he thought. *Buz will be around, all the time, and just his sheer presence will have to influence Burt and Donald. The show will still have the Berkeley "look." I know it will.*

*It will.*

*It must!*

To celebrate the signing of the new contracts, Cyma arranged a small party at her museumlike town house. There was another reason for the party. The principals who had arrived in New York to work under the great, legendary Busby Berkeley had to be introduced to the man who would replace him. It was a ticklish situation, since the star of the show—Ruby Keeler—had been lured back to Broadway in the belief that she would be working with an old friend. Now she had to be told that plans had changed.

Ruby took the news unemotionally, once she was assured by Harry that Buz would be around at all times for guidance and help. After *all,* Harry emphasized, it wasn't as if she was all alone in New York. Ruby's sister, Gertrude, was with her, taking a respite from the occasional jobs that were a result of Al Jolson's largess and legacy. Still on the Warner Bros. list of preferred "extras," Gertrude had last worked in the crowd scenes of *They Shoot Horses, Don't They?* A tiny, enthusiastic woman, recently widowed, she had come along from the Coast as Ruby's secretary. What if she went onto the backstage staff as Ruby's dresser?

And there was Ruby's son, John Lowe III. Back from Vietnam, John did not want to return to college to finish his education. He was engaged to a tanned, blonde California divorcee who had two active and beautiful youngsters. Suppose he gave up his small, struggling photography business in California and came to New York to work on the show as an assistant stage manager?

And what if Ruby's lean, sun-bronzed youngest daughter, who had just graduated from UCLA at Berkeley, went into the chorus of *No, No, Nanette?*

Would that—all that—keep the star happy?

Delighted to be able to have part of her family around her, Ruby agreed. Her daughter, Kathy, a sober, pretty girl with thoughts of going into social work, turned down the chorus job. "None of us kids sing or dance," she said. "John did a little acting in school, but none of us really ever thought about going into showbusiness." She decided to watch rehearsals only long enough to see that her mother was secure, and then return to the Coast to find a job. John Lowe, however, flew from California to report on the first day of rehearsal, and plans were made to put Mrs. Gertrude White on the payroll.

A crisis thus had been averted when the principals assembled at the Rubins' home for the dinner party. Among them was Hiram Sherman, the consummate actor whose penchant for professionalism in the theater already was causing him sleepless nights. He had met Berkeley previously, and was worried.

"When I first met him," Sherman recalls, "I thought he was an old, ill man whose name was terribly important to everyone. Not his body, or his physical presence. But when you are trying to put a show together, the physical presence of someone who is *not* going to be part of it—well, that can be exhausting for everyone else. You have to remember to be extremely agreeable, extremely politic. And there are times when you can't *afford* to be."

The performer pauses, carefully considering the blue veins of age that show on his own hands. "The terrible thing is that I, too, was around in the 1920s. Oh, not the early twenties, perhaps, but later. I was playing in Chicago at the Goodman Theater . . ."

"Chubby" Sherman remembers the party at the Rubins' in detail. "There was Helen, and Bobby Van, and Ruby . . . Ra-*ool* . . . Busby and his wife . . . myself . . . everyone, I guess." He and Burt Shevelove spent much of the evening laughing over amusing things that had happened to them in London, where Shevelove lives and Sherman often performs. Harry, witty as always, was visibly elated at being surrounded by a galaxy of stars and so many of his old theatrical friends. Cyma was playing the gracious hostess to the hilt, barely able to contain her own giddiness at finally being ready to start rehearsals on her very own Broadway musical, her very first Broadway musical.

"And then," recalls Sherman, "we finished dinner and were ready to go home. As we got up from the table, Busby rose—and slid right down to the floor.

"It was just an old man rising suddenly. His pins, you know, just gave way. It really was nothing. I've been through a lot with geriatrics—I *am* one—and it was nothing unusual.

"But to Cyma, it was just as if he had *died* on her living room carpet."

The scene instantly turned into hysterical confusion. Harry and Etta, who had seen it all happen before, helped the aged director to his feet. They moved him quickly out to a cab, holding his arms despite his protests of "I'm all right, I'm all right." Cyma ranted behind them, trying to speed them along and at the same time apologize to the embarrassed guests who were hoping to slip away unnoticed.

"From that moment on, there was a whole change of pace, a whole different feeling, about the production," says Sherman.

# 13

*Oh, dear heaven, dear God, would rehearsals ever begin?*

Harry Rigby chewed his thumbnail and tried to appear nonchalant as he studied the miniature set Raoul had constructed for Act One of *No, No, Nanette* out of bits of cardboard. At first glance, Harry saw that it was perfectly detailed—and beautiful. Precisely the kind of living room that could never be seen outside of a musical comedy, it was flawless, and right, and *beautiful.*

The cardboard scraps were glued together to make a spacious room whose furnishings consisted only of a minuscule

> "When the day comes that I can't take my stars out to lunch or send a car for them, Mrs. Rubin can have the theater to herself."
>
> ALEX COHEN

grand piano and a circular ottoman. At each side, a wide staircase rose in a graceful, curving sweep to join in a balcony that semicircled the entire stage halfway up the distance between floor and glittering chandelier. A wrought-iron railing up one staircase, across the balcony, and down the other staircase . . . a pair of French doors beneath the balcony at the rear, with the effect of their curtains repeated on another pair above . . . floral-patterned wallpaper bursting with giant blossoms—*heaaaavens*, it was just too much! Harry closed his eyes and saw a miniature Ruby Keeler making a slow, graceful entrance down the steps. And then the stage, the stairs, the balcony—*everything*—exploded with a dozen, no, a *hundred* tap-dancing boys and girls! It was too much, too much.

God, if rehearsals would only begin.

The set was left to gather dust on the wide window sill of the rehearsal hall, perhaps to be peopled by its cast of elfin singers and dancers magically after nightfall. But the singers and dancers in the rehearsal hall this hot September afternoon were full-sized, and perspiring as they battled once more for the few spots still open in the chorus of *No, No, Nanette.* It was less than a week before full rehearsals were to begin.

His back against the mirrored wall of the room, Donald

Saddler leaned with his arms folded lightly across his chest. Tall, thin, lithe as a ballet dancer, and garbed in blue from head to toe—slacks, shirt, necktie—he resembled a gray-haired corporate executive who strives to appear casually dressed at the country club, but not *too* casually dressed.

Saddler kept his eyes on the small groups of dancers who pranced before him. Once more they were shown tap dance steps by the wizened, muscular little man—that same balding little man who had put some of them through the earlier tryouts—but now he was wearing an ill-fitting toupee that sat precariously atop his bald pate. As he bounced into the steps he wanted the dancers to copy, they smiled behind him in expectancy that the hairpiece at any moment would fly off and float to the floor.

Behind the dancing girls, Busby Berkeley sat on a hard wooden folding chair, his hat pulled low on his forehead. He stared soberly at the dancers' backs. Occasionally, his eyes would meet those of Donald Saddler, who was facing him on the other side of the room, and Saddler would smile quickly, as if to say, "Am I doing all right, Buz?" Berkeley would glower in silent reply and nod his head.

Sitting on either side of the aged director were his wife, Ruby's sister and daughter, and a half-dozen others who had come to watch the final audition. Harry Rigby slouched against the wall, his face looking gaunt in the flood of hard daylight that streamed through the long windows and bounced off the mirrored wall. He brushed his hair out of his eyes to get a better look at the row of dancers who tapped nervously in the center of the room.

Buster Davis watched them, too. On rubber-soled canvas sneakers, he bounded around the rehearsal hall, crossing to say a few words to Saddler here, a few to Harry there, and then a few to Cyma Rubin who herself was keeping a steady eye on the auditioners. Davis, in a short-sleeved blue sports shirt and red Bermuda shorts, with the dark glasses he wears indoors and out, looked as if he were about to attend a fathers-and-sons Cub Scout picnic.

Costumed in a plaid, high-collared midi-dress and mannish hat, Cyma chatted amiably with a *Business Week* editor who had come to talk about the economic state of the theater. It was her first interview as a Broadway producer, and she tried to choose her words carefully so they would not be misunderstood against the background of tapping feet and the rehearsal piano.

"There is just no reason why a musical should cost as much as most producers spend nowadays," she said. *"Follies*—$800,000! *The Rothschilds*—$850,000! That's ridiculous. We've budgeted our show at $500,000. And we have only a 10 percent overcall, instead of 20 percent."

"How do you intend to keep the costs down?" the editor asked.

"Why," Cyma said, "you just have to take the red pencil to all the little extras. For example, you don't pick up the lunch tabs for your stars. You don't send limousines to take them to the theater and chauffeur them around."

"And that will save $300,000?"

Cyma laughed. "Maybe not, but if you watch all the little details, you'll come out all right. There are other producers who don't, you know. They figure it doesn't matter how they spend the investors' money so long as they themselves look important. This may be my first Broadway show, but I've done a lot of events to raise funds for charity, and I know how to hold down the costs."

"Speaking of investors, Mrs. Rubin, money is tight these days. Did you have any trouble raising the $500,000 for *Nanette?*"

"Oh"—and there was a pause—"we're putting up half of it."

*"We?"*

"The producers."

"And the rest?"

"Uh—friends. We had people *begging* us to invest once they heard what kind of show we were doing. The climate is perfect now for a show that offers—oh, *relief*—just relief from all the pressures around us. There's no message in *Nanette*, just loveliness. We have three beautiful sets, 270

192

beautiful costumes. And the costumes are so much in fashion right now. The 1925 look, the midi-skirts—they just endorse the whole idea of feminism."

"Why did you ever decide to revive *this* show, though, out of all the—"

"Well, Harry wanted to do something with Busby Berkeley, and I sent him to the library to look through all the old scripts until he came upon this one, and it was just right. It has such great music—'Tea for Two' and 'I want to be Happy'—and we're having *new* songs written to some unpublished music too. Then I thought of getting Ruby Keeler, and I put Harry on a plane and told him not to come back without her."

The editor scratched a line in his notebook. "But do you think you can make money on Broadway today? So many shows lose money—"

Cyma smiled and interrupted. "It's all a matter of setting the budget realistically and sticking to it. The way it's worked out, we should pay back the production costs in six months and make about $20,000 a week."

The newsman started to ask another question, but Cyma was moving away, hurrying across the studio to whisper to Saddler. He turned and stared at a tall, long-legged brunette whose hair floated wildly about her face, Paula Prentiss-style. The girl obviously could not tap-dance, but was trying to copy the steps of the other girls in the line. Moments later, when she was asked to sing, it was apparent that she could not do that, either. She fit perfectly, however, into that wonderful chorus-girl category, "Beautiful girl who does not sing, dance, or act—but wow!"

"Wait until you see her in those costumes," Cyma said as she sat down again to continue the interview. "We *have* to have her."

Buster Davis took over the piano keyboard and began hearing the girls Donald Saddler had weeded out of the crowd. Some had brought music with them, but several were not even sure which key they sang in. Friendly, grinning, Davis asked them to sing "Happy Birthday," cutting most of them off after the first few notes and sending them, sheepish and giggling, back to the far side of the room. One girl began "Just in Time," and got halfway through it before she hesitated as if afraid that she had been told to stop and had not heard the command.

"Is that all right?" she asked timidly.

"Oh, fine, fine," said Davis. "That's a Jule Styne number and he once made me promise never to cut off one of his songs."

The girl laughed, recovered her poise, and finished the song—to applause.

An hour . . . two hours . . . and the final selections for the *Nanette* chorus had been made. The assembled girls were told to report back bright and early, at 10:00 a.m., on September 21st. At that time, their contracts would be ready.

Ruby's sister Gertrude sat, amused, through the entire process. "My sister Helen and I were in all the pictures with Ruby," she told the inquiring editor, "and we used to watch the other girls go through auditions like this years ago. Of course, these little girls can dance and sing so much better than any of us could." She paused, watching as a young dancer moved from the group of rejected applicants and held out a folded piece of paper to Busby Berkeley.

Berkeley reached out slowly, took the paper, and handed it to Etta. His wife opened it, leaned over close to his ear, and read the words to him. Berkeley nodded at the girl, saying nothing.

She smiled, embarrassed, and walked away. Swiftly she picked her dancing shoes and sheet music from a chair and hurried out of the studio.

Gertrude leaned over to take the note from Etta. Carefully printed, it read: "My mother was in the chorus of *No, No, Nanette* in 1924."

"A bunch of us Berkeley girls," said Gertrude, as she folded the paper, "still see each other and get together from time to time. We even thought about a half-dozen of us flying in and getting up there with these young people to audition. Without telling Buz, of course. But then we

**194**

thought the shock might upset him. Probably, though, he'd just growl, 'What are you doing up there? Get out of the way.' That's the way he's always been."

When the last of the chorus girls had left, only a small knot of people remained behind. There was a sense of expectancy in the sunlight-and-resin-filled air. Cyma waited, hoping for a miracle. Harry waited, knowing he would see one. And Donald Saddler, flanked by his two assistant choreographers, waited—with no idea of what lay ahead.

Ruby Keeler was about to dance professionally, for the first time in some twenty-odd years.

She got out of a taxicab on the corner of 56th Street and Broadway, an elderly woman who looked like a middle-aged one, and stared at the brilliantly lighted automobile showroom before her. Then she saw the small glass door at one side. She pushed it inward, walked a few steps toward the self-service elevator, and rode up four floors, carrying a purse in one hand, a shoebox in the other. The door of the cramped, four-passenger cage slid open and Ruby Keeler stepped into a small foyer. Directly ahead stood a Coke machine and a peanut dispenser. A cheap black plastic sofa backed against a crowded office with a small switchboard. In front of her were the doors leading to the two studios that were to be her home—and that of the *No, No, Nanette* company—for the next six weeks. She stepped through the door that was open.

"*Ruuuuuby!*" Harry was there, holding out his arms, running to her side, reaching to take her purse and the box, starting to help her off with the white sweater slung about her shoulders. "You look wonderful!"

"The cab was very hot. The *city* is very hot," she said noncommittally, and Harry laughed.

"Oh, you'll get used to it. Let me get you to Donald and his people right away." He took her by the arm across the studio, where Saddler held her hand warmly for a moment. He introduced his assistants. The man in the bad hairpiece was Ted Cappy, a tap-dance professional with a long list of credits. The short-haired girl, wearing an artist's smock over a pair of dancer's black tights, was Mary Ann Niles. Once she had been married to choreographer Bob Fosse (who later wed Gwen Verdon) and they danced as "Niles and Fosse." Cappy had been hired to assist Saddler throughout the rehearsal period and the first weeks of the out-of-town tryout; Mary Ann was on a "temporary" contract.

"Well," said Saddler, "why don't we start by having you show us what you remember?"

"I hope I remember *something*," said Ruby. She sat easily in a chair, slipped out of her shoes and took a pair of worn low-heeled pumps from the shoe box.

"No taps, Ruby?" said Harry, obviously disappointed.

"Oh, not yet. Not until we're ready with something." She tossed the box casually onto the window sill behind her, slid her feet into the shoes, and stood up. From her bag, she took a pack of Parliaments. Harry rushed over with a match. Then, the cigarette dangling from the side of her mouth, Ruby Keeler said, "Well, there was this—"

And she began to dance.

Exactly the way she danced in *42nd Street* in 1933 . . . and *Footlight Parade* a year later . . . and *Dames* . . . and all the rest. Time and again, she used her left hand to shove back a wayward lock of hair falling over her forehead. And, even in the soft leather shoes, the tapping sounds seemed crisp and staccato.

"Hey," said Mary Ann, "what was that?"

Ruby looked at her feet, then repeated the funny little hop-step she had just done. "That?" she asked.

"I've never seen that step. Do it again, will you?"

Ruby repeated it. "Everybody used to do that one," she said.

The younger dancer grinned and said as she tried it, "Boy, it's so old it's brand new." She tried it again. "This—and this—and, I've *got* it. What else?"

As Ruby continued to demonstrate—almost flawlessly—dance steps dredged from the dim recesses of her mind, Saddler's two assistants sought to copy her choppy, buck-and-wing style. Donald Saddler stepped back, folded his arms across his chest, and gently tapped the forefinger of his left hand against his lower lip.

"Isn't it marvelous?" said Harry, almost fainting with delight. Cyma, who had been sitting quietly on the hard wooden chair, nodded.

"Hmmmmm," she said. Harry took it for an enthusiastic assent.

It had been decided that Ruby Keeler and the chorus would dance the show's "big" tap routine to "I Want to Be Happy," rather than the song that the audience might expect them to use, "Tea for Two." As Ruby varied the steps and repeated the ones she knew in different rhythms, Ted Cappy turned to Donald Saddler and nodded his head, enthusiastically.

"She can practically do a whole routine now, Donald," he said. "About all we'll have to do is work the chorus in behind her."

Harry's eyes went wide. *Ruby. The chorus behind her.* It was coming true. His dream, *coming true.*

"Ruby," he called, scurrying with another match to light the new cigarette she had placed between her lips, "we're all going to dinner tonight. You and Gertrude and Kathy. There's a marvelous place you just have to see. All the young kids in the Village hang out there. Kathy'll *love* it."

Ruby Keeler smiled at him. "It sounds nice, Harry," she said. And when she went back to work, brushing her toes and heels against the hard wooden floor, her smile burned in Harry's mind, and the woman he saw floating before him was nineteen years old and there were no lines etched across her forehead or at the corners of her eyes.

"Harry," called Cyma, straightening from her chair, "I'm going to go over and see Raoul's costume sketches for the beach scene."

He tore his eyes away from Ruby's dancing figure. "Oh, yes," he said, "I'll come along."

"Harry," Ruby called as he started to leave. "When do I get a script? I'm not sure how long it will take me to memorize my lines."

197

"Don't worry, Ruby, you won't have any trouble. But I'll check with Burt and Charlie Gaynor this afternoon, and tonight you'll know all about everything." He looked over his shoulder at Cyma, waiting impatiently. "Have to run. Be ready about 8:30."

That evening, as Harry proudly took Ruby and Gertrude and Kathy to Max's Kansas City—a dark, crowded restaurant catering to long-haired artistic types—Cyma and Sam dined quietly at home.

"You just watch, Sam," Cyma said, between quick mouthfuls. "You just watch Harry now. He's going to turn on me. He's a faggot, and he's got Ruby, the Queen of the Camp. So he's going to be the King. I've given him the Queen, and you watch his relationship with me. You just watch. He's going to—*turn.*"

Sam Rubin stroked the left side of his mustache and chewed thoughtfully, thinking about more important things.

**14** By the time the first day of full rehearsal arrived on September 21st, Ruby Keeler had virtually perfected the tap-dance that she would do to "I Want to Be Happy."

And she was bored.

Each day for nearly a week, she had arrived at the Broadway Arts rehearsal studio and had gone over the steps with Ted Cappy and Mary Ann Niles. After the first two days, even Busby Berkeley—who was determined to be on hand as much as possible—stopped coming to watch her. Her plaintive requests to see a script seemed to fall on deaf ears.

> "Of course I learned something. Never sign anything without a lawyer at your side."
>
> **HARRY RIGBY**

"Ruby, darling," Harry said, "don't worry your head about it. Charlie Gaynor and Burt are thrashing it out this very minute."

Actually, Burt was thrashing it out—alone.

"I had two meetings with Gaynor, and we didn't see eye to eye on the script," says Shevelove. "He'd seen the original play, I don't know how many times, and he wanted *that* to be on the stage. I asked for rewrites and they weren't forthcoming, and they said they'd get me somebody else, but nothing happened. So I started to rewrite the script myself, just so I would have *something* to rehearse with the cast."

Shevelove's idea for *No, No, Nanette* was to pare the original script to its barest essentials. With barely six weeks to go before the opening in Boston, he had little time to do anything else. He had signed to *direct* the show, and rapidly was coming to the realization that he would also have to write it. Harry and Cyma had both said they did not want the show "Camped." That was good, he thought, because the cast members all had different acting styles (or lack of style) and it would be difficult to blend them into Camp. He decided to provide a simple script—all innocence and warmth, the way most people remember the Twenties to have been—and the simplest direction possible.

**199**

Maybe in six weeks, it could be done. A script could be written, a "star" who had not worked in four decades could be rehearsed, and enough of a show could be gotten onstage so that it looked like he had earned his money. Maybe, with Buster's help, it could be done—and the notices would not be too bad. Maybe.

But Burt Shevelove would not have bet on it.

The director was not present on the first day that the entire company gathered at the rehearsal studios. He was in his hotel room, working on the script. Shevelove knew the first day was a time for the cast and chorus people to get together, for W-2 forms to be filled out, for names and addresses to be registered. Little actual "work," he knew, would be done. This first day would be different from others for another reason. Once again, the news media had been invited to be on hand—to carry the full story of *Nanette*'s first rehearsal to the eager public.

The hot lights of the TV cameramen brightened the studios, and flash bulbs exploded like Fourth-of-July fireworks as the dancing chorus gathered in one room, the principals in the other. In one corner, Bobby Van told an attractive young interviewer from a women's magazine, "I always do my own choreography for my numbers, and Ruby and I will be working on a tremendous challenge dance for the second act." In another corner, Patsy Kelly got laughs by telling a newsman that her favorite recipe, when she entertains guests, is for instant coffee. Then she preferred to talk more about what a warm and gracious woman is Ruby Keeler than about her own career.

At the center of the room, Ruby and "Buz" sat side by side and posed fondly for the photographers. In answering questions, Ruby said no, she *wasn't* terribly nervous about coming back to Broadway after all these years—and if things didn't turn out to make the show a hit, "I can always go back home." Buz growled out that the show would be a hit, no doubt about it.

Young leads Carole Demas and Roger Rathburn posed for publicity photos with avuncular Hiram Sherman, who would play Carole's guardian. And Helen Gallagher confessed to a reporter that she was terrified at the thought of having to sacrifice her trademark bangs for a softer, 1920s hair style.

In the chorus studio, the girls and boys busily signed their contracts and "riders" which guaranteed that they would stay with *Nanette* for at least six months. "But I don't understand," squealed one girl. "Why are we staying on the road for so *long*? Eleven weeks! And maybe we don't even come back to New York then?"

Bob Becker, the show's boyish dance captain, had a ready answer. "We don't want to come into town until we're absolutely certain the show is 'right.' And we won't come in until we get the right theater."

"Oooh," the dancer said. "then we'll be sure to be a hit." She put her name to the six-month agreement.

Not every girl did. Eleven weeks away from Broadway, through Thanksgiving and Christmas, is a long time, and it can be expensive when you're spending money for a hotel room on the road and keeping an apartment in New York, too. Some of the girls had husbands or boyfriends—or, more important, chances at lucrative TV commercials—that could not be left behind for three months. Three girls rejected their contracts and prepared to make the rounds of other shows that were auditioning.

John Lowe III, Ruby's son, had arrived from California. Muscular, tanned, and extremely open, he told an interviewer that his first job as assistant stage manager on *No, No, Nanette* was to move a piano from one studio to the other. "I guess that shows how much preferential treatment they're giving the star's son," he laughed.

The producer's daughter, Loni Zoe Ackerman, similarly got no special attention on this, the first day. She sat quietly on a chair alongside Pat Lysinger and K. C. Townsend, waiting until M. J. Boyer signaled publicity photographer Sy Friedman to shoot the three gold diggers draped around Hiram Sherman's neck.

Two television cameramen tried to get Ruby on her feet to dance just a few steps, but she refused. Previously she had warned Merle Debuskey that she would not dance for any pictures.

"I don't want them to see anything until it's all ready," she said.

Debuskey shrugged. "It's up to you." Then he tried strategy. "Some people will start rumors that you can't dance any more," he said with a laugh.

Ruby ignored the challenge. "When I'm ready, and am wearing something that's more presentable than these rehearsal clothes," she said, "I'll dance."

The TV photographers eventually packed their newsreel gear and carried it to the tiny elevator. "That Keeler dame wasn't much," said one. "She just sat in the chair through the whole interview."

The other cameraman nodded. "It'll be all right. Van was colorful. He moved around a lot."

Now Sy Friedman gathered the entire company around a piano. Buster Davis played "Tea for Two" and the group sang lustily as the photographer clicked away with three cameras. Then someone noticed that Ruby was not in the group—she was in the other studio taping a radio interview —and M. J. went to get her.

"Oh, they don't need *me*," Ruby said. "They've got Patsy and all the others."

Through all the excitement, Harry Rigby stood quietly, ecstatically, at one side and let the stars and Cyma Rubin do all the talking for the press. He did not listen to the interviews. Already that day he had heard plenty—from Cyma.

"Those girls you picked out in California, Harry, were dogs. Just *dogs*. Donald Saddler agrees that we just can't use them in the show. I've paid them off—it cost me $5,000 to buy up their contracts—and I've sent them back to the Coast. They were dogs, all of them."

Harry bit his lip and said nothing. What difference did it make? Besides, he had seen Raoul's costume sketches for the chorus—the girls would be in pastels and the boys in bright, multicolored sweaters—and Harry felt that in this show, the boys would be more attractive than the girls. And what would be wrong with that?

Now Cyma was telling one of the newsmen who straggled behind that Raoul would dress Ruby and Helen Gallagher in magnificent bugle-bead dresses for the finale. "I got a bid on making the dresses from Brooks—the people who do all the Broadway shows—and they wanted *$2,000* apiece," Cyma exclaimed. "Can you imagine that? Well, other producers might have taken that price. Not me. I've found a wonderful little woman who will do them for $500. All handwork. Just beautiful! Wait till you see them!"

Harry cringed at the hopelessly vulgar attack. *Oh, dear,* he thought. *There are Ruby Keeler and Busby Berkeley and all those wonderful people—ready to make* magic*—and this woman is bragging about saving money on a dress! What have we all gotten ourselves into?*

As he turned away, he caught sight of a middle-aged and husky woman who moved with a dancer's grace. "Oh, there you are," Harry called. "You're not ready to start so soon?"

"Not yet. I just came to see what the girls looked like."

"You *will* be able to teach them, won't you?" Harry had searched his mind and memory for something that would look onstage like a Busby Berkeley film routine, and had decided he wanted the chorus girls to dance on top of huge beach balls in one number.

Now the instructor, a former circus performer, looked at him with assurance. "All I need is one girl who can do it well. It's been a long time since I taught anyone, but give me one girl who can do it well—and we'll fake some falls that will have the audience screaming."

Harry screamed at the very idea. "Wonderful, wonderful!"

Cyma, all smiles, came over. "Let's go to the house," she said. "Everything is finished here, and we should talk over some things. Ruby keeps asking when she's going to get a script, and I'm tired of telling her it's not ready."

"I'll take care of it, I *will*," Harry replied. He hurried to say a few consoling words in Ruby's ear. "And, Patsy," he called, "just wait till you hear the comedy song that Charlie Gaynor's writing for you. You'll love it, just love it!"

Patsy, frowsy-haired and tired from the long day and the

203

crash diet she had been on for the last month, waved a careless hand at him. "Who cares if *I* love it when I hear it?" she barked. "Let the audience love it when I sing it—and with my voice, buster, that's askin' a lot."

Harry doubled over, giggling, and Cyma laughed, too. Then the two of them crowded into the elevator with the last of the departing newsmen.

A few minutes later—just the length of time needed for a cab to get from 56th and Broadway to the Rubin town house in the sixties off Fifth Avenue—Harry Rigby signed away his dream.

\* \* \*

Until that day, September 21, 1970, Harry Rigby and Cyma Rubin had no contract between them. As they had worked together during the previous year, Cyma had provided Harry with spending money and allowed him to live in the "office" on East 17th Street. Harry, in return, had rounded up the friends and acquaintances that he knew could put a musical production together.

True, a corporation known as Rubin & Rigby Productions, Ltd., was in existence—but Harry had no control of it. It had been formed by Cyma, who naturally was chairman. In negotiations with the various copyright holders of *No, No, Nanette,* the "producer"—Rubin & Rigby, Ltd.—had explained that any corporate profits would be split three ways: One-third would go to the corporation itself; one-third would go to Cyma Rubin individually; and one-third would go to the Limited Partner investors, who, in this case, was Sam Rubin. Although Harry had signed contracts with various stars of *Nanette* as president and as vice president of Rubin & Rigby Productions, Ltd., he had no official title.

Now, here, on the magical first day of rehearsal, when he was as excited as a five-year-old at his very first circus, Harry Rigby was about to get a title—and a contract. He took the piece of paper that Cyma Rubin held out to him. He tried to study it, but he was too giddy to concentrate. He flipped quickly through the pages, hardly seeing the words. It all looked very legal and proper. There were four pages, neatly triple-spaced for easy legibility. And there were plenty of "Whereas" and "Therefore" clauses. And it said he would serve in the office of vice president. And he would get one-third of the net profits of the corporation. And he would get a yearly salary. And he couldn't be fired for six months. And even if he did get fired, he would still get 20 percent of the profits from *Nanette* and the other properties he had brought into the corporation.

At least, that is what Harry thought the words said.

What could be simpler?

He picked up the pen to sign beneath Cyma's name on the fourth page.

"Mmmm, just a minute," said Cyma, turning back to page two. "This last sentence was supposed to be changed. See, here where it says 'Rigby shall not be obliged to repay the amounts paid him as a draw against profits'—that's your salary—'in the event no profits are realized.' That should be changed to read '*unless* and *until* profits are realized.'"

Harry squinted his eyes, thinking. Heavens, it was all so complicated, after all. Let's see, here. The way it read now, he didn't have to pay Cyma back anything if the show did not make any profits. And she wanted it changed so that he would have to pay back the money she gave him to live on *when* he got his profits. That seemed fair, didn't it? Why, the mere idea of making profits from a Broadway musical seemed remote. If he made *anything* off his precious dream, Cyma was certainly entitled to get back some of her investment in him.

He nodded his head excitedly, his long gray hair falling over his forehead. He tried to pay attention as she took the pen and drew two fine lines through the last seven words of the sentence. Then she wrote in the change, put her initials next to it, and handed him the pen.

Harry initialed the change. He wrote his name at the end of the last page. With a flourish.

Theoretically, there was nothing at all *wrong* with the agreement between Harry and Cyma. It had been drafted by Sam Rubin's attorney, and then had been revised by Harry's lawyer (whose expenses were paid by Cyma), and then revised once more by Sam's lawyer. A copy was mistakenly sent to Sam, who scribbled "Why me?" across one corner and passed it on to his wife. It was all very legal.

What was *unusual* about the agreement is that it did not contain any number of things that are usually part and parcel of most theatrical agreements.

Billing credit, for example. There was nothing in the "Employment Agreement" that Cyma presented to Harry that said how large his name would appear—or where, if at all, it would appear—in programs, posters, or advertising. To anyone in the theater, billing is a critical matter, and in the case of *Nanette,* the discussions of credits reached such depths that artist Hilary Knight had difficulty squeezing everyone's name—twenty-eight in all—into the first newspaper ad. And when the show was set to open in Boston, the names of such minor "artists" as the production manager, stage manager, and piano players had to appear on the title page of the *Playbill,* along with Ruby Keeler and the other stars, the authors, and the directors.

Also missing from the agreement that Harry signed was any mention of "house seats"—the number of tickets reserved for his personal use at each performance. A pair or two of nightly seats to a hit musical can be extremely valuable, and the contracts of most important stars and production people ordinarily spell out how many front-and-center tickets they are entitled to get at each show.

Most importantly, perhaps, there was nothing in four pages of legal gobbledegook that said Harry Rigby had any artistic control over *Nanette* or any of the other projects that Rubin & Rigby Productions, Ltd., might present. He was not empowered to hire people, fire people, or give orders as to how *Nanette* or other productions should appear. His duties, said the agreement, were to "propose properties for production, sale or other use by R&R . . ." and to "assist in the production, sale or other use of such properties. . . ."

What it came down to, says Cyma Rubin, is that Harry Rigby was simply an employee of hers who worked for a salary of less than $10,000 a year after taxes. He was never a co-producer of *No, No, Nanette*, she says, and the fact that she often called him that, or that the newspapers and publicity releases identified him as such—well, that was just one of several titles she bestowed on him at various times to keep him happy. But *calling* someone a co-producer doesn't *make* him a co-producer, she insists.

Harry laughs, more than a bit embarrassed, when he thinks back on it. "I don't know—my name was in the corporation, and the paper said I was vice president, and all. It just never occurred to me—I never thought . . . Anyway, it *did* say that if there were any disputes, that we could both go to the American Arbitration Association, and iron them out. It all seemed all right to me at the time—and I signed it. That's all. I signed it." He rolls his eyes skyward and pushes a stray lock of hair from his forehead.

"Oh, if I had only *imaaaaagined*—but Mrs. Rubin and I had not had any important disputes before. Why should we have any now?"

**15** Looking back on it now—at the blend of dreamers and schemers, of major and minor talents who were to put *No, No, Nanette* together—it seems incredible that a sizable explosion did not take place on the first day of rehearsal.

Several occurred on the second day to make up for it.

The dancers, scheduled to work from ten in the morning until 6:30 at night, managed in a few hours to learn most of the steps they would do behind Ruby in the "I Want to Be Happy" number. They ran through the routine several times for Cappy and Niles while Donald Saddler stood approvingly by. After one particularly complicated pattern of steps had been absorbed and practiced, Mary Ann gave an instruction that was to be repeated many times during the next few weeks:

> "I was never sick a day in my life until I took that damn shot."
>
> **PATSY KELLY**

"All right, kids, now turn around and do it for Mr. Berkeley."

And, like obedient children in a dancing school class showing their latest accomplishments to proud, visiting parents, the entire chorus did an about-face to repeat the steps for "Buz," who had been staring at their backs. When they finished, the director soberly nodded his thanks, and the group swung around once more to face its instructors.

Cyma turned angrily to Harry, who was grinning on the sidelines. "I want him *out*," she hissed. "He's paid to be a director, not an audience!"

Harry grimaced, waved a nervous hand. "Shhhh, he'll *hear* you." He began to argue as forcefully as he could in a whisper. He pointed out that Berkeley could handle publicity interviews and leave Shevelove free to work on the script and direct the cast.

"Buz understands *perfectly*. He'll work hard. I told M. J. to line him up for all the interviews she can, and to book him on all the TV and radio shows. *Everybody* wants to talk to him. They want Ruby, too, y'know. But she doesn't want to do *anything*. All M. J. has to do is tell me when and where she wants him, just an hour ahead of time. I'll get him all steamed up and see that he's there. You'll be surprised what he can do when he's enthusiastic."

Cyma was dubious. If she had her way, the old man and his wife would be shipped back to California. But Harry loved Berkeley, no doubt about it. And everyone who was working on the show liked Harry. No wonder, of course. They were all one of a kind.

She was the outsider, the "lady with the checkbook." They were *theater*.

But she would show them. All of them.

She looked around, and her gaze fell on the funny little man with the horrible toupee who was up there sweating in front of the chorus line. Cyma shuddered.

Ted Cappy. How much longer would he be needed? There was only one tap number in the show, and it was nearly finished. Hmmm, let's see, now. Ruby did her own steps. Bobby Van would do his. Why pay a tap-dance supervisor $300 a week after his work was finished?

She would have to think about it. Right now, there were still three dogs in the chorus line to be considered. Cyma had learned that any girl who signed a six-month contract less than a week before the first day of rehearsal could be fired during the first three days. Donald Saddler still was looking for a couple of girls to replace those who had refused to sign for six months. He might as well find a few others who were attractive.

Donald would do it if she asked him. She liked Saddler. "He's easy," she said. "He doesn't fight back. He's willing to take suggestions." Cyma went off in search of him, to make suggestions.

The *Business Week* editor was coming in the door, a copy of the current issue of his magazine under his arm.

"Oh, I've already seen it," Cyma said. "And all those things you quoted me on, about holding down costs by cutting out lunches and limousines—well, it's absolutely *true*. But, oh, the trouble! Our so-called 'star' saw it"—and she cocked her head toward the other studio where Ruby Keeler was working—"and, would you believe it, they're calling me *cheap. Me!*"

It was only a minor problem. There were bigger ones to worry about. The general manager that Harry had suggested, for example. He was never around when she wanted him. He had lined up the out-of-town tour, with all those insane two-week stops, and then just *disappeared.* She had so much to find out about putting a show together, so many questions to ask. Well, Harry would just have to talk to him and tell him that when Cyma Rubin laid out money to someone, she wanted to know what he was doing for it.

And where the hell was Burt Shevelove with the script?

Burt Shevelove, two weeks out of the hospital, sat in his hotel room and pecked at a typewriter. Slowly. Painfully. He had already fought his way through the original *No, No, Nanette* book several times. He had carefully memorized the lines that might still get laughs, even if they were forty-five years old. There were not many of them.

Keep it simple, he told himself. Keep it simple.

After a morning's work, he had finished fewer than a half-dozen pages. He read them over. The scene that began the show retained the flavor of the original, but it moved along much more rapidly. He read it again.

It would do, Shevelove thought. He had eliminated the meaningless opening chorus. He had quickly brought on Lucille, the lawyer's wife, so that the plot could begin to unfold. Maybe "Too Many Rings Around Rosie" was not an opening number, but the lyrics made good sense, and Helen Gallagher had a big, brassy voice, and with a small group of boys and girls behind her, it would get the show off to a fast start. Harry and Cyma would like the period touches he had added—"Banana oil," for example—that would get a laugh from the geriatric set.

He tucked the few pages of script under his arm and hurried to the rehearsal studio. The principals were there, waiting for him.

In a chair against the windows, Ruby Keeler tapped an

impatient foot and took a thoughtful drag from the ever-present cigarette. Patsy Kelly slumped on the window ledge alongside her, tired but expectant. Hiram Sherman began chatting amiably with young Carole Demas to cover up the fact that he had been studying his watch when Burt hurried in. Bobby Van sat opposite Helen Gallagher at an angle, like a prize fighter waiting for the gong, and coolly wondered if her Irish temperament was all that he heard it was.

The attitude of the group was wary, as it always is when work first begins on the script of a play or musical. The actors did not know one another. They did not know how their individual styles would mesh with those of the other performers. They did not know what the director would expect from them. Ordinarily, they should have had a good idea by the end of the day, after they had read through the script aloud, feeling out their parts and getting an under-standing of who the various characters are and where the plot is going.

But this show was different. There was no script.

Shevelove tried to outline the plot of *No, No, Nanette*. He said that he would have to be hazy about some of the details, because—well, frankly, he was not sure which lines and songs would remain and which would be discarded. All that he knew for certain, he said, was one thing:

"The world today is not a pretty place. It is filled with ter-rible news every day of Vietnam, campus riots, pollution, crime, inflation. The audiences that will come to see our show will have heard enough—much too much—about all those things. We must take their minds off those problems and make them concerned only with this: Will Nanette, this innocent little child, get her wish and spend a week end in Atlantic City? Nothing else, nothing else at all, is important. This warm, sunny, lovely little show must be our valentine to the audience."

The speech, which would be given many times during the weeks of rehearsal and would come to be known as "Burt's Valentine's Day Address," was a pretty one. But Ruby Keeler was thinking only of speeches on paper. She looked at the few pages of script that Bob Skerry, Shevelove's young assistant, had pulled from the mimeograph machine. "Oh, dear, I have *twenty-two* lines to remember in the first scene," she said, incredulously. "How many more will there be?"

Shevelove, who had sweated out every one of her few lines, looked at her. "I—don't—know," he said, with an edge to his voice.

"Well, I just hope there aren't too many," said Ruby. The little laugh on her lips did not conceal the fact that she meant every word of it.

Shevelove glowered, then turned to the others. "Let's begin," he said softly.

In the adjoining studio, John Lowe watched the dancers work on "I Want to Be Happy." As they turned about to show their prowess to Busby Berkeley, he explained that his daily assignment was to see that Berkeley got picked up each morning at his hotel and brought by cab to the studio.

"I was really surprised," he said. "I'd heard that Buz could hardly move, but he's always up and waiting for me. He says he doesn't need me." Like his mother, Lowe is an unflappable, low-key individual who takes things as they come. (Ruby told an interviewer that she did not know her son had won a Bronze Star in Vietnam until the medal arrived in the mail one day. "Why didn't you tell me?" she asked. "Well, mom, I wasn't sure the package would ever get here," John answered.)

"I'm not out to make a career in showbusiness," he said. "If this show flops, I'll probably open my own advertising agency in some small city."

He looked at the line of chorus girls and boys. "Did you hear, three of the girls got fired this afternoon? The idea is that we're supposed to have twenty beautiful virgins up there on the stage." He thought it over for a moment. "I don't think they'll find them in New York."

Cyma Rubin, having chased the dogs from her chorus line, approved five new girls the next day. Funny, she thought, but hundreds of girls had been auditioned for months and months to uncover a precious few who were

212

"not just beautiful, but gorgeous"—and she and Donald and Buster had found five overnight. Now the chorus was perfect.

Or, it *would* be once the girls had their hair cut.

The news that all long-haired dancers would have to have their locks shorn into 1920s styles hit the chorus like a bombshell. To many a dancer, long hair is part of her very own choreographic style, as well as an expression of her personality. Some of the girls—who ranged in age from sixteen to their late twenties—had never cut their hair.

Several of the dancers, with tears filling their eyes, went to Harry Rigby in protest. "I know," he said. "I *know*. But Mrs. Rubin wants everyone to look authentic 1920s, and she'll *fire* anyone who doesn't have the right hair style. I argued with her *all* night, but—"

The girls scurried to check their Equity contracts. Yes, most of them *had* signed an extra piece of paper, a "rider" that gave the producers the power to restyle their hair. But *cutting* it? The girls, who first learned of the shearing when the stage manager handed them a schedule of hairdresser appointments, threatened a mass walkout.

The next afternoon, Cyma agreed to discuss it with them. She had her reasons, she explained, for wanting them to have their hair done by a fine stylist. She wanted the girls to be the most beautiful on a Broadway stage. She wanted people everywhere to admire them, to worship them, to recognize the loveliness that a "Busby Berkeley Girl" possessed. In fact, Cyma said, she thought it might be nice if every girl in the show wore modified 1920s make-up—pale face and bee-stung lips—on the street at all times, along with midi-skirts and flowing 1920s styles, so that people would stop and stare and say, *"There* goes a Busby Berkeley Girl!"*

In the back row, a red-haired dancer in a boy's sweat shirt and a pair of faded dungarees turned to the brunette beside her, who was dressed in a long-sleeved blouse and hot pants. Simultaneously their lips puffed outward and two pink tongues showed.

"Bleeaaah!" they said softly, gagging.

Cyma's explanation did little to win over the reluctant

ponies. But her obvious willingness to fire any girl who refused to cooperate did. One by one, the girls thought it over, realized that it was getting late and the other shows that might provide jobs were already in rehearsal—and agreed.

One girl refused to submit to the stylist's shears.

Joanne Lotsko, the first chorus member to sign a contract, had not been asked to sign a "hair rider." She explained her unwillingness to have her hair cut short. "I like it this way, long," she said. "And I get other jobs—TV commercials, for instance—where long hair is an asset. Besides, in *Mame,* we had a Twenties number and we all just put up our hair or wore wigs."

Cyma, noting that the dancer had a firm six-month contract, said testily, "Well, maybe something can be done." But she insisted that the strenuous dance routines planned for the girls would not permit them to wear wigs.

Precisely six months later, when Joanne Lotsko's contract expired, she was informed, "Your 'look' isn't right for the show," and she was fired.

"The little girl came into my dressing room," said Patsy Kelly, "and told me they said her 'look' wasn't right. Wadda they want her to do—have plastic surgery?"

Patsy's own discussion with Cyma over hair styling was short. "She wanted my hair dyed black," the comedienne recalled. "I said no, I wear a maid's cap in every scene, so who sees my hair anyway? And so what if it's gray? Mrs. Rubin insisted I get it dyed.

"Then I told her, in my opinion hair that is dyed black makes a woman look hard.

"And she smiled and said, 'I dye *my* hair black.'

"And I looked her right in the eye and said, 'Exactly.' "

The near-traumatic experience of the stylist's scissors going snip-snip-snip upset Helen Gallagher, too. According to Cyma, she almost had to drag the performer by the hand to Vidal Sassoon's salon and pat her shoulder while the trademark bangs were removed, and her hair was shaped into a 1920s bob.

One long-haired performer escaped having her tresses

trimmed. She was Loni Zoe Ackerman, the producer's daughter.

Almost from the beginning of rehearsals, Loni found herself in an unpleasant situation. She was one of the cast, and yet she was inescapably a part of the production team, too. When things went wrong at rehearsal, when a performer complained about something, should she tell her mother—or not? Would telling help solve problems, or would it create new friction?

For example, should she tell Cyma that the producer's penchant for severe, black clothes, her anxiety to save money, and her haste to dismiss people had led some of the chorus kids to dub her "The Black Witch"? Would it make her mother angry? Or would she take a less dictatorial attitude toward others?

Loni wondered. And considered.

And, like a dutiful daughter, told her mother what was going on.

"She's a beautiful girl, and very talented," said one of the *Nanette* chorus boys, "and we all realized that she was in an awkward position. And we felt sorry for Loni, *very* sorry, at first. But after the record-album incident—"

The "incident" was to occur shortly after *No, No, Nanette* opened on Broadway. One of the chorus boys—with encouragement from the others—scribbled an anonymous letter to Cyma Rubin. The letter complained that the stage managers were neglecting their duties. A few days went by. Nothing happened. The stage managers seemed unperturbed. The letter was forgotten.

"And then one evening," said the member of the chorus, "Loni put her head in the door of the boys' dressing room and asked if she could come in for a minute. Her mother, she said, wanted to present Leopold Stokowski with a copy of the original cast album of *Nanette* as a birthday gift.

"And she wanted everyone in the cast to autograph it.

"I remember Loni saying that we shouldn't just write our names, that her mother wanted us all to write a personal message to Stokowski—something like, 'Dear Maestro, congratulations on your 90th birthday.' Well, like fools, we all wrote our little notes—and it was *days* later before we realized we had given Mrs. Rubin large samples of our handwriting.

"Even then, we couldn't believe Loni's own mother would have not told her what she was up to. But we asked Ruby if she had autographed the album for Stokowski, and she said, 'Well, gee, I don't *think* so—' And we went to the girls' dressing room, and they hadn't signed it. Well, we didn't bother going any further. Mrs. Rubin had us. She *knew* who had written the note, and the only thing to do was wait for the axe to fall."

But all that came later, after *Nanette* was a hit. In the first week of rehearsal, there was no time for Cyma or anyone else to play games.

But there was plenty of time for complaints.

"Where's the director?"

"Where's the script?"

"How many times can we go over 'I Want to Be Happy' before we start screaming?"

"What do we do next?"

Like a mother hen, Harry Rigby fluttered from rehearsal studio to rehearsal studio, pleading for patience and understanding. Ruby's daughter, Kathy, cornered him with tanned, clear-eyed forthrightness: "Mom is looking for a different hotel. That one Mrs. Rubin recommended is impossible. Turn on the air conditioner and the fuses blow—they blew three times the night I arrived. And how can mom cook on a hotplate? The location—well, you just can't get a cab up there. Did you see that article about not getting picked up in a limousine? Well, that's how it's being done, all right. Mom would never say anything, but when she was invited to the film festivals, she always had a car . . ."

Cyma, overhearing, rolled her eyes upward in despair. Oh! That woman! She was never happy about anything. The hotel was good enough for the Berkeleys. Well, she couldn't worry about it now. She had just gotten word from the hair-

**216**

dressers that the stylist who came over to check each girl's hair was in the hospital with hepatitis! And he had touched every one of her girls!

The entire company was ordered to report at four o'clock for gamma globulin shots—a free gift from the producer.

One problem was solved early in the first week of rehearsal. The general manager whom Cyma could seldom find decided he did not *want* to be found, and gave his two weeks' notice. He was promptly replaced by another professional who had worked on a show that Harry Rigby was associated with previously. Two weeks later, after noting that "Mrs. Rubin is driving me crazy, wanting to cut the budget," he was out of the picture. Cyma turned to Merle Debuskey for a successor, and he suggested that two young men—Tyler Gatchell and Peter Neufeld—be assigned to manage their first Broadway show. Cyma, realizing that she would have a strong hand with them, accepted the proposal.

The one man who seemed to be always on hand during those first hectic days was Donald Saddler, the choreographer. But his presence, instead of acting as a steadying force for the nervous chorus members, produced a reverse effect on some. Always courteous, supple, and thoughtful in appearance, Saddler perpetually seemed to be on the verge of announcing a breathtaking choreographic idea.

But as the days dragged on, the idea seemed to remain just out of reach. To inspire the dancers, the choreographer brought in ads and pictures clipped from magazines of the 1920s and taped them on the walls. In legendary Busby Berkeley fashion, he began relying more and more upon his assistants—Mary Ann Niles and Ted Cappy—to furnish the actual dance steps. Frequently he would spot a chorus girl (often Mercedes Ellington) who did a particular step or gesture with grace, and he would ask her to teach it to the rest of the chorus.

Dancers, however, who had worked in Broadway shows with more forceful and dynamic choreographers were confused by Saddler's easygoing style. At times, one dancer related, the director talked so softly at one side of the studio that his instructions had to be passed from member to member across the line.

"It was like the game called *Whisper*," the dancer said, "where the sentence gets mixed up more and more with each person who passes it on. Donald would say, 'Hold your arms —so!' And the person next to you would ask, 'What did he say?' And you'd answer. 'Fold your arms.' Then he would fold his arms and the guys on the other side of him would follow and fold theirs, too.

"I remember that it was about a week before we opened in New York, after we had been on the road for a couple of months, that one of the boys got sick and couldn't do the show. He sat out front to watch it. Afterwards, he came running backstage, to tell us that he had seen for the first time that we were doing different things—*different steps*—on each side of the stage."

Saddler's work proceeded slowly. But not so slowly as Burt Shevelove's.

It was not only that Shevelove had a difficult task in trying to write a script each morning, and direct it in the afternoon.

He was meeting resistance from some of the cast members. Certainly, they were nervous. Certainly, they were worried. Certainly, they were all temperamental children. And it *was* unusual—decidedly unusual—to go into rehearsal without a script.

Shevelove knew all of that. He also knew that he would have to tailor the parts in the script he was writing to the talents of the performers, and that some of those talents were limited.

Still, Helen Gallagher was definitely fighting his attempt to change her from a wisecracking tart to a sophisticated matron. And Hiram Sherman was making much of the fact that he was not used to being handed his part like a daily ration, a page at a time, a *line* at a time.

As for Ruby Keeler—well, she could not act and that was that. She saw nothing funny in the joke lines that she was given, and, rather than argue with her, Shevelove began to

218

cut her lines to a minimum. And to cut her, personally.

"What upset me most," said Hiram Sherman, "was Burt's downright rudeness to Ruby. I know he was working under a lot of pressure, but I couldn't bear it. I don't know if it is just age or experience, but I thought, 'This lady sitting here is your meal ticket. Nothing else really matters, because she is the one who is going to sell the tickets.' Ruby is not our most adept actress, true, but she's a gentle woman and her instincts are right. Now, Burt and I had the same frame of reference—we've both lived and worked in London —and I was the only one around that he could tell certain stories to, and we should have gotten along beautifully.

"But I just could not forgive his basic rudeness to Ruby."

Shevelove—with Harry pleading on one side, Cyma demanding on another, Berkeley glowering on yet another— had little thought of politeness. The show, he knew, must go on—and it must go on in Boston in less than four weeks for its first preview. He would give orders, and others would have to take them.

And, with a bit of luck, *No, No, Nanette* might just make it.

In his hotel room, he turned on the radio, dialing for a bit of soothing music to help him get into the mood to attack the typewriter. He heard the familiar tone signal of NBC's *Monitor* program, and then the voice of Gene Rayburn introducing a guest: Ruby Keeler.

"Gee, no, I'm not terribly excited about being back to do the show," Ruby's flat voice said from the loudspeaker. "As a matter of fact, sometimes I feel like I just want to go home to California."

The radio announcer laughed, then told his listeners, "Say, wouldn't it be ironic if Ruby Keeler quit her show on opening night? And they had to put her understudy on, and the unknown little girl turned out to be a big star?" He laughed again. "Oh, no, it *couldn't* happen. Ruby Keeler's a pro. She would never walk out on a show."

Burt Shevelove stared at the blank page in his typewriter, thinking.

Wouldn't she?

**16** The second week of rehearsal began with good news.

Danny Kaye in *Two by Two*, the Richard Rodgers musical about Noah, had opened in Boston to unflattering reviews. The one show that seemed to be the guaranteed hit of the season—the musical that could not miss—had missed.

In the competitive world of Theater, where the chances of bringing in a hit are better than ten to one against you, the news of a flop is always encouraging. If Boston audiences did not like *Two by Two*, the chance was increased that they would like *No, No, Nanette*, which would follow it into the Shubert Theater. After all, they had to like *something*.

> "I knew someone was going to get fired, but when I found out it wasn't me, I didn't worry about it."
>
> ROGER RATHBURN

Or so Cyma Rubin reasoned.

But time was speeding by so swiftly. How did that Cole Porter song go? "Another op'nin', another show. . . . Four weeks, you rehearse and rehearse. Three weeks, and it couldn't be worse." That was it. But *No, No, Nanette* now had only three weeks before its Boston opening—and rehearsals had barely begun.

The chance for a momentary reprieve came with word from Boston that *Two by Two* wanted to remain longer at the Shubert while the authors and director tried to whip it into shape for New York. Could *Nanette* delay its opening for a week? If it could, there was something like $25,000 in it for the producers, to cover any additional expenses.

Cyma considered the proposal. But moving back the Boston opening—God knows, the show *could* use the rehearsal time—would mean moving back the dates in Toronto, Philadelphia, Baltimore, and Washington. Contracts had been signed, newspaper ads were scheduled, tickets were printed. No, it couldn't be done.

*Unless* the Rodgers show wanted to pay three times what it said was its final offer.

(It did not. *Two by Two* subsequently moved to New York as scheduled, played ten days of previews, opened to lukewarm notices, and—by virtue of its star's popularity and some heavy promotion—eked out a moderately profitable ten-month run.)

It was early October. The shadows of the buildings along Broadway were beginning to lengthen, and daylight was scarcer now that the summer had slipped by. In the dusty rehearsal rooms of the Broadway Arts, a nervous pattern had developed.

In one studio, Hiram Sherman and the three gold diggers worked diligently on a song entitled "Fight over Me," in which the wealthy Bible publisher amusingly advises the girls to "battle, like cattle" for his affections.

Bobby Van and Helen Gallagher, in another room, started working on a medley of dances—the Castle Walk, Turkey Trot, Tango, and Maxixe—that they would perform after singing a chorus of "You Can Dance with Any Girl at All." Van's attitude was energetic, self-important; Gallagher's was coolly professional, as if she was about to burst into a chorus of "Anything You Can Do, I Can Do Better."

Carole Demas and Roger Rathburn, neither of whom were dancers, practiced a soft-shoe to "Tea for Two." At Cyma's instructions, a special dance teacher had been hired for Carole. "I don't care what Roger looks like onstage," the producer said to the young ingenue, "because he plays a clod and people won't care if he's clumsy, but I want you to look good."

And, in the large studio, the chorus began learning the lengthy, elaborate soft-shoe dance that would follow the initial duet by the two young leads.

Luther Henderson, a heavy, jovial Black man whose usual costume is a colorful dashiki flapping over a pair of slacks, with several strands of love beads around his neck, sat at the piano, seemingly in all of the various rooms at one time. As dance-music arranger, he composed on the spot, changing the tempos and adding or subtracting notes as the dancers and choreographers ordered.

221

Also gliding from room to room was Donald Saddler. Working with the chorus on "Tea for Two," he would wave his arms in wide, sweeping circles to give Ted Cappy and Mary Ann Niles an idea of the kind of patterns he thought the boys and girls should move into—and then he would dash off to a smaller studio to check on the principals. Left behind, alone with the dancers, Mary Ann developed the steps that set the dancers into the proper designs. Then, the chorus practiced the steps until Saddler returned to nod approvingly.

Dutifully, Ruby Keeler arrived at the studio each afternoon around three, as she was ordered to do on the daily "call sheet." After running through her "Happy" tap dance, she would wander from room to room, watching the others rehearse.

"I have nothing to do," she murmured several times each day, until Cyma grew tired of hearing it. The "audience"— Berkeley and his wife, Ruby's sister and daughter—bothered Cyma, too. So many people seemed to be sitting around, doing nothing. The idle chitchat they offered by way of conversation did not help.

"Buz has been working on his autobiography, you know," said Etta Berkeley one afternoon during a ten-minute chorus break. "Of course *now* he's too busy. But every major publisher has contacted him about it. And last year, he was asked to go on a lecture tour of fifty schools, or maybe a hundred. It would just be too much for him, so he had to turn it down, even though they said they would furnish us with a private car and driver. We have to take cabs here."

Gertrude White, Ruby's sister, caught the exasperated Cyma as she hurried away from Etta's monologue.

"Ruby's worried about the script, Mrs. Rubin. She *knows* Burt is working on it to build up her part, but still—I mean, isn't this delay going to make us postpone the opening?"

Cyma smiled quickly, condescendingly. "Oh, no, no," she said. "Our original plan was to work the dancers six weeks and the cast five. You'll see, when it's all said and done, we'll only have missed a few days."

"But there's a whole week lost, isn't—" Gertrude stopped in midquestion. Cyma was already halfway down the corridor, where artist Hilary Knight stood showing his poster design to Harry Rigby.

"It's just lovely, Hilary, just lovely," Harry was saying. The drawing featured a sextet of bobbed-hair flappers, clad only in strings of beads, frolicking in a fountain of champagne bubbles.

"It took a little longer to make up than I expected," said the diminutive, soft-voiced artist. "I wanted the letter 'e' in everyone's name to have this special look, y'know, and each 'e' had to be pasted in by hand."

"It cost a small fortune," Cyma said quickly. "But it does look wonderful" She studied the artwork. "There's just one thing, Hilary. I said before that I thought the girls should not be nude. Now I'm *sure* they shouldn't be. This show isn't *Oh! Calcutta!* We don't want anyone to think it's sexy."

Hilary Knight sighed deeply. "Well, I *could* cover them—"

"Have it ready by Monday," Cyma ordered, starting to move away.

"I was going to spend the weekend in Connecticut," the artist called after her, but she was already out of earshot. He turned to Harry, who shook his head in a hopeless gesture. "But I guess I'll work on this first," Knight concluded weakly. And Harry nodded.

Harry, in touch with Burt Shevelove and Buster Davis about the script, was growing increasingly anxious. He had become a hand-holder for Ruby and Patsy, for Hiram and some of the chorus kids, but he didn't know how much longer he could convince them that everything was going fine, just fine. And now Raoul was complaining that Mrs. Rubin's suggestions for costume changes were driving him frantic, and he had asked that Harry keep her away from him.

How could Harry do *that*?

Well, he had tried. One morning—*could it really have been at 2:00 a.m.?*—when he had drunk enough to get up the nerve, he had dialed Cyma's number. When she answered, he had screamed at her: "You're everything I hate in a

223

woman!" But then he couldn't remember whether or not he had been coherent enough for her to understand what he was talking about.

It had been a hectic week.

Monday began with word from Burt Shevelove that he had finished writing enough of Act I—with two acts to go—to begin daily rehearsals. The announcement was applauded warmly by the principals and by Busby Berkeley, who promptly asked when he could have a copy "of Strangelove's script." His slip of the tongue did not amuse Shevelove, although Berkeley's memory lapses were frequently funny to others. He once had referred to Buster Davis as "Butch."

"I've been called a lot of things in my lifetime," laughed the quiet musical director, "but no one has hung that on me before."

"Ted Cappy got fired today," John Lowe told a visitor in a whisper. "One day's notice." Cappy, whose original contract called for billing as "Assistant to Mr. Saddler" on a back page of the *Nanette* program, got a new title, "Tap Supervisor," on the front page to salve his wounded pride.

With Cappy gone, the burden of the choreographic work fell more heavily on Mary Ann Niles. Her tireless energy and perpetual smile stayed intact as she worked with the boys and girls on routine after routine.

"I don't *want* to be a choreographer," she said one afternoon, echoing the incredulity that young Valerie Bettis had had in her voice twenty-five years previously, when Busby Berkeley ordered her to "have the girls do one step over and over until they applaud." Mary Ann shrugged, grinned. "I don't even want to be a *dancer*. I want to act—Shirley Booth parts. I can do them."

But now she was teaching a chorus of sixteen girls and eight boys tricky little steps for the show's finale, "Take a Little One-Step." And she was running them day after day through "I Want to Be Happy." And "Tea for Two."

And she and Saddler were mapping out the big second-act opening, "Peach on the Beach," in which eight girls would walk—maybe—on top of giant beach balls.

Like everything else about *Nanette*, the ball-walking rehearsal got off to a slow start. Only one of the huge balls, weighing about eighty pounds, was built, so the girls had to line up and take turns trying to stay atop it. Ernestine Mercer, the instructor, ordered three of the boys to form a triangle around the rolling sphere and lock their arms to catch any girl who slid off. The boys were kept busy.

At the end of the day, one of the girls most proficient—who could keep her balance and make the ball roll a few feet forward—was Carole Demas.

Harry and Bob Schear, the stage manager, came into the studio where the girls were toppling off the ball with embarrassing rapidity. After a giggling fall, each would retire to the sidelines to play cards or knit until called for another attempt.

"The ball's too light," the instructor complained. "It's only 80 pounds."

"They're going to make them 150," said Harry.

"It should be 300."

Harry laughed. "*Heavens*, how could we carry them?" He turned to a chorus boy dripping with sweat after an hour of girl-catching. "What do you think?"

The boy studied the situation. "If you could weight them on the sides, but not in the middle—"

"Oh, no," said Harry, "they have to roll around in all directions. Know what Buz suggested? He thinks we should put them on tracks. That's what he would do in Hollywood."

The chorus boy chewed his lip. "Yeh," he said, "but we're not in Hollywood."

Burt Shevelove, continuing to tap out the script in the morning for the cast to rehearse with in the afternoon, appeared one day with a bit of unpleasant news for Hiram Sherman and the three gold diggers. He had decided to eliminate the "Fight Over Me" number.

"It doesn't fit with my idea of the show," he explained. "The character of Jimmy Smith, as I see him, is too innocent to dally with the three girls, even momentarily."

Hiram Sherman, who had spent long hours to learn and

rehearse the song, was irritated at the waste of time. In the dance that the girls had worked out to compete with one another for Sherman's admiration, Loni performed a wild routine à la Isadora Duncan, K. C. Townsend did a show-it-off shimmy, and Pat Lysinger whirled about the stage wielding a prop violin like a weapon. All the effort now went down the drain. Sherman, the veteran, commiserated wearily with his young supporting players: "That—as they say —is showbusiness." But his usual smile was absent as he said it.

Cyma Rubin did not take it lightly. "But, Burt—that number—it's ..."

Burt Shevelove knew what she was thinking. "Fight over Me" was the only number in the show in which Loni got to do a solo dance. The only other musical chance for the three gold diggers was a song, "Telephone Girlie," where they would back up Bobby Van as a trio.

"Burt, if you cut that number," Cyma continued, "the second act will only have three songs and the finale. Is that enough?"

Shevelove looked at her. "I think it is," he said flatly.

As the writer-director had worked on the script, he had begun to wonder about the number of songs that were needed. In addition to the original score, which had fourteen songs, the jaunty third-act "Take a Little One-Step" had been added from *Nanette*'s London production. And Charles Gaynor had written several others to the Youmans tunes.

Shevelove tossed out all but one of Gaynor's numbers, a duet for Ruby and Hiram called "Always You." Then he and Buster Davis compressed several isolated numbers into the first-act and second-act finalettos. When he was finished, the score again had fourteen separate songs—and needed one more number, the socko comedy song that had been promised Patsy Kelly.

Daily, Patsy was told that her song was in the works. She waited.

Ruby Keeler waited, too. Shevelove was delivering more script pages now, but there were no lines for her on them, so

226

she did not read them. In Hollywood, where she had worked on several pictures at one time, and often filmed the end of a picture before the opening scenes, Ruby seldom knew how other actors or scenes fit into the story. She saw no reason now to start learning.

The chorus kids felt differently. John Lowe asked M. J. Boyer if she could provide him with, at the least, a synopsis of *No, No, Nanette,* so that he could give the chorus an idea of the story and how their numbers fitted into it.

"I don't know if we'll see a finished script before we open in Boston," John said with a hollow laugh.

Busby Berkeley was grateful for the daily ration of script that Shevelove brought to the studio. Diligently he stapled the pages together and shuffled them on a desk before him while the dancers worked. His wife, Etta, had been asked not to attend rehearsals—her continual chatter made it hard for some people to concentrate, she was told—but Berkeley did not seem to miss her. He nodded soberly as M. J. told him that she had lined up a half-dozen interviews with Boston newspaper and television reporters.

To the boys and girls of the chorus, Berkeley was looked upon as another avuncular figure to be tolerated with kindness. A male dancer remarked, "It's funny, but every once in a while he starts yelling at us—telling us to smile and work harder. He probably has a lot of ideas, but no one is asking him for any."

Ideas were in plentiful supply, and that was the problem, according to Hiram Sherman. "Cyma Rubin gave one direction," he said. "Burt gave another, and Buster Davis gave another. All at the same time."

More and more, the mood of the company became one of utter confusion.

Ruby Keeler's daughter, Kathy, bored with the rehearsal routine, had returned to California. Now Ruby's sister Gertrude talked of going back, too, at least until there was a script and something for her to do. Ruby herself would not be happy alone in New York, and everyone knew it. The chorus members began talking to her at every opportunity, adopting her as a surrogate mother, and Ruby responded. Several times she told interviewers that she was worried more about the jobs of the chorus kids than about her own future on Broadway—and *that* was why she stayed with the show. The interviewers laughed, thinking she was being modest. One laughed even when she noted painfully that, "Producers were different in my day. They were more—organized."

Because of the similarity in their ages and long-time acquaintance with one another, Patsy Kelly and Ruby Keeler huddled together to wonder about the snail-like pace of the production. Patsy's "the-hell-with-it" attitude balanced Ruby's worried frown, which Patsy frequently tried to erase with a story.

"The other night after rehearsal, I'd had a few belts," Patsy said, "and Mrs. Rubin came up to me, friendly-like, and said she wanted to ask me something.

" 'What?' I said.

"And she said, 'I was wondering if you could tell me why some of the people call me *The Black Witch*.'

" 'Lady,' I said, 'you caught me on just the right drink!' "

Hiram Sherman found it difficult to laugh, even at Patsy's broad comedy. He was beginning to feel familiar vague pangs of regret. Was Burt Shevelove directing the show with any sense of style, with anything in mind other than getting the characters on and off the stage? There was one particular scene, where Burt wanted him to pretend to be looking for his cap—which eventually was to be found sticking out of his pocket.

"Burt, it isn't *funny*," said Chubby Sherman. "I'm standing on a bare stage, the audience can see there is no place for my cap to be, they'll see it in the pocket immediately. There will be no surprise when I pull it out."

Shevelove had a simple answer. "It's funny. Do it the way I tell you."

Sherman bristled, then shrugged his shoulders. "All right, but if they laugh, I'll eat the hat."

The director, too, was having second thoughts on what he

had gotten himself into. He was still tired and weak from the long siege in the hospital, and everywhere he turned he had to resist someone ready to give him advice. Take such a simple thing as his staging of "Tea for Two," for example. In the original *No, No, Nanette* of 1924, the song had been done as a gentle ballad between Nanette and her boyfriend, Tom. Only in later years had it become a standard tap dance number. Now, Shevelove again wanted it staged very simply —as a romantic ballad—with the boy and girl standing absolutely still and singing the lyrics to each other.

"Burt," asked Cyma, "are they just going to stand there and sing?"

"Burt," said Berkeley, "don't you think there should be some movement? The boy should go this way, and the girl should follow him; and then she should go that way, and he should follow her."

"It looks—well, static, doesn't it?" asked Cyma. "I mean, just the two of them, *standing* there."

The director did his best to smile. "Let's try it my way," he said as gently as he could. "It will be fine." He did not have time to argue about it—not with a much bigger problem facing him:

Shevelove had made up his mind that Carole Demas would not do as Nanette.

It was one thing that the cast that had been handed to him included an aging non-actress who interrupted rehearsals and stepped out of character to say, "Good morning, John," when her son entered the studio, or to point out that the prop telephone she was using had no cord. It was something else that Helen Gallagher was only just beginning to drop the brassy quality from her reading, and that Hiram Sherman seemed to be growing more bitter with each passing day. Bobby Van was willing to do whatever he was told, as was Patsy, but their roles were natural ones for them and did not call for an excess of direction on Shevelove's part. He could work with the performers that he *had* to work with—such as Ruby. He could work, too, with the ones who were professionals and would take orders, who could adapt

229

themselves to last-minute changes and suggestions. But he did not have time—no one had time—to work with an ingenue in her first Broadway role, who really could not dance, and who was singing in a voice that was obviously not comfortable for her.

No matter how pretty she was.

When Shevelove told Cyma that he wanted Carole Demas replaced by someone more experienced, she was aghast.

"But, Burt, we've got all these *old* people, these creaking stars in the cast. We have to have *someone* who is new and exciting and delicious. I've got a dancing teacher working with her . . ."

"Harry and Buster both think Susan Watson would —"

Cyma snorted. "Harry's a friend of her husband, isn't he?" she asked, putting an end to the conversation. "You watch, Burt. Carole will be delicious."

"We'll argue about it later," the director said, moving off to join Harry and Donald Saddler, who were trying to form several chorus boys into human letters that would spell out, "No, No."

Cyma watched him go, her eyes narrowing. "Argue about it," she repeated to herself. That was what Shevelove and Harry and Buster enjoyed doing. They delighted in arguing, in bickering, in quibbling about every little detail. And, meanwhile, nothing was getting done. "I can't stand it," she said. "I like to make decisions and go on to something else. *They* love to fight among themselves."

"Harry," she called, and watched as he scurried over.

"*Yes?*"

"Let's get hold of the managers and have them check the Hamptons for some wicker chairs for the second act. The antique shops out there are practically giving things away."

"All right. But by the time someone goes all the way out there, wouldn't it be just as inexpensive to buy some here in town?"

"I don't think so. The stores out there are dying. Did you hear anything about the costumes?"

Harry waved his hands. "Yes, they won't be ready until

the 26th. We'll have to hire a special truck to rush them to Boston. We seem to be running out of time."

Cyma's voice was flat, angry. "We're *out* of time," she snapped, looking across the room where Saddler and Shevelove were giggling. The contortions of the chorus boys had resulted in "On, On," rather than "No, No."

"Let's forget it," laughed Donald Saddler, and another fifteen minutes of rehearsal time had been wasted.

M. J. was at Harry's side now, pleading that the printer in Boston *had* to have copy for the programs immediately in order to have them ready for opening night. "But we're not sure about the sequence the songs will be in," Harry said. "I'll have to talk to Burt about it."

Cyma winced again. "Talk about it, talk about it," she muttered. Oh, God, if Sam only knew what was happening. She had asked him not to come around, to stay away from rehearsals—such as they were—because she knew what his reaction would be. Sam was a businessman, used to making quick, forceful decisions. If he saw how things were going, he would tell her to drop the whole project at once.

Cyma was sure of it. Absolutely.

Already she had worried whether or not to tell her husband about the $500 beaded dresses whose price had climbed to $900. And the dresses did not look right, in spite of the increase. Had she made a mistake, trying to cut corners? "If you deal with amateurs," Merle Debuskey had said, reminding her of her father's remark about fleas, "you get crap." Well, Cyma Rubin would not settle for crap. She would make the costumer do them over and over until they were right.

But everything was beginning to cost so much money. The beach-ball instructor said she had to have more practice balls for the girls to work with. Buster Davis reported that the "Peach on the Beach" number was so bouncy, with so many notes to each bar of music, that the copyists would have to go onto overtime if the orchestrations were to be ready for the first Boston preview. At Barbara Matera Ltd., one of the three shops working on the wardrobes, a silver

231

dress for Ruby should have been made by two women in two weeks' time—but, because so many costumes had to be made so quickly, "It will take two women and a lot of overtime," Cyma had been told.

And the comedy song for Patsy Kelly. Gaynor's number, "My Doctor," was unusable. Another writer, Marshall Barer, said he would do a song called "Don't Turn Your Back on a Bluebird" for $300. Barer, who had written marvelous lyrics for *Once upon a Mattress*, was given a go-ahead—"and then," said Cyma, "his agent got into the act, and the $300 was forgotten." She refused to go higher.

"He'll have to stick to his original deal. Or else we'll use Gaynor's songs. I don't understand it—Harry and Buster and everyone raved about Gaynor's numbers for all these months, and now suddenly they're no good. Gaynor can be worked with, y'know. I called him the other day to ask him to change one word in 'Always You.' The first line goes 'Who's the one that I'll spend each day with?' Well, Hiram Sherman can't say 'Who's'—it comes out 'Who'sa.' So I asked Gaynor to change it to 'Who' and you would have thought I asked him to write an entire opera. He argued. He refused. He almost cried.

"And today he delivered the new lyric. It goes 'Who—do I want to spend each day with?' Big deal."

During the next few weeks, several other songwriters—including Johnny Mercer, who had come from Hollywood to New York on other business—were reported at various times to be hard at work on the comedy number for Patsy. Finally, a few days before the Boston opening, with the last few grains of sand trickling through the rehearsal hourglass, Shevelove thought of something:

"Who made the law that says, if Patsy Kelly is in the show, she has to sing?" he said. "She would have had to follow the 'I Want to Be Happy' tap-dance and try to top it with a small, little comedy song. The first act was running long anyway, so I told her that her number would have to go."

Patsy, who by this time would not have been perturbed if

the rehearsal hall collapsed in an earthquake, took it casually. "I didn't want to sing in the first act anyway," she said.

Ruby Keeler, on the other hand, did not want to sing in the first act, the second act, or the third act. Despite Buster Davis' protestations that she had a perfectly adequate singing voice, and would do fine, she resisted any vocalizing.

"She was nervous about everything," said Buster Davis. "Perhaps she didn't show it outwardly, but I always felt in rehearsal that she was panicky. I treated her with kid gloves, really, because I sensed that right below the surface was pure panic. With anyone else, I might have said, 'Aw, come on,' but I empathized with her so much, and I like her so much that I went out of my way to be very gentle with her."

Ruby's singing talents were to be restricted to two songs —the first eight bars of the "Take a Little One-Step" number, after which the chorus would pick up the words, and "Always You" as a duet with Hiram Sherman. She memorized the "Always You" lyrics quickly, then began rehearsing a few dance steps with Sherman to finish off the number. Donald Saddler and Mary Ann Niles demonstrated some steps that Ruby and Hiram might do, but Ruby did not like them. "The dance should be lighter, with more humor," she said. Saddler agreed and tried some alternate steps. Watching, practicing the movements by herself, Ruby nodded, and then changed places with Mary Ann. She had the steps down perfectly, and in ten minutes the number was complete.

"Well," Ruby Keeler said as she took off her dancing shoes, "if I only had something *else* to do." Everyone, it seems, was busy except her.

And the one man who was closer to *No, No, Nanette* than anyone else.

Irving Caesar.

**17** A half-dozen blocks down Broadway from the studios where the company of *No, No, Nanette* was slowly trying to breathe life into a forty-five-year-old musical, seventy-five-year-old lyricist Irving Caesar sat in an office crammed with yellowing newspaper clippings and dusty stacks of phonograph records and sheet music. For more than thirty years, the songsmith had kept an office—first a small one barely large enough to hold a piano, and then a four-room layout with space for filing cabinets and bookshelves—in the Brill Building, headquarters of Tin Pan Alley.

> "If a person isn't a bore, I forgive 'em for anything. I love the villains and the angels, but not bores. They consume me."
>
> IRVING CAESAR

Once the corridors of the building had echoed with the sounds of dozens of pianos jangling and thumping as song pluggers performed their latest tunes for publishers. Today, while rock-and-roll writers play "demo" records of their new compositions for record-company executives in office towers throughout the city, the Brill Building houses bookkeepers, lawyers, dentists, real estate agents . . .

And ghosts.

On first meeting, Caesar himself appears specterlike—a figure out of the past. Short, stocky, with a thick cigar dangling from pudgy fingers and with his eyes magnified by half-inch-thick glasses, he stands in the doorway of his ninth-floor office, stretching an eager hand to grab a visitor's arm before he might escape. The booming voice that comes out of his barrel chest is a sound of welcome, but also a cry of joy at having captured an audience.

For Irving Caesar, like the man who made his "Swanee" famous, must have attention . . . and applause. He lives to perform.

Once he had had plenty of eager listeners. The songs he wrote—"Tea for Two," "Is It True What They Say About Dixie?," "Just a Gigolo," and a thousand others—brought the producers flocking to him. And the women. Party invitations poured in, along with requests to sing his songs on vaudeville stages and at country club affairs.

Something happened, though, imperceptibly, after the feverish activity of the 1920s and 1930s. Other songwriters —his friend Irving Berlin, young Richard Rodgers and Lorenz Hart, Youmans, Gershwin, "Yip" Harburg—went on turning out Broadway shows and a steady stream of hits. But Irving Caesar sat back, divorced from the hit parade scramble, and wrote a series of children's songs—about friendship, safety, health. He published them, performed them on radio, and toured the various school systems around New York to play and sing them—*in person*—for wide-eyed third-graders.

Ask Irving Caesar today why he did not go on writing Broadway scores after his hit with *Nanette,* a milder success with *Nina Rosa,* and a flop with *Yes, Yes, Yvette,* and he has a ready answer: "I never found one composer whom I could work with consistently, the way Hart worked with Rodgers."

Unlike Busby Berkeley, however, Caesar in recent years did not sit and brood over the fact that he was outside the theatrical mainstream. He did not pine for another chance to show he still had the old stuff. Hell, once you have written "Tea for Two" and "I Want to Be Happy," and the others, what more do you have to prove? After the vogue waned for his children's songs, he contented himself with spending his afternoons at the track, his Sundays at the Turkish baths, and a few hours every day at his office, where he worked at turning his fifty-year diary into a memoir. Even when his "girlfriend" of the past thirty years succumbed to an illness, and other acquaintances and friends from his youth slipped away in an endless stream of funeral processions, Irving Caesar was not distraught. There were still two or three cronies at the Friars Club who would play low-stakes poker with him one or two nights a week. And occasionally, an awestruck young songwriter from Ashtabula or Kansas City would walk hesitantly into his office, to sit transfixed in delight while the great author of "Tea for Two" studied his lyrics and solemnly said, "You have definite talent, my boy, but your songs are too good to be commercial."

Money? Caesar had enough. A half-dozen of his songs

were "standards." They were played on radio and television year after year, and he collected comfortable royalties and performance payments from the American Society of Composers, Authors, and Publishers. He lived frugally, economically, in the same hotel he had lived in for thirty years. No, there was no worry about money. Irving Caesar had time to relax, to read heavy texts like *Pentagon Capitalism*, and occasionally, because it came naturally to him, to make up a lyric—a short novelty song or a long series of quatrains set to "Yankee Doodle" and poking fun at the military-industrial complex. He did not compose to compete with younger writers; their rock-and-roll was no competition for him. He had not gone to see a Broadway show in years. Irving Caesar at seventy-five had just about everything he wanted.

Except an audience.

These last years, before *Nanette* was announced for the 1970-71 Broadway season, things had been extremely quiet. But now the phone began to ring—not frequently, but often enough to put a sparkle into Caesar's eyes. One writer wanted to interview him for an article in *New York,* another wanted to write him up in *Playbill,* and there were others after him for TV and radio talk shows. He never turned down a request. He could *not* turn down a request.

"What time can you get over here?" Caesar asked an interviewer who called out of the blue. "I'm in my office every day. I *love* my office. How about this afternoon?"

An hour later, the interviewer was swallowed by a huge leather armchair in the inner sanctum of the energetic songwriter, and the words began pouring out of Caesar's heavily lined face like an explosive string of midget firecrackers—*pop-pop-poppity-pop-pop!*

"There are no *songs* today! No songs, *period!* There are no songs of inspiration. There are no boffs! For Christ's sake, when DeSylva, Henderson, and Brown wrote a show, they came up with *five* hits—in *Scandals* and so forth and so on. There are no *hits* now. What the hell, everyone knows the pattern of how to write a song. The craftsmanship is there—this goddamn thing, radio and television, is the greatest teacher of how to do things. This is an age of imitation. Everybody knows the *pattern*. All right, so what? One song is just like another. Oh, occasionally a great song comes along, but considering the hundreds and millions that are put into the business, there's very little to show for it. I mean, after all, what has *emerged?* What has really emerged that you can say in five years they'll be digging up and playing? I mean, these producers don't know. They don't *know!*"

His cigar jabbed fiery periods and exclamation points between each sentence. His short arms stretched out of the sleeves of the rumpled suit jacket in expansive gestures, making it look as if the coat was several sizes too small. "These kids today," he continued feverishly, "they think they're writing propaganda songs. For Christ's sake, I *started* songs of propaganda! I was just out of City College, on Henry Ford's Peace Ship, and I was writing peace songs *then."*

He paused, taking a drag from the cigar, remembering. "I was going to Columbia at night, working on Ford's assembly line in the daytime. Studied Russian for three months—kick myself for not going on with it—but I only took it because there was a girl who was taking it and I wanted to be near her." His eyes flashed behind the thick lenses, then narrowed again, quickly.

"But you want to hear about *Nanette.* Here's something funny. This Mrs. Rubin—she said that she took Spanish in school from my sister, who was a marvelous teacher. She said my sister was tough on her. Funny. Not one *other* person ever said that, to my knowledge. All the students *loved* my sister. That right, Dick?" The question was addressed to a poker-faced, elderly man who functions as a one-person switchboard operator, secretary, file clerk, and errand boy for Irving Caesar Music Co. He nodded affirmatively, and announced that he was going downstairs to the lobby restaurant for a sandwich. Caesar waved him out.

"Look," he said, relighting the cigar, "they're going to spend five or six hundred thousand dollars on *Nanette.* So I sat back and said to myself, 'Why should I frustrate them in any way?' In the contract, however, I insisted that they cannot change the *tone* of the show. But I don't want to butt in or interfere in any way. They're putting up six hundred thousand dollars for a property of 1924. They're entitled to have their own swing at the thing."

He paused just long enough to shove back the glasses that were slipping down on the broad nose. "I will say this, though"—and his voice had an edge to it—"in the beginning they neglected me. Oh, I was invited twice up to Cyma Rubin's house—a very nice woman—but they neglected me. They shouldn't have. I think I might have been helpful. But I said nothing. I didn't feel too badly about it. Lately, Rigby has been in touch with me. He called me the other day and said they needed a line to finish 'Too Many Rings Around Rosie' with a big ending."

Caesar pointed the cigar. "You know the song?" Suddenly, a forceful Jolsonesque baritone boomed from his throat: " 'Too many rings around Ros-ie will never get Rosie a *ringggg*! Too many beaux where she should have one' "— and now he was speaking again—"and so on and so forth. Well, I thought about it for half an hour, and it came to me, just like that. It's a very important line, an inspiration. Listen to this, now."

He *dum-da-dum-dummed* himself an introduction by slapping the ancient desk and began singing: " 'If she can't make up her mind, Rosie will stay behind, *all alone,* She'll be *all alone*—with never a ring on the phone!' " When he reached the words "all alone," he clasped his hands before him, rolled his eyes skyward in mock mourning for a lost love, and switched from the jaunty Youmans melody to the familiar bluesy notes of Irving Berlin's classic "All Alone."

"Get it?" he asked, grinning from ear to ear. "Rigby loved it, but he was worried about getting permission from Berlin to use his song. I said, 'It's only two bars, don't worry.' But Rigby said he couldn't go ahead, and the orchestrator was waiting on it, so I dialed Berlin—he's on the phone with me all the time—and he said, 'Aw, for Christ's sake, use the whole song if you want to.' So they put the line in at rehearsal, and everybody thinks it's wonderful. It's an inspiration to get something like that, y'know. It looks easy, but it's not."

He got up in an energetic bound from behind the desk and pulled the dust-covered Venetian blind from the grimy window. He stared out at the silent Broadway rooftops below. "It's not easy," the seventy-five-year-old man repeated. "You know what bothers me?" he asked after a second of deliberation. "I told Rigly, or Rigby—whatever his name is—and Mrs. Rubin, 'Here are all my telephone numbers. I'll get on a plane or a train within an hour after you say you need me. Otherwise, just tell me when you think the show's ready for me to see.' " His tone became confidential. "But they signed a very silly contract with the Youmans estate. It forbids any music that isn't Youmans'—and they're supposed to work with a lot of things out of his trunk. Well, they're not going to get a writer like myself to work with a *dead man's* tunes. I'm a singing lyric writer, I work without a piano, make up my own melodies. I couldn't take a dead man's tunes. It wouldn't inspire me at all. Who the hell gives a good goddamn about a dead man's tunes? *I'm* not going to write to them. Rigby knows that, so he's got some friend of his—you know how *they* stick together—writing songs. What a mistake!"

Caesar strode rapidly about the office, pausing to point out a framed picture of himself in several dozen poses, singing at a benefit of some kind. "Hell, I've got *three* songs that would be sensational in that show. I've got a love song that was done in England, a comedy love song. *Sensational!* Listen." He began to sing, acting out both parts of a duet, frequently interrupting himself to point up the cleverness of a rhyme with a wink or guttural growl.

When he finished the long number, ending up on one knee in the center of the faded rug with his arms extended to embrace an imaginary girl, he looked up, ready for applause. "Great? Wild?" he asked. "I mean, on the *stage*. It isn't a *commercial* song."

Youthfully, buoyantly, he jumped to his feet. "I've got another one that Ruby and that Sherman fellow could do.

It's the only six-eight love song ever written. It was done in England, too, not here, and it sent the people marching out after the show was over, marching right down the street, singing, like this." Suddenly, he was singing again, accompanying himself with "Rum-a-tum-tum" sotto voce beneath the melody, and marching about the office, keeping time with an invisible baton.

" 'I'm a little bit fonder of you,' " sang Irving Caesar that still October afternoon, " 'than of myself, it's true. (Rum-a-tum-tum.) Things that I never do for myself, I do for you. I do.' "

"Talk about a hit song!" he exclaimed. "Biggest hit I ever had. The show was *Mercenary Mary*, and it played in Manchester. And the orchestration—*Daaaa, da-da-da-da-da-bum-bum-bum!*" He acted out trombones, trumpets, drums, the entire orchestra. "Oh, dynamite!" he shouted. "Dynamite!"

Irving Caesar was panting now, winded, catching his breath as he waved an impatient hand to clear the air of cigar smoke. "But I'm not going to write words like that to a dead man's tunes. I *couldn't* do it. I don't need the dough so bad that I—well, I *couldn't* do it. I'd be very unhappy. And what right have they got, anyway, to tie up a show with a dead man's tunes? They'll have to get out of it if they want me."

Caesar's "boy" returned from the restaurant, empty-handed. He knew from long years of experience that his employer preferred to skip lunch when he had things to talk about. "If I go out for lunch," said Caesar, "I eat like a pig, drink a couple of bourbons, and a bottle of beer—at Gallagher's or Moore's—and then get sleepy around three o'clock and fall down in this chair. Then I wake up around 4:30, conscience-stricken that I haven't read a book or made an entry in my diary or some fuckin' thing."

He shook his head angrily, disturbing the wispy crown of silver-gray hair, and scratched behind his right ear. "Let's see, now," he said, trying to remember, "where was I?" He scratched harder.

"Oh, yeh, the *songs*. Listen, I've got a comedy song for Patsy Kelly—she was in a show I did for Jolson, y'know. *The Wonder Bar*. Wonderful girl. Jolson was one of my best friends. He was a son of a bitch, a no-good double-crosser, but if you stood up to him every once in a while, you got along. I went out to Hollywood to do a picture for him. *Hallelujah, I'm a Bum*. The bastard fired me halfway through, and Rodgers and Hart wrote the score finally. Only picture Jolson ever made that was a failure. Wait a minute. lemme tell you about the comedy song. It's one that I did for Durante—y'know I did 'Umbriago' for him—and this one's better. Listen, now—"

Caesar was on his feet now, in the middle of the office, sticking his thick nose into the air and turning into Jimmy Durante. The song was funny, and he built it through chorus after chorus with a professional showman's skill.

"Hell, why *shouldn't* I know how to put a song over?" he turned aside the compliment. "I headlined five years straight at Loew's State—headlined *over* Red Skelton. And I've done my one-man show dozens of times, for all *kinds* of organizations. I can do an hour, hour and a half, *two* hours, without a piano even. I'm going to do it off-Broadway, y'know. Lyle Stuart—the book publisher, he's a good friend —he's going to rent a theater for me, and if he can't rent one, he's going to buy one for me. For my one-man show."

Now the songsmith, who once had written the words to what might be the most-played American popular song, dived into a box of phonograph records. "Here, lemme play this for you," he muttered. "I set the Pledge of Allegiance to a tune that just came to me one morning. This is a record with the Army Band that they played in Congress for a special presentation. It'll knock you out of your seat."

He worked several minutes at the old portable phonograph in the corner of his office, shoving his glasses up on his forehead to peer at the record label. As he fussed with switches and tried to set the needle into the proper groove, he talked about *No, No, Nanette* in its new life.

"Rigby says they pulled out the song called 'Fight Over

241

Me.' It was in the original, y'know. Very weak song. They had so many namby-pamby numbers in the score when I was called in. There was one that went like this—he slid scornfully into the melody—" 'Santa Claus, everyone da-da-da-dum should be a Santa Claus.' Nothing! But I hit it right on the nose, didn't I? 'I want to be happy, but I can't be happy—' "

As he sang his song, he emphasized each "happy" with a martial downward swing of his right arm. "Hey," he asked, "do you know if they do this little gesture when they sing the song in the show? I did it when I first demonstrated the song for Frazee, and everybody picked it up in the original. We had the whole audience doing it—look, it's a real swing of the arm, like this. 'I want to be *happy*,' see that? It *makes* the whole song. Jeez, I hope they don't leave it out. I'll have to tell Rigby."

He went back to the phonograph. The 45 record of the Pledge of Allegiance needed an adapter disc for the large spindle hole, and Caesar had trouble fitting it in. He went on talking. "These people putting on *Nanette*, y'know, are taking a hell of a gamble. Maybe they sense something in the air, a backlash against all the nudity and junk around. If the pendulum is ready to swing back—and it *has* to swing back one of these days—they can't miss. It all depends on their timing."

He stopped fiddling with the record player long enough to relight the cigar. Then he adjusted his glasses one more time, sighed, and pressed the record onto the phonograph with a *click* of finality. He reached for the switch, but let his hand rest on it.

"I've had a lot of friends who wanted to put money into the show. I told them, 'Go right ahead,' but I had to point out some of the drawbacks. These people putting it on are making a lot of mistakes. They're spending five or six hundred thousand dollars, right? Now, listen, they don't have the picture rights—*they* belong to Warner Bros. They haven't got British rights. They've got no *residuals*. All they've got is what's on that stage. No *residuals*!

242

"I don't understand why they'd do it. All that money—don't get me wrong, I'm glad as hell they did it. I want it to be a hit, Jesus, but I don't understand. What a gamble! What a *gamble*! Sure, they can make an album, but what the hell is *that*, f'Christ's sake! And putting Ruby and Patsy in the show—well, sure, they're nice people—but who wants to see them *now*? I wouldn't use either one if it was *my* show. Y' think these producers know what they're doing?"

His hand left the switch, relighted the cigar. His tone became serious, philosophical.

"Listen, I believe most people basically stink—but I love 'em. If they're *interesting*, don't y' understand? I don't think people are the most noble things in the world. When I was a kid, I was a Walt Whitman-lover of people. But I don't idealize 'em to that degree any more. I know people are expendable. But I love 'em. I can *talk* to 'em. F'Christ's sake, I can't go to the zoo and talk to a *monkey* or an elephant. If an elephant just had ten words that it could say, what chance would most people have? I think all human beings are inherently honest. You take these wealthy people who are stingy bastards—I'm not demeaning them—that's just the way they are. It's their way of seeking perfection, without being able to paint like Michelangelo on his back. These people don't know how to write a song. All they know is making and hanging onto the most money they can. That's the rationale for what they do—for being stingy bastards. Maybe the miser, in the final analysis, is some form of an artist: He wants to get the maximum out of what he does best."

The ebullient, untiring songwriter nodded to himself, thinking it over. It seemed to make sense. Then he looked up.

"Here," he said, "let me play this for you." As he turned on the machine, he added over the rush of the military music, "And then I want you to hear some of my children's songs—

"You've got time, haven't you?"

**18** The Sunday drama section of the *New York Times* carried the first public advertisement that there would be a "new 1925 musical" called *No, No, Nanette* during the 1970-71 theatrical season.

It would open, said the relatively small three-column ad, on January 28th.

Somewhere.

Unlike the usual announcement ad for a new musical, the one that ran for *No, No, Nanette* did not list a theater where the show would play on Broadway. And it did not list

> "Loni? I didn't want her in the show. If I'd wanted her in the show, wouldn't I have made her the star?"
>
> CYMA RUBIN

the prices of tickets. Theatergoers interested in seeing *Nanette* were advised to call a phone number—Harry Rigby's office—and inquire about arranging a theater party.

If potential patrons were puzzled, Broadwayites were amused at the producers who had no theater, no seat prices (since prices could not be determined until the size of the theater was known), and—if the loud rumors were to be believed—practically no show.

One thing the *Times* advertisement did have was a multitude of names. Twenty-eight of them. Everyone was listed, from Ruby Keeler to Loni Zoe Ackerman, Frank Mandel to Charles Gaynor, Busby Berkeley to Burt Shevelove.

And up at the very top of the ad, it said, "Cyma Rubin and Harry Rigby present...."

Harry loved it, of course. He looked at the newspaper page again and again. "Cyma Rubin and Harry Rigby present ... RUBY KEELER ... PATSY KELLY ... Production supervised by Busby Berkeley." It was beautiful, just beautiful. And the Hilary Knight drawings, the fanciful females, clad now in bubbles and beads and feathers, looked fine. Cyma had wanted to leave some of them out on the poster, to make room for all of the names, but Harry had argued, suggested printing the names so that the figures showed behind them—and it had worked.

Production Manager May Muth was not pleased. "I was told my name would be in the ad," she said.

Burt Shevelove was not pleased. "Too many names," he muttered the next afternoon at rehearsal. "Too many, and too big. It looked terrible."

Harry giggled nervously. "Mrs. Rubin made your name larger—and Donald's too. As a surprise. It was supposed to be 50 percent as large as the title, but she thought 60 percent made for better balance."

"Well, *everybody's* name can't be that big. I talked to Donald and he's perfectly willing to have his name smaller. It will look a lot better."

Cyma appeared suddenly, and Burt told her of his discussion with Saddler. Her face darkened.

"But if you two want your names reduced, I'll have to talk to Raoul and Buster. Everyone's billing is in relation to everyone else. I just can't—"

Burt held up an impatient hand. "I'll talk to the others and they'll agree. Don't worry about it."

Cyma tightened her lips, then nodded. "All right," she sighed, "I'll call Hilary again."

Harry Rigby threw his hands up in mock terror. "Just so long as *I* don't have to get involved," he shrieked, and opened the studio door where Donald Saddler and Mary Ann Niles were running the boys and girls through "Peach on the Beach" one more time.

Eight of the chorus girls, after a week of practice, had mastered the trick of staying on the rolling balls for a few minutes. The instructor had made it easier by placing a strip of red tape around the spheres so that the center balance point was easily defined. The chorus broke into giggles when she brought in the tape and said, "All right, let's operate on the balls."

Now the boys, who would be dressed as lifeguards, began to develop a fancy routine in which they threw heavy rowboat oars back and forth. The studio was promptly christened "the 'oarhouse," and the dancers tossed and spun the long shafts like a drum majorette's baton—while Donald

Saddler stood watching to latch onto particularly effective movements.

Buster Davis dashed in, sheet music in hand, the inked notes still damp. "Let me hear how this sounds," he said, handing the music to the rehearsal pianist. Instantly, the chorus boys burst into the song:

"What a peach of a girl! She is charming!
"What a peach on the beach she will *beeeee*!"

Davis grinned, cut them off with a wave of his hand.

"Oh, boys," he breathed in comic delight, "that was so butch it frightens me!" He gathered the music and hurried off. In another studio, he found Cyma Rubin, impatiently waiting. Quickly, he put some sheets of music on the piano and began playing. The song was called "One Girl," and it was a joint effort of his and Shevelove's. Cyma listened attentively.

"I don't like it," she said.

"Don't like it? It would be perfect for Ruby and Hiram."

"No. It doesn't fit the period, Buster."

"It does, it *does*. It sounds just like the number of Charlie Gaynor's that we threw out yesterday."

Now Cyma nodded. "Hmmm," she said, "it does, doesn't it? Maybe we ought to use Gaynor's after all."

Davis sighed. "Yes, I guess so," he said. "Burt and I are writing new introductions and second choruses for 'Too Many Rings Around Rosie' and some of the other things. I think you'll like them."

"What about that ending Irving Caesar gave Harry?"

"We worked with it to make it fit," the musical director said quickly. "This is how it goes now—" He brought the piano to life and sang:

"Those flirty-Gertie girls you know will end up unknown,
"Just wait and see, they will be—
"All alone, by the telephone,
" 'Cause too many rings around Rosie
"Will never get Rosie a ring!"

He closed the piano cover and began gathering the music.

"It will do for Boston, but we'll change it afterwards. Burt has some ideas. We're going to talk about it later."

*There it is again,* Cyma thought, as Davis hurried off to work with Helen Gallagher on her big number, "Where-Has-My-Hubby-Gone Blues." *We'll talk about it later.* Everything was later ... later ... later. Didn't these people understand that her money—Sam's money—was going out faster and faster? That she wanted results *now*? If they would just settle down and do one thing at a time, without talking so much about what they were *going* to do, the show would be a lot further along. She *knew* it.

Cyma smoothed her midi-skirt with an angry brush of her hand and stepped into the hall. Burt, Harry, and Donald were having a whispered conference outside the large studio. They looked up as she approached.

"She's got to go," Burt said flatly.

Cyma knew exactly what he meant. *Carole Demas.* Her fresh, delicious new face.

"I can't do it," Shevelove said. "I cannot work with her."

Cyma looked at Donald Saddler.

"Well," he said softly, "she's coming along, but it would take a lot of time ..."

"What does Buster think?"

Harry laughed. "Buster says that when a show is in trouble, you always fire the ingenue—it's a very dangerous part to be in. Everybody knows"—and he nodded toward the studio where the principals were rehearsing—"that Carole is singing in a voice that's strange to her. Of course, there's Ruby and Patsy to *think* about."

"What do you mean?" Cyma snapped.

"Ruby and Patsy," Harry repeated. "They love her. They've *practically* adopted her. She's like a daughter. I don't know how they'd take to her leaving."

"What difference does that make?" said Cyma, a new light brightening her eyes. "If the show needs somebody stronger in the part, we'll get somebody stronger. The first thing to do is to get rid of that dancing teacher I'm paying good money to."

"The *first* thing is to get a replacement," Shevelove said.

"Any ideas?" Cyma asked.

"I'll call Susan Watson," Harry offered quickly.

"No, wait a minute," Cyma said, thinking very fast. "Let's let the new general managers talk to her, and find out how much money she wants. That's what they're paid to do."

The three men nodded soberly. Then Burt Shevelove spoke in a low voice. "I wouldn't say anything to anyone about this. Something might happen and we may be stuck with the little girl." He rubbed his beard with the back of his hand. "But, God, I hope not."

The director opened the door of the rehearsal studio and walked in to face the anxious performers. "I've got news for you," he said. "Last evening I finished a new scene and we'll work on it right away."

Chubby Sherman's voice was frigid. "Why don't we start where we left off yesterday?" he said, biting off each word. "We barely got started before quitting time."

The other actors almost simultaneously drew in their breath as Shevelove's face darkened. "I'd rather start on *this* scene," he said, carefully, "but if you—"

Sherman spread his hands out wide. "Oh, what difference does it make, the shape we're in? Whatever you want to do—"

Shevelove looked at him. "We'll go from where we left off," he said.

The rehearsal was a glum, tight-lipped affair that afternoon, and the dour glances of May Muth seemed perfectly in keeping with the atmosphere. At six o'clock, Bobby Van and Helen Gallagher strode exhausted from the rehearsal studio, bundling themselves into scarfs and coats to ward off the chill October winds.

Van nodded with a slight smile to his waiting wife, Elaine Joyce. A young looking and wide-eyed blonde who had flown in from Hollywood for a brief visit between tapings of her appearances on Don Knotts' television show, she had been sitting patiently in the tiny area cluttered with soda and candy machines. Her husband seemed to listen only partly to

her tale of an unsuccessful shopping search for a coat at
Bendel's.

"I'm depressed and down, but I'll snap out of it," Van said
as he leaned against the elevator button.

"*You're* down?" Helen Gallagher said, incredulous. "I'm
so tired I should do nothing but go home and rest. I really
should."

"Why don't you?"

Her Irish eyes flashed, tired or not. "Because I'm going to
my group and tell them what I've been going through, that's
why! I work everything out there on everybody else. That's
my relaxation."

As the principals squeezed into the elevator, Hiram Sherman hurried out of the studio to catch it. Behind him, Harry
Rigby called cheerfully, "Don't look so worried, Chubby. It
will turn out all right."

Sherman was in the elevator now, turning to face front.
"Will it?" he asked.

Harry giggled. "Doesn't it *always*?"

"No," Sherman said, as the doors closed him from view.

The hours and days were beginning to blur into a downward spiral of frustration and anger on the part of almost
everyone connected with *No, No, Nanette*. Only one aspect
of the entire production—the publicity campaign—seemed to
be going well. Everyone, it seemed—every television and
radio station, every newspaper and magazine—wanted to
talk about nostalgia, wanted to interview Ruby and Berkeley, wanted to discuss how Raoul Pène du Bois' costume
designs would stir the entire fashion world.

But there were difficulties, even here. Ruby hated to be
interviewed, grew bored quickly, preferred to chat con-
cernedly about such things as the recent kidnapping of a
Canadian diplomat rather than the show, and modestly—but
firmly—refused to pose for more than one or two pictures.
Her disdain for photographs of herself, her unwillingness to
spend a half-hour sitting for a portrait, forced the publicity
office to cut her head from a rehearsal picture in which she
appeared with Hiram Sherman, touch up the facial lines and
wrinkles with an airbrush, and print it as a "head shot."

Berkeley, on the other hand, *was* willing to sit through lengthy interviews—but the logistics of getting him back and forth were complicated, and his age and physical weakness meant that interviews had to be spread out so he would have time to gather his strength between them.

And there was resentment from others associated with *No, No, Nanette* because the publicity spotlight was barely touching them. A harried M. J. Boyer found herself in the awkward position of trying to explain to reporters that Ruby Keeler really was "too busy" to talk to them, but Bobby Van would gladly consent to an interview if he could be assured that a sizable story would appear. Or, since Mr. Berkeley was busy "supervising" the show, wouldn't they like to talk instead to the three girls who played the gold diggers?

Each publicity turndown only seemed to whet the appetite of the media for more about *Nanette*. *Life* magazine said it would cover the show as part of a big spread on nostalgia. *Newsweek* announced it would beat *Life* with its own nostalgia article, and would feature *Nanette* on the cover. *Look* sent Entertainment Editor Louis Botto to rehearsals and made plans to photograph the Boston opening. And everywhere that M. J. went—to Boston, Philadelphia, Toronto— weeks before the show was scheduled to arrive, editors began to talk about *Nanette*.

From Boston, where a local publicist named Guy Livingston had been hired to keep the editors' enthusiasm at a high pitch, word came that the advance sale of tickets was over the $50,000 mark, and climbing. The news should have cheered Cyma, who had calculated that *Nanette* would break even if it took in $70,000 a week.

But she had problems to think about.

Shevelove, for one. He had dismayed the principals by taking an entire day off—to work at home on the script, he said—and then had spent most of the following day apologizing to the cast for being absent, and lecturing them on what difficult, tiring work *writing* is.

And Ruby, for another. When Shevelove had not shown up for rehearsal, she had been the one who cornered Cyma and told her in that tired, little-girl voice. "Today was just a waste. I do hope that man is here tomorrow." And those interviews! Couldn't Ruby ever say *anything* to make the show sound like it was fun and exciting? Just yesterday she had told a radio newsman that when she had gone backstage to visit Ethel Merman after a performance of *Hello, Dolly*, the great Broadway star had asked if she was excited about doing *No, No, Nanette*. "I said, no, not yet," Ruby announced over the air in bored tones.

And then there was the whole Carole Demas matter.

Once Cyma was convinced that Burt simply would not direct the young ingenue, she had a brilliant idea. Harry had sparked it in her mind when he argued that Carole Demas would have to be cut loose. "Good *heavens*," he had said, "this isn't a movie musical where you can bring in a tap dance teacher and teach someone how to dance overnight! And her voice just isn't right, no matter how good she looks onstage!"

In the back of Cyma's mind, something clicked. There was someone already in the show who *could* dance . . . who *could* sing . . . who looked good onstage . . . and who was a fresh Broadway face.

Her daughter Loni.

Cyma reached for the telephone in her town-house bedroom. She dialed the number of the apartment on West 17th Street.

"Hello?" Harry's voice was sleepy. Did it have a slight alcoholic blur?

"Harry, Cyma. I know it's late, but I've got a wonderful idea. I want Loni to try out for the part."

"For *what* part?"

"For Nanette. She could do it!"

Harry was wide awake now. "But I thought we agreed on Susan Watson."

"Yes, I know. But we're having a terrible time finding her."

"What? What do you mean, finding her? I've got her number right—"

"I know that, Harry. But who knows if she's available?

Or interested? Look, I want Loni to try out for the part. That's all, let's just let her try out."

The phone clicked in Harry's ear. He hung it up slowly, wondering. It rang almost immediately. Harry lifted it, half afraid that Cyma's voice would crackle out at him again. "Yes?"

"It's Burt, Harry. Cyma just called—"

"I know. She wants Loni to try out for Nanette."

"Oh, she got to you already."

"Yes, what are we going to do?"

"Harry, I know one thing. Never in our lives have we done a vanity production. We can't start now."

"I *knowwwww*. Loni wouldn't even be in the show if her mother wasn't the producer. She certainly can't do the lead. Hiram thinks she has talent and she works hard, but he'll quit if Loni got that part. And Ruby and Patsy—well, there's no telling what they'd do."

"What's happening with Susan Watson?"

Harry cackled gleefully. "You won't believe it. Cyma says she can't *find* her!" Burt's laugh was also a groan. "Don't worry, I'll think of something."

The laughter was gone from Shevelove's voice. "You'd better, Harry. Fast."

The next afternoon, after he had gone over the words a hundred times in his mind, Harry called Cyma aside. He took a deep breath and began speaking rapidly.

"It's not that we don't think Loni couldn't do it—or that she wouldn't be very good in the part. Really. But as her mother, think of the position she'd be in. She would want to please her director, and her fellow cast members, but she would also be *desperate* to please you. That's a terrible burden to place on a young and inexperienced girl. I mean, she possibly could do it—but the strain. . . ." He caught his breath, and plunged on. "And, if anything happened, and she couldn't pull it off, it would be dreadful. *Dreadful!* She is your daughter, and I don't see how you, as her mother, would want to place such a strain on her. . . ."

Cyma appeared to think it over, judging his performance.

252

Then she nodded slowly. "Well—" she said, "maybe—let's see what happens with Susan Watson."

That evening, Cyma called Harry again. "I don't think Susan Watson will work out," she said. "She's making all kinds of demands. But Loni—"

"What kind of demands?"

"Oh, she's worried about her baby or something. Loni could—"

"Let me talk to her," Harry said quickly. "Her husband's a friend of mine—we were going to work on a film together —and I know Susan. Maybe we can work things out."

Cyma sighed. "All right, all right. But if not, Loni—"

"I'll call you tomorrow."

Susan Watson got a call from Harry. And then a visit. And she agreed to step into the part, with less than two weeks to rehearse before the first preview in Boston. *If*.

*If* her salary was more than twice the amount paid Carole Demas.

*If* she only had to play two weeks in Boston, Toronto, and Philadelphia—with an understudy taking over in Baltimore and Washington, so that she would not be required to spend too much time on the road with her infant son.

The demands dismayed Cyma. It was not just the question of paying Susan Watson more money than the budget called for, or that it would be highly unusual to have a star step out of the show during the last important weeks before the production came to Broadway. It was something else: The part of Nanette called for a girl who was practically a teen-ager, and Susan Watson had been around on Broadway for years, since 1960, when she had played a teen-ager in *Bye Bye Birdie*.

And then there was the fact that Carole Demas had a run-of-the-show contract, which meant she would have to be paid as long as the show ran in New York—whether or not she was in it!

Cyma sighed. Well, the way things were going, it looked like the show would not run very long anyway. What difference did it make? There was no choice, at any rate.

She picked up the telephone and called Peter Neufeld, one of the general managers who had just been hired.

"Peter? Go ahead with the Watson contract. But keep it quiet."

The rumor spread around the Broadway Arts rehearsal halls that *someone*—probably Carole Demas—was going to be fired from the company. One chorus boy, who was friendly with one of the members of the production team, even forecast positively that Susan Watson would be the ingenue's replacement. But a day went by, and another, and another—and Carole Demas continued to rehearse "Tea for Two" with Roger Rathburn, and the beachball walking routine with the chorus. Maybe she wasn't going to be fired . . . *maybe* . . . but—

Carole herself heard the rumors. "Listen," she said one afternoon to a friend in the chorus, "this show is in so much trouble that I think somebody's head is going to roll."

Nerves began to jangle as everyone waited for the expected-unexpected to happen. One evening, the nervousness broke to the surface like a festering boil. An angry chorus boy noticed that a final rendition of "Tea for Two" had ended at 6:03 p.m. Under Equity rules, the company had to be dismissed at 6:00, or else be paid overtime. The chorus member placed a phone call, and the actors' union promptly placed a claim for $300 in overtime pay.

Cyma was furious. "I'm going to fight it," she snapped. "We let the kids off an hour early the other night to attend an Actors Fund benefit, and they didn't appreciate it." She chewed her lower lip thoughtfully. "It was John Lowe's fault," she decided. "He should have called time, even if they were in the middle of the number. It's his inexperience, that's what caused this trouble."

Carole Demas had another explanation: "When there is so much disorganization," she said, "when there is so much frustration that you can't do *anything* about—all the standing around at rehearsal and nothing getting done—sometimes people feel they have to take some kind of action just to let others know they can't walk all over them. Some of the gypsies have been in more shows and have done more performances than a lot of stars, and they resent being treated like animals."

Rehearsals, which had never moved rapidly, now seemed to be grinding to a standstill. After a particularly ragged run-through, during which the principals once more went over lines in the first act that they had done many times before, a magazine writer started to interview Harry Rigby. "I'd like to ask you when you first had the idea for the show," he said.

Rigby, leaning against the wall and looking like a dissipated Lee Marvin, smiled feebly. "Right now I wish I'd *never* had it." Glumly, he turned and sidled over to Donald Saddler, who was whispering to Cyma. Suddenly the studio door opened a crack. Carole Demas poked her head through it and looked around at the tired, unhappy figures huddled in groups under the yellow ceiling lights.

"Is it okay if I come in?" she asked with an attempt at humor. "Nobody will yell at me?"

The people in the room smiled limply and waved her in. "My mother's coming in from Breezy Point tomorrow. She's bringing a heavy coat that I'll probably need in Boston," Carole said.

No one answered. Everyone was suddenly busy, discussing costumes, and dance routines, and music. With a shrug, the young ingenue pulled up a chair, opened a magazine on a table and began reading it, while she licked a Fudgicle. With her hair in braids, and dressed in blue jeans and a floppy sweater, she looked like a teen-ager.

The next afternoon, Ruby Keeler and Patsy Kelly met a stranger, a motherly-looking woman sitting on the black plastic sofa in the rehearsal hall's waiting area. The three women chatted while the performers waited for Shevelove to call them into rehearsal.

"My daughter's in the show," said Carole's mother. "She's playing Nanette. I brought this coat for her. It gets cold in Boston."

"Oh, I know," said Ruby. "It's cold everywhere in the

East. That's another reason why I wish I were back in California."

Patsy started to say something when Burt Shevelove threw the door open. "We can use you two now," he said. Then he looked curiously at the third woman.

"This is Carole's mother," Ruby smiled.

Burt's face broke into a friendly grin. "Really?" he said. "She looks so young, I thought she was in the chorus. Why don't you come and sit inside and watch your daughter work?"

Flushed with pleasure, the smiling woman followed Ruby and Patsy into the studio. She sat between them on the hard wooden folding chairs.

"Attention, everybody," called Shevelove. "We have a guest. In the show, as you all know, Nanette is watched over by her guardian angel, Ruby Keeler, who treats her like a daughter. Well, this afternoon, we have Nanette's *real* mother with us."

He waved a hand at the blushing matron. Laughing, she stood up and took an awkward bow. Her daughter, the chorus, and the entire company laughed and applauded, as the warmth flooded throughout the room.

The next morning Carole's agent called to tell her she was fired.

**19** In 1924, when young Phyllis Cleveland was fired from the title role in *No, No, Nanette*—largely because her tiny voice could not be heard past the third row of the theater—and the experienced Louise Groody was brought in to replace her, the winsome Miss Cleveland smiled bravely and vented her anguish in a single sentence:

"Harry Frazee is a lying, no-good, double-crossing bum."

In 1970, when young Carole Demas was fired from the title role in *No, No, Nanette* and the experienced Susan Watson was brought in as her replacement, Carole was

> "Ruby just likes to 'kvetch.'
> She saw the third act."
>
> CYMA RUBIN

speechless. It was three days before she could bring herself to talk about the disappointment. And then, the words flowed out in short bursts of sound, punctuated by teary sighs.

"The sadness comes in waves, y'know. I wake up in the morning or sit at lunchtime and suddenly I start wondering what the kids are doing at that moment. 'Peach on the Beach,' with those crazy balls? 'Tea for Two'? . . . Then I try to forget it, and I *do*, until I look at the clock and realize that it's about the time Ruby—that classy lady—should be dancing her number. Is the cigarette still there? Is Patsy Kelly crying the way she does when she watches Ruby dance?"

Carole's face forced a weak smile, but the spark that lighted the large brown eyes was gone. "Ruby and Patsy both called me—such wonderful, wonderful people—to tell me how sorry they were. I didn't call anyone to say goodbye. I *couldn't*." She paused, biting her lip, trying to remember. "No, wait. I did call Roger. I thought he would be upset if he came to rehearsal and found Susan there. But—well—he sounded like he wasn't surprised." Now she laughed, ashamed of herself. "I guess I was a little disappointed that he took it so matter-of-factly."

Her voice edged knife-hard for just an instant. "I didn't

even get the satisfaction of shouting at anyone. No one had the guts to call me personally. They were all so friendly when they hired me, but now they had the new company manager—he had just been *hired*—call my agent. Then, as I actually was putting things in a suitcase to take to Boston, my agent called and said I was through. I *laughed*. 'Lester,' I said, 'with the way things are going, that's not a funny joke. I have enough problems.' "

Her long braids swung limply back and forth as she shook her head. *"Problems.* There were so many that some people would chase Harry and Cyma down the hall to complain. A friend said I should leave the producers alone, that they usually don't have time to get involved with petty squabbles. But maybe . . . maybe if I had talked to them . . . I might have had an inkling they were dissatisfied. No one *said* anything. And now, this way, I don't know why I was let go. What was wrong? If you don't *know,* you can get afraid to try *anything."*

Her run-of-the-show contract? Her agent settled for the amount of salary she would have been paid during the ten-week road tour and a few weeks on Broadway. "I was in such a state that I told him to do whatever he thought best. If I'd held them to the contract, he said I might have to appear in person every week to collect my salary. That would be difficult if I went into another show or film . . .

"Besides, I'd come out ahead only if the show ran longer than a few weeks. And that was a gamble . . ." Now she laughed, remembering something. "You know what Roger said when I told him they had paid me off? 'Maybe you better spend the money on acting lessons.' Can you imagine! And I called him hoping for some *encouragement."*

Her mahogany-brown eyes misted over suddenly. "One of the kids phoned today to tell me how things were going. She said Susan was doing very well—I didn't need *that.* But Susan's very good, a very fast learner. She'll be—" The rest of the sentence would not come. She changed the subject. "I'm sorry about one thing: I won't get to work with Burt Shevelove. I really respect him as a writer and a director.

He turned out script pages like a machine. And, at rehearsal, he never lost his temper. His standards are very high, y'know, and—well, I just wish I could have met them."

* * *

When Ruby Keeler appeared for rehearsal on the Wednesday afternoon that Susan Watson joined the cast, Patsy Kelly stopped her outside the studio.

"Well," the comedienne said in the same flat brassy voice that she would use to announce the end of the world, "I'm maid to a new Miss Nanette."

Ruby sensed the chagrin beneath the simple statement, and her own unemotional face fell with the realization. It was not just that Carole, that sweet little girl, had been fired on the eve of her big chance—but now there would be someone *new* in her place. Ruby, who tended to forget her lines over a long week end, now would have to get used to saying them to a different girl—and that meant more work. She started to say something—perhaps it was only "Carole?"— but then her eyes filled with tears.

Harry Rigby was there, suddenly, patting her shoulder, whispering that it would be all right, it would be just fine, it would be better. Burt Shevelove, fresh script pages in his hand as always, stood nearby and waited until Ruby's face was calm once more.

"It was one of those things that had to be done," he said. "For the good of the show. For everybody's good."

Ruby's voice was colorless. "Everybody?"

The director stroked his beard, matching her gaze. "Yes— I think so." He reached for the knob on the studio door. "Well, let's get to work. And, everybody, please forgive me if I'm a little abrupt today. I was up until 5:30 this morning trying to finish the second act. I took a pleasant pill just before I came over, but I don't feel very pleasant."

* * *

The dismissal of Carole Demas drove through the *Nanette* company the way an asbestos curtain separates performers from audience. The sides now were cleanly drawn. Cyma, The Black Witch, had drawn first blood, and the chorus kids

259

rapidly spread the word that her diabolical plot to fire Carole and replace her with Loni had somehow gone awry. It was assumed that Harry, Burt, and the others—including Busby Berkeley—had somehow managed to foil her scheme (or part of it, anyway) by forcing her to hire Susan Watson. The moment had its heroes.

But the atmosphere was charged with tension. What scheme—for surely she had one—would The Black Witch come up with to get revenge? On guard, everyone.

One chorus boy prepared for trouble by starting to keep a day-by-day diary of the seeming disaster that was *Nanette*. "When Carole was fired," he says, "I had a feeling that this was going to be the first and last Broadway musical for me, and a lot of others. I thought the survivors might want a record of what happened."

As did Bobby Van and Helen Gallagher—who wisely, politically, kept busy throughout the long weeks of rehearsal and thereby avoided having to take sides (or being much noticed, for that matter)—Susan Watson stayed aloof from the resentment and curiosity that flowed to meet her in those first days. She had no time to think about it. In exactly nine days, the musical would open in Boston, and she would be onstage—as Nanette.

It had taken Carole Demas more than four weeks to learn —partly—seven songs, a long and involved dance to "Tea for Two," and (Good Lord!) how to walk on a beach ball. Could Susan Watson learn it all in just over a week, and memorize the two-thirds of the completed script and a third act that was still to come?

During a twenty-minute cast break on the first day of rehearsal, Mary Ann Niles and "Billybob" Becker taught the entire "Tea for Two" routine to the new Nanette. Learning to stay on the spinning beach ball took a little longer—an entire afternoon. Watching Susan, awed, the chorus kids grinned, applauded, were completely won over.

And the events of the final week of rehearsal seemed to rush upon one another, a kaleidoscopic picture with its myriad parts jumbled together and constantly changing in a rapid sequence of jump cuts, as in a Richard Lester film.

\* \* \*

*Cut!* New ads for the Boston papers are prepared, with Susan Watson's name placed above the title in "star" position along with Keeler, Sherman, Van, Gallagher, and Kelly. Patsy's agent agrees that Susan's name can precede her client's if the ads read *"and* Patsy Kelly."

\* \* \*

*Cut!* Ruby Keeler refuses to wear one of the costumes that Raoul has designed. Helen sees the sketch, loves the dress, gets it for her third-act blues number. Both performers ask for duplicate costumes because the strenuous dance routines will leave the gowns damp with perspiration and grime. Cyma says she will "take care of it." Then, a costumer lets slip that no duplicates will be made until the show is clearly established as a hit, which might not be for months, if ever.

\* \* \*

In a bare studio, Bobby Van rehearses with buxom K. C. Townsend, slender and comedic Pat Lysinger, dark and earnest Loni Zoe Ackerman. They are working out the dance routine for "Telephone Girlie." Van, who once had been told that he and *Ruby* would do a "challenge dance," is trying to develop the idea with the three girls. He does progressively more difficult steps as the girls try to match him.

Donald Saddler looks on as Bobby leaps nimbly into the air and clicks his heels together. The girls cannot do it, so Bobby suggests that K. C. and Loni get a laugh by lifting Pat up high while she does the heel-clicking business. Saddler asks the girls to "look this way, that way, this way—and then lift," but they fail to do it, as he suggests, on four counts. "It's more feminine," shrugs Saddler. He then suggests a comic bit that Groucho and Harpo Marx once did with a nonexistent mirror: Bobby whirls around and stamps his foot, thinking the girls are following him—but they ignore the whirl, and copy only his final stamp as he ends up facing them. They all work on it, trying for the right laugh-provoking effect—but never quite getting it.

*Close-up.* Cyma watches the budding routine, fire flashing in her eyes. She storms out of the studio, cornering Harry in the corridor.

"Harry! Do you know what Bobby's doing? He's taking the whole number away from the girls. It's the only dance they have in the show—and he's hogging it."

"But he says the girls can't do the steps—"

"Maybe the other two can't, but I know Loni can!"

\* \* \*

*Cut!* The chorus kids are now working from ten in the morning until ten at night. They get a one-hour break for lunch, another hour for dinner. Several boys and girls complain to Bob Schear that they would rather have ninety minutes for lunch, thirty for dinner.

\* \* \*

*Cut!* Burt, battling to complete the script, tells Cyma and Harry to cancel the Friday-night preview in Boston. The first preview is rescheduled for Saturday afternoon, October 31st, Halloween.

\* \* \*

*Cut!* Like an anxious mother at baby's first haircut, Cyma hovers over the Vidal Sassoon stylist as he works on Ruby's and Helen's hair. "Please," he finally shouts, "you're making me *nerrrrrvous!*"

Photographers and reporters are in the salon from *Look*, *Women's Wear Daily,* and United Press International to get material on "the return of the Twenties bob." They get more than they bargained for. Ruby announces loudly that the show seems to be in considerable trouble. "The first act is cute, the second act is terrible, and the third—well, none of us have even *seen* the third act!"

\* \* \*

*Cut!* Harry Rigby suggests that Merle Debuskey book him for publicity interviews on radio programs. "I won't say anything *outraaaageous,*" he promises.

\* \* \*

*Cut!* Cyma is worried about the opening night party to be

given by Mrs. Cornelius Crane at the Ritz-Carlton in Boston. It will take place on Election Eve, after midnight, and she wonders if liquor can be served. "If there's any problem, we'll run it like a speakeasy. That would fit the period," she says.

\* \* \*

*Cut!* The beach balls have multiplied like rabbits and now there are six filling a corner of the rehearsal studio. Some of the girls can roll them out in a straight line, gingerly form them into an X, and execute a few dance steps before slipping off. The instructress, having taught the basics, has long been dismissed—and her plan to stage some scary-looking fake falls has gone with her. The girls' falls look—and are—quite real.

\* \* \*

*Cut!* Shevelove shows up for Saturday's rehearsal with a few lines for Ruby. She is to phone her friend Lucille. Ruby takes the prop phone and says, "Hello, operator, give me the Hotel Traymore (*Pause*) Hotel Traymore? (*Pause.*) Mrs. William Early, please. (*Pause.*) Lucille? . . ." Her readings are flat, and it is obvious that she is not talking to anyone on the other end of the phone.

Burt asks her to leave out the pauses. "Just read it all in one breath."

"But I have to wait for them to answer."

"No, don't wait. Read it like this: 'Hello-Operator-give-me - the - Hotel-Traymore-Hotel-Traymore - Mrs. - William - Early-please-Lucille-can-you-come-over-right-away?' "

Ruby looks confused. "But—"

"It will be funny," Burt promises. And it will get the lines over with quickly.

\* \* \*

*Cut!* Cyma says that Raoul has "flipped out" and won't return her phone calls. She can't understand it. He has been so cooperative till now. "Do you know what he wanted Helen to wear for 'You Can Dance with Any Girl?' " she exclaims. "An Irene Castle chiffon dress. *Pink* chiffon." But she had set things right.

*Fade to a flashback as she talks.* "I said, 'Raoul, I want

263

Helen in a gray suit with a gray fedora.' He said, 'I'm not dressing her—she's got a fat ass. Look what she looks like. She's ugly.' I said, 'Raoul, I promise you, I know how to dress her.' He said, 'How?'

" 'Remember how young Swanson used to look? I went through old magazines and looked at stars from the period, and she was slightly—*over*-chic. Just enough. Raoul, I will *show* you. I will change her hair—those bangs, that stringy hair—and get her a bob. We will dress her in stunning clothes and teach her how to walk so she doesn't swing her ass all the time.' He came up with the pink chiffon, and I said, 'No, I want the gray fedora. It's a *look*. *Ultra*.' And he said, 'You're right.' "

\* \* \*

*Cut!* In a studio, Helen Gallagher is working out the graceful dance movements to accompany her singing of "Where-Has-My-Hubby-Gone Blues." The chorus boys pose like John Held figures in a semicircle behind her. Donald Saddler sits on a folding chair facing her. She sings a line of the song at the left side of the room, and as she begins the next line, makes a slight gesture toward the right side with her hand. She looks questioningly at Saddler.

*Close-up.* Saddler nods.

Helen crosses slowly to the right side, singing, and then gestures toward the center of the stage, questioning the choreographer once more.

*Close-up.* Saddler nods.

The singer crosses to the center . . .

\* \* \*

*Cut!* Harry Rigby tells Cyma that he needs an assistant, and has found a tall, good-looking young man named Steve Beckler who is perfect for the job. Cyma grudgingly signs him on as "Assistant to the Producers." He is assigned the task that John Lowe is now too busy to handle—getting Busby Berkeley up, and in, and out.

*Close-up.* Cyma watches the new young assistant chatting with the old showman, and beneath her breath: "Now I've got to get rid of the old man *and* the kid."

\* \* \*

264

*Cut!* At the costumer's, Raoul Pène du Bois, who has dressed Broadway's biggest stars for four decades without Cyma's advice, is checking the individually handmade flowers that decorate the chorus girls' tea dresses. A photographer asks if he may take a picture of one of the dancers modeling an unfinished dress.

"Oh, heavens, no," Raoul laughs. "Not with my hair in a mess like this."

\* \* \*

*Cut!* Cyma has decided that the banners on the buses that will carry the chorus to Boston should have orange lettering to match the color Hilary Knight used on the *No, No, Nanette* poster. The sign company says there is no time for special colors—and it will give her red lettering, period.

Her disappointment is assuaged when M. J. tells her that a skywriter wants only $400 to spell out the show's title over a crowded football stadium in Boston. "Oh, we *have* to have it," she says excitedly.

\* \* \*

*Cut!* Busby Berkeley is in his hotel room wrapped up warmly against the growing October cold. He has missed several days of rehearsals and the chorus kids whisper two explanations: He is ill, and/or Shevelove ordered him out because Ruby and Helen asked his advice on some lines in the script.

\* \* \*

*Cut!* Ruby finishes dancing "I Want to Be Happy" for the ten-thousandth time and wonders aloud how she will have time to catch her breath before saying her next line of dialogue.

"Don't worry," Helen Gallagher says, "you'll have plenty of time during the applause."

*Close-up.* Ruby's eyes narrow in surprise. "Oh, do you think they'll applaud?"

\* \* \*

*Cut!* Cyma, increasingly worried about the lack of a Broadway theater, has set her eye on the 46th Street Theater where *1776* is playing to progressively smaller audiences. If the crowds get below a certain point, the show will have to move. Perhaps *Nanette* could get the theater, which is just the right size—not too big and not too small—in mid-January. That would mean canceling the tour to Baltimore and Washington, which would solve the problem of having Susan Watson's understudy play Nanette in those towns.

                       * * *

*Cut!* Burt calls the entire company together for a run-through of Acts I and II, and what there is of Act III. He spends considerable time explaining the curtain calls. After "Take a Little One-Step," which will be done in darkness so that ultraviolet lights can make the dancers' shoes glow, the entire company will come out on stage with ukeleles hidden behind their backs. After the first bow, they all will play the ukes and sing "Tea for Two" and Ruby will ask the audience to join in. The chorus laughs delightedly.

*Close-up.* A gloomy Hiram Sherman, muttering, "If we don't have the third act, maybe we should do the curtain calls after the second?"

                       * * *

*Cut!* Charles Gaynor's credit line is removed from the Boston ads and program. Shevelove's credit now reads: "Adapted and Directed by Burt Shevelove."

                       * * *

*Cut!* A distraught Cyma Rubin, her skin breaking out with a rash from nerves and worry, approaches her husband anxiously. Thus far, the show has cost $300,000 and it is going to take more to open than she originally counted on. No other investors have come forward. Sam, who has been kept away from rehearsals, wonders if his wife's health is being harmed, and if he should take his loss and forget it. Cyma pleads, charms, wheedles, *promises* that it will be all right.

And Sam agrees to put up the rest of what she needs . . .

                       * * *

*Cut!* A remote-controlled vacuum cleaner that will chase Patsy around the stage in one scene is delivered from the prop shop. The old-fashioned upright cleaner can be turned on and off and moved about from a switchbox offstage, but the dust bag on it does not inflate. The bag can be made to puff up realistically for $200. It is decided that the effect is not worth the expense.

\* \* \*

*Cut!* At a run-through, Ruby Keeler finally—albeit momentarily—explodes after reading a new line handed her by Shevelove.

"It's one thing to look bad onstage because I'm an old woman," she says hotly, "but it's another thing to look bad because I've been given bad material."

*Close-up.* An angry Burt Shevelove, biting back a retort. *Freeze frame.* And *Fade-out.*

267

**20** The week that was to include the first public performance of the 1970 version of *No, No, Nanette* began with the confusion and rancor of the weeks that had preceded it. The entire company gathered at the Broadway Arts studios on Monday at 10:00 a.m. to get last-minute instructions for the trip to Boston, check baggage tags and hotel reservations, and learn the rehearsal schedule for the four days prior to the Saturday preview.

Ruby Keeler, as always, showed up promptly at ten— and by noon was complaining to Cyma, "I've been here two hours and all we've done is sit and listen to that man talk."

"I have one word to describe the success of 'No, No, Nanette'. It's 'infuckingcredible.' "

ALEX COHEN

"That man" was Burt Shevelove; his "talk" consisted of changes he had made in some of the performers' lines.

A *Newsweek* reporter was on hand, and two newspaper men had trekked from Philadelphia and Toronto to get advance interviews with the stars. Harry caught Ruby as she was making a quiet exit—"Oh, Harry, I don't have time now. I have to pack and get to a costume fitting"—and he pleaded that she answer the writers' brief questions.

"I always do what people want," sighed Ruby.

The following afternoon, two chartered busses—with gaudy red-on-white banners proclaiming *No, No, Nanette*— were parked, solely by chance, in front of Irving Caesar's hotel. The chorus kids crowded aboard while John Lowe snapped candid pictures. Cyma and Sam Rubin posed at each end of the banners, pretending to tack them into place. As the bus drivers checked their watches, eager to beat the city's evening rush-hour traffic, a cab screeched alongside. Out of it stepped Harry Rigby, a tiny poodle under his arm. The wind of the blustery, late October day blew both Harry's gray-white locks and Cyma's long black hair around their faces as they, too, posed at opposite ends of the banner. John Lowe's camera clicked off its last frames.

Then Harry—who had checked into Boston's Ritz-Carlton

on Sunday with his assistant, and had then flown to New York—climbed on board the bus "to ride up with my company." As the busses pulled away from the curb, Sam and Cyma waved to Loni at a window seat. The effect was one of worried parents sending their children off to summer camp.

The principals and production staff made their way to the train station in the afternoon and evening, using tickets purchased for them by the Nanette Company. Now it began, Cyma knew. Now the travel expenses, the per diem payouts, the orchestra costs, the stagehands—the *big* expenses would have to be met. She tried not to think about it.

"I'll go up tomorrow afternoon, Sam," she said. "I want to be there for the first orchestra rehearsal to hear those tempos. I think they're too slow, but maybe it's because people are still learning them."

Buster Davis put the orchestra through its paces Wednesday afternoon on the roof of Boston's old Bradford Hotel. Under a clear blue sky, the cast listened and suddenly realized that, no matter how much ineptitude or confusion reigned in other parts of *No, No, Nanette*, here was professionalism. The music was big, exciting, richly orchestrated in what Davis called "an MGM movie-musical sound."

Had the original orchestrations from 1924 been used, he added, "the effect could only have been one of Camp." His idea had been to remove all sense of period from the music —"it's not Twenties, Thirties, Forties, Fifties, and it's certainly not rock"—and simply to use as much *lushness* as possible. "Audiences today are musically sophisticated," he said. "Their ears have been conditioned by listening to thousands of hours of Mantovani, Percy Faith, Andre Kostelanetz, even Nelson Riddle backgrounds for Sinatra. No one who sees the show would know that the harmonies the orchestra plays are too complicated to have been used in 1924, any more than movie audiences who heard Judy Garland sing 'The Trolley Song' in *Meet Me in St. Louis*, which took place at the turn of the century, would think to complain that the MGM harmonies were too advanced for 1900."

The rich and soaring melodies brightened the day some-

269

what, for the five-hour bus and train ride the preceding afternoon had worn everyone out. Burt Shevelove, attempting a brief run-through with the principals, discovered that the one-day layoff caused Ruby to forget most of her lines. And Hiram Sherman, who ordinarily was letter-perfect in his lines, fluffed many either through weariness or worry.

Only Busby Berkeley, who had dozed on the train trip while Etta admired the New England scenery out the window, seemed enthusiastic. He taped a television interview for a Boston station that contained the following conversation:

> INTERVIEWER: Mr. Berkeley, in the film where pianos danced across the stage, there were men in black beneath each piano, pushing them around. Did you have to rehearse much with them to get the pianos into the right position?
>
> BUZ (*with a laugh*): Oh, no.
>
> INTERVIEWER (*puzzled*): But then how did they know where to go?
>
> BUZ: Well, we just told each one where to go and then we practiced a lot before we filmed it.

When the sets arrived late Wednesday night to be installed on the stage of the Shubert Theater, the excitement began to mount. The chorus kids, who had practiced their tap-dance to "I Want to Be Happy" hundreds of times on the flat studio floor of the Broadway Arts, suddenly saw the height of the two staircases they would have to climb when they did the number onstage. Bobby Van, who intended to whirl up one staircase, across the balcony, and down the other when he danced to "Call of the Sea," began to wonder if it was worth the effort. (He later decided it was not.)

Thursday afternoon, while the stagehands practiced changing Raoul's three massive sets, the principals and chorus put costumes on, took them off, and put others on in frantic sequence to check for poor fit and ripped seams. Beneath the stage, a battery of wardrobe attendants worked at sewing machines and ironing boards to remedy any problems.

A full run-through of the production was scheduled for
8:00 p.m. Harry agreed that Busby Berkeley would not be
present "because Burt might blow up if he sees him—and
then Buz would want to take over. Y'know, he says they
used to call him 'Dr. Buz' whenever a show was in trouble."
There was trouble that evening.

Cyma Rubin appeared in Hiram Sherman's dressing room
shortly before the first act curtain was to go up. In her hand
was a bunch of flowers. Furiously, Sherman said, "We're
dying for lines—for a script—and we get flowers!" He
stormed onto the stage—a meek, soft-spoken man whose
ordinarily warm, humorous face was livid with rage—and
confronted the other performers.

"I *cannot* take the frustration any longer," he said. "You
can't be expected to perform when you're handed your lines
almost as you're stepping on the stage! Even if an actor can
ad-lib his way out of a paper bag, he likes to have something
to hang onto! I'm about to—flip!"

Ruby Keeler's voice was steady, almost childlike.

"Please don't, Hiram. Not until we've seen the third act."

Sherman's chubby face relaxed into a smile, a grin, and
suddenly he was laughing along with everybody else. "All
right, all right," he said as tears of amusement filled his
eyes, "let's get on with it. But, Burt, please—can we have the
end of Act III at least an *hour* before the curtain goes up
Saturday?"

Shevelove laughed, nodded, promised to try to finish even
sooner. He delivered the last lines of the script the next evening, minutes before the last rehearsal of *No, No, Nanette*
was to begin.

This was to be a complete dress rehearsal—with all the
costumes and set changes, all the lighting cues and performance details that would be part of the show some fourteen
hours later when an audience was out front.

The last notes of the overture were still echoing from the
walls of the near-empty, gloomy auditorium when the curtain rose to reveal Patsy Kelly leaping nimbly over her vac-
uum-cleaner cord. She had no costume—just her usual

271

rehearsal clothes of baggy slacks and a loose overblouse. Her several maid's uniforms were still in various stages of construction.

Helen Gallagher, wrapped in a fox-fur stole, entered, and immediately stopped the proceedings to ask if she *had* to wear the furs. Burt Shevelove had already gone through a lengthy discussion of the subject with Cyma.

"He told me, 'Only hookers wore red fox in the Twenties,' " Cyma said, "and I came right back at him. 'Okay,' I said, 'I went to Paris. Here are the *Vogues*. The most elegant ladies wore them.' "

"I don't care who wore them," Helen shouted from the stage. "*I* don't want to wear them!"

Slowly, Shevelove stood up in the middle of the theater. "I don't want to be dramatic, children," he said in a calm, well-modulated voice, "but you know I recently was in hospital. I have doctor's orders to leave the theater if there is going to be any display of emotion."

Angrily, Helen Gallagher tossed the fur around her shoulders and stood aside for Ruby Keeler's first entrance. From the rear of the theater, from the dark corner where Harry Rigby sat with his assistant, came an audible scream. "What have you *done* to my star?" wailed Harry. "What have you done to her?"

Onstage, Ruby Keeler carefully picked her way down the staircase and walked forward to the orchestra pit. She had not bothered to put on make-up. Her hair had been set, but a backstage dryer had not worked, and now the silver-brown locks seemed glued to her head. Girdle-less, she bulged in her first-act costume like a Long Island housewife in a Korvette's dress. Her first line in the script was a simple greeting to her friend Lucille, but instead, out of her mouth came a stern warning.

"There will be no pictures taken of me tonight."

It was unnecessary. Sy Friedman was on hand to take the "official" production photographs of *No, No, Nanette*, along with a photographer from *Look* magazine. Both had dropped their viewfinders from their eyes in stunned surprise. Cyma was already adding up in her mind the cost of another

272

photo call when Harry snaked through the rows of seats and hissed in her ear:

"That dress was supposed to have a *coat* with it! What happened to the coat? Raoul's sketch had a coat! You're trying to save *money*—on the star's clothes!"

"Shhhhhh!" The order from Burt Shevelove cut through the darkness, and Harry stumbled back to his seat, shaking his head in disbelief. The Ruby Keeler that he saw in his mind's eye—the young, pretty, *ratatapping* Ruby—was not up there onstage. That was an elderly, unglamorous grandmother, dressed from Lane Bryant.

Hiram and Ruby timidly ventured into their duet, "Always You." Ruby's voice did not carry past the third row.

Now Susan Watson was on, sounding good, but—in costumes that had been designed for a slenderer Nanette, for Carole Demas—looking bad.

Bobby Van's first-act dance was energetic and appealing, but his third-act routine seemed repetitious. His acting style appeared slick and mechanical, particularly in contrast to Ruby's amateur technique and Hiram Sherman's casual warmth.

Sherman, who throughout rehearsals had been dismayed whenever a performer stepped out of character to voice a complaint, stopped the run-through several times himself to point out that either he or Roger Rathburn had on a wrong costume. The searching-for-the-lost-hat bit, which Burt had *guaranteed* would be funny, wasn't.

Patsy Kelly's laugh lines—"I'm Pauline from Peoria" and "I'm going to quit this job"—seemed about as funny as the beach-ball routine in which three girls toppled to the floor and one of the heavy spheres rolled into the orchestra pit.

Of the three gold diggers, only K. C. Townsend—her awesome breasts overflowing her costumes' low-cut necklines—looked as if she would get laughs from a regular audience. Loni Zoe Ackerman, singing in a powerful, heavy contralto and posing like a high-school Duse, seemed obviously miscast as a scheming young flapper.

The "Tea for Two" number, which Saddler had tried to

"build" à la Busby Berkeley, appeared nothing more than overlong as the boys and girls soft-shoed their way through chorus after chorus of the simple tune. "That number should be cut," Sam Rubin said loudly to his wife on seeing it for the first time.

Midway during the third act, Patsy Kelly managed to get an unscheduled laugh when she appeared onstage in a costume that had hastily—finally—been stitched together. Primping like a fashion model, she showed off for the tiny knots of grim-faced people scattered throughout the theater until she drew applause.

The laughter faded immediately when "Take a Little One-Step" began. The luminous dye on the dance shoes gleamed only faintly in the feeble ultraviolet glow. All that could be seen of the complicated routine were hazy purplish blurs moving vaguely about the stage. At one point, Ruby—who had sworn a week earlier that she would not dance "one more step" in the show—was left standing in the middle of the stage as the chorus whirled about her. "What am I supposed to do for four choruses, Donald?" she shouted into the darkness. "Just stand here?"

The third-act curtain fell, almost miraculously, to end the torture at almost one o'clock in the morning.

A concerned-looking Donald Saddler turned to the assistant sitting beside him, who had held a pencil and clipboard ready to note the choreographer's whispered corrections on the dances throughout the evening. The paper on the board was blank. "We'd better fix up 'One-Step,'" Saddler said dryly, as he waved the company back onto the stage.

It was several hours later, a chorus boy recalled, when Hiram Sherman's self-control cracked.

"We had been there eight or nine hours," the dancer said. "We were standing on stage, and we were standing—and standing. Donald couldn't decide what he wanted to do. Cyma and Harry were arguing. Burt was running around like a chicken with his head cut off. Ruby and Patsy looked like they were ninety years old. It was total chaos, there's no other word for it.

"Finally, Chubby walked forward and said, very quietly,

'Mrs. Rubin. *Mister* Rigby. What is all this about? Why are we standing here? If we're going to do something, fine, let us work. But if we are not going to do anything, we are all exhausted. Let us go home.' And then, he looked at them both, and said, 'I love the theater—but I hate showbusiness.'

"And with that, he walked off the stage. It was the first time that anyone questioned anything publicly, in front of the whole cast. All of us wanted to applaud."

After a hurried conference among the producers and directors, the cast was dismissed. Donald Saddler was the last to leave the empty theater. He was not sure that "One-Step" looked any better—but what difference did it make, since the black-light bulbs were too weak to illuminate the dancers anyway? Halfway up the aisle of the deserted house, Saddler stopped to turn off a single gooseneck lamp burning at a small desk. It had been placed there for Busby Berkeley to use at an earlier run-through, while he sat nodding over the pages of the script and dozing through thirty-minute intermissions as sweating stagehands struggled with the heavy sets.

Now Saddler glanced back at the stage that in just a few hours would hold the theatrical debacle to be forever known as the last show to be "supervised by Busby Berkeley."

Saddler put a finger to his lower lip thoughtfully. He nodded his head in a slow movement.

*It's all yours, Buz,* he whispered. *It's all yours.*

\* \* \*

On that most marvelous of days, Matinée Day, clusters of aging Boston matrons chattered excitedly over coffee and vanilla-ice-cream-for-dessert in the homely, brightly lit atmosphere of The Union Oyster House. It was twenty minutes after two, and the ladies were fairly trembling with excitement. In just a few moments, just across the street at the Shubert Theater, there would be music, colored lights, gaiety. Far behind, in the distant areas of Burlington and Peabody and Natick were tired husbands and noisy children and bawling grandchildren. But inside the Shubert, there would be magic. *Magic.* And Ruby Keeler.

The ladies rose as if cued by a silent signal, lined up

before the restaurant's cashier to pay their checks (after first determining whether or not Jane's dessert cost more than the extra coffees for Marian and Dorothy), and then helped each other across the street. Briefly they examined the orange-and-purple marquee, their mouths almost watering perceptibly as they saw the names.

"Look, 'Ruby Keeler'! The first one, up on top!"

"And, see, I *told* you. 'Production Supervised by Busby Berkeley.' "

"I just *know* I'm going to love it! I *do* wish Charlie had come with me."

As the ladies—and a sprinkling of elderly widowers and fading fags—crowded into the lobby, Burt Shevelove was on the telephone in an upstairs office. He had placed a call to a friend, choreographer Jerome Robbins, who was ill in New York.

"Well, Jerry," Shevelove said, chuckling, "I wonder how far back we're going to set the theater with this one."

It was precisely 2:40 when Buster Davis snaked his way through the musicians and stepped onto the conductor's platform. His dark glasses looked like a mask beneath his longish red hair, and the audience buzzed. Was this man some kind of hippie? Was this going to be a different kind of *No, No, Nanette?*

And then Buster poised his baton in the air, like a diver preparing to arc from a springboard. He brought it down in a swift curving movement. From the trumpets came the clarion notes:

" 'I . . . want . . . to . . . *be* . . . happy!' "

And the crowd was clapping, chuckling, answering the orchestra with its own overture of sound.

Backstage, in Ruby's dressing room, where a huge bouquet of roses from Busby Berkeley scented the musty air, the echo of welcoming applause brought a moment of incredulity. Of wonder. Of realization.

The audience was ready to *love* the show—*before* it had seen it, before the curtain went up.

The growing realization was reinforced a moment later

when the twin pianos in the pit rippled into the first notes of
"Tea for Two"—and the applause welled up again.

But wait. The spectators liked the *music*. But the show
had long arid stretches ahead, without music, without those
great old familiar tunes. At the rear of the theater, Cyma
and Harry and Burt and Donald sat stiffly in their last-row
seats, waiting for the dullness and labored humor that had
been onstage last night to reappear.

The curtain slid silently upward in the drumming of
approval for the overture, and, as the clapping died, the
audience saw that the bulky figure behind the vacuum
cleaner was Patsy Kelly, alive and well and actually—*"Did
you see that?"*—dancing over the cord in a comical leap. The
applause welled again in another crash of sound.

Helen Gallagher, hidden behind a mountain of purple
shopping boxes from Bergdorf's, came on, apologizing for
spending so much money, but excusing it with a flip "I had a
bad week at mah-jongg." The audience squealed in delight,
and squealed again at its first look at Raoul's flapper dresses
and cloche hats for the chorus girls. "Banana oil!" caused a
wave of laughter, then a continuing ripple as woman after
woman repeated it to her hard-of-hearing companion.

Now Helen and the chorus were into "Too Many Rings
Around Rosie"—Irving Caesar's new ending and all—and
the ladies were pounding their palms together enthusiastically. They enjoyed the number, but each had looked at her
*Playbill*, and knew that the *next* number, "Always You,"
was to be sung by "Jimmy"—Hiram Sherman—and "Sue"
—*Ruby Keeler!*

Wait, now, Patsy Kelly was gesturing toward the staircase. A door at the top was opening . . . and *she* was coming
through it, coming down the steps, coming toward the audience out of time and memory. Traces of gray were in her
hair, yes, and there was a matronly thickness to her girdled
waist, but—"Oh, just *look!*"—the legs were long and smooth
and slender beneath the salmon-pink pleated skirt, and the
face, unlined and youthful behind the make-up, had the
familiar fresh innocence of yesteryear.

The applause swept, thundering, to meet the figure half-way down the staircase, but Ruby Keeler, unconcerned, moved through it as a swimmer dives into a wave. She said her first line—"Lucille, are all those packages yours?"—in that voice that once again told the audience, "I'm not an actress, you know, but they asked me to say this, and I hope you'll all understand."

The audience understood, and loved her for it. Everyone in the theater who had ever been forced to take the *tiniest* of roles in a show at grade school, or high school, or a PTA affair—and who had been scared senseless, but had gone doggedly through with it to please doting parents or friends —well, every man and woman in the theater *knew* how Ruby Keeler felt up there onstage. They had gone through it themselves—and knew she was not doing it for her own pleasure. She was there to please them. That was all that mattered.

But, oh dear, oh God, *when* would she dance? *How* would she dance? *Could* she dance? The crowd leaned forward, waiting . . .

Yes, there was Hiram Sherman now—all warmth and fumbling embarrassment and good humor. And he was at the fake piano, pretending to play, while Ruby leaned across it, smiling at him. They began the duet—a weak little song— in weak little voices that could barely be heard over the orchestra. And then they did a few quick little dance steps, ending up in a tentative, old-folks' embrace on a bench upstage.

The murmur of disappointment matched the crowd's perfunctory applause.

Was that *it*? Was that the dancing that Ruby would do? *Could* do?

The comment that crept through the minds of the men and women in the audience hung, heavy and tangible, in the air: "Well, what can you expect? After all, she *is* in her sixties—I mean, she *has* to be, 'cause I used to see all her movies. Anyway, she's doing *wonderfully* just to be able to get up there, and look *that* good, and dance that much."

But the smiles on the faces of the audience now were smiles of resignation, of acceptance. Nothing more. No anticipation. No pure pleasure.

The mood became more critical. Susan Watson and Roger Rathburn came on, all giddy and bubbling, to duet to a lush Youmans melody, "I've Confessed to the Breeze." But the tune was unfamiliar and the applause was routine. Bobby Van raced energetically through "Call of the Sea," getting appreciative nods when he drew the chorus line from the wings with the crook of his song-and-dance-man's cane. But it was plain that the spectators wanted something else, something more.

Then Susan Watson and Hiram Sherman sat side by side on the circular sofa in the center of the stage. Pleasantly, they did a softly sung chorus of "I Want to Be Happy." ("It's all wrong," Irving Caesar had said when he first heard how the number was directed. "In the original *Nanette*, Charlie Winninger danced all over the stage, finally ending up with a back-flip into the orchestra pit. And he always used this gesture—")

As Hiram sang the first words of the refrain, applause spattered like raindrops from the audience—but when the song ended, without back-flips or exuberant thrust of the right arm across the body, the audience reaction was friendly, nothing more. Again, the murmur of disappointment crept through the half-filled theater, almost drowning out the few lines of dialogue that Susan and Hiram had to speak before they cleared the stage.

And, then, while the audience sat there, staring at the bare stage, wondering if someone had missed a cue and was late coming on—the *plink-plunka-plink* of a single ukelele was heard. Through the French doors at the rear stepped a half-dozen chorus boys in knickers and wildly patterned argyle socks and sweaters ablaze with color. To the accompaniment of the uke, they sang the first eight bars of "I Want to Be Happy" while the memory-struck men and women in the rows of seats drank in the costumes.

The door at the top of the stairs—that wondrous portal—

279

opened once more, and Ruby Keeler walked nonchalantly, smiling, down the steps. She wore the same long-sleeved salmon-pink dress with its scarflike collar, her hair was the same, her nerveless manner was unchanged.

But there was something different about her—the way she moved, the way—

The audience spotted it before she had taken three steps down the long staircase. And the whisper raced from seat to seat.

"Look! She's got her tap shoes on!"

Ruby Keeler waved to the chorus boys, gestured for them to go on with the song, and—to the rhythm of the uke and their Glee Club voices—she began to tap.

She started easily, gently, holding one side of her skirt with one hand and flipping the other hand out in a graceful gesture. By the time the boys had sung the first line of the song, her taps had clicked eighteen times against the wooden floor—and the audience was thundering its applause.

Ruby smiled, danced on, lightly finished the chorus, picked up the tempo now, brushed back the hair that tumbled over her forehead, waved on the rest of the chorus boys and the girls in their whirligig dresses, and *ratatatatapped* faster and faster as the kids moved up the staircases on either side and across the balcony to frame her in a blur of color and motion.

Then, on the stage of Boston's Shubert Theater, a miracle took place. It was one of those showbusiness miracles that happens only in a script, like *Light Up the Sky* or *Room Service* or *The Producers* or—of course!—*42nd Street*.

The woman onstage, a sixty-year-old grandmother who was tap dancing in a salmon-pink high-necked gown, disappeared. In her place was a dewy-eyed Irish youngster named Ruby Keeler, with jet-black hair, tapping furiously in a homemade costume of tiny shorts with a bib-top. And her co-stars were not people with prosaic names like Hiram Sherman or Susan Watson, but magical people named Jimmy Cagney and Warner Baxter and Ginger Rogers.

The ticket buyers that afternoon in Boston might as well

have closed their eyes while they watched Ruby dance, for they did not see what was on the stage. They saw what their memories and minds and hearts wanted them to see. They saw their own youth, alive once more. Alive and dancing.

And when the number ended, after Ruby and the chorus had grinned as they raced in place for what seemed like hours, their arms and legs shooting forward and back like pistons on a railroad engine, the audience cheered and stamped and screamed for more. They could *not* let the young lady, the "old" Ruby Keeler, get away. Their youth might vanish with her. So they held her tight.

They held her through the bows taken by the pink-clouded woman onstage, that Ruby who had disguised herself for some unknown reason as a sixty-year-old grandmother ("But, look, she isn't even out of breath!"). And they held her all through the rest of the show.

Never mind that the intermissions took twenty-five minutes while the backstage crew shoved the sets into place. Never mind that Susan Watson's costumes made her look as if she was wearing a bustle. Never mind that chorus girls tumbled off beach balls and scrambled to mount them again. Never mind that "Take a Little One-Step" was invisible in the black light.

No, nothing mattered now that Ruby Keeler was back.

Let Patsy Kelly say, "I'm Pauline from Peoria," as she clumsily tossed a suitcase over her shoulder, and the house exploded with laughter. Let Bobby Van and Helen Gallagher show off their fancy interpretation of the Turkey Trot in "You Can Dance with Any Girl," and the crowd buzzed with recognition and amusement. Let Helen pour her heart out in the blues, and the ladies wept for their own lost, strayed, or stolen mates. Let chorus after chorus of "Tea for Two" lap gently against the audience, like a soft ocean wave, and the men and women grinned with unbearable pleasure. ("Now, that's what I call *music*—not that rock stuff the kids play today!")

And the ending—with sixty ukeleles *plinkety-plunking* onstage and the entire company swaying to a joyous chorus of "Tea for Two"—brought them out of their seats, up on their feet, trying to remember the words, trying to sing with the vigor and energy and youth that seemed once more to be part of them. They *wanted* to sing, to thank all those wonderful people on the stage—Ruby and Busby and Patsy and, oh, gosh, *everybody*—for making them young again.

The final curtain came down, went up, came down, went up. The audience would not let go. It held on for a minute longer. A moment longer. An instant longer.

Dazzled, awed, struck speechless by the applause, Cyma Rubin turned to her husband in the seat beside her. Her eyes flashed with accomplishment. She tried to say something over the roar of the crowd. He could not hear her, but she knew he was pleased by the laughter in his eyes. They both heard a shrill cackle of joy behind them. It was Harry Rigby, leaping to pound first Burt Shevelove and then Donald Saddler joyfully on the shoulders, and then hugging Busby Berkeley in an affectionate embrace.

"They love it!" Harry screamed over and over. "They love it! They just *lovvvvve* it! Ruby! Patsy! Buz! They love *everything*!"

The smile faded from Cyma's eyes, and her mouth tightened as she watched him dancing in the aisle of the theater. *Dancing* like some kind of maniac, like some kind of screaming—

She looked at Sam, whose smile also had become intense as the realization came to him of what a Broadway "hit" might mean—financially. Her husband's expression was thoughtful.

No one knows for sure, of course, but in that moment—as Mr. and Mrs. Sam Rubin watched the curtain descend for the last time on the first performance of *No, No, Nanette*— it is possible that they first thought seriously of taking Harry Rigby's dream for their own.

# 21

The movie would end here. *Forty-Second Street. Babes in Arms. Summer Stock.* They all would end here, with the crowd on its feet cheering the kids who had worked so long and hard to put on the show, the wonderful, wonderful show!

And Warner Baxter or Mickey Rooney or Judy Garland would say, "See, what'd I tell you? I knew all along it would be a hit. I wasn't worried for a minute!"

After *No, No, Nanette* opened in New York as the smash of the 1970-71 season, there were people who said they knew it would be a hit almost from the beginning: A lot of people.

> "I guess it doesn't matter whether or not we like the book, Don, so long as it tells the truth."
>
> RUBY KEELER

BUSTER DAVIS: "With Vincent Youmans' music, and Burt Shevelove—even though he put it all together on scraps of paper, racing against time—I felt sure that any problems would be overcome. And as soon as we did an afternoon preview for the gypsies—all the other chorus people working in Broadway shows—and those *kids* dug it, I felt sure we were in. I'll take their barometer of acceptance or rejection before anybody's."

HARRY RIGBY: "Abe Burrows taught me years ago that if you can stop a show three times, you have a hit. Now, I knew 'the beach balls' was going to create havoc, I knew they'd love that. And Ruby's 'I Want to Be Happy' dance was number two. And I thought that 'You Can Dance with Any Girl at All' was *awfully* good, and maybe would be number three. Then Helen sang 'Where-Has-My-Hubby-Gone,' and I thought we had four stoppers! I knew the book, of course, was nonsense—but it always *was*. And the audiences found it *endearing*, because Burt Shevelove kept it from being dull and *long*."

CYMA RUBIN: "I never lost faith. I always felt easy—from the time I talked to Buster. Because I had said to Buster, 'I think the music should be—big! It shouldn't be—*this*.' And he said, 'Absolutely!' Buster and I never disagreed on where we were going. I mean, there were lots of things I did not know, which I learned as I went. But the basic *idea*—I always believed in the whole crazy thing."

Belief, sheer unadulterated belief, was not plainly evident backstage after that first Saturday preview in Boston. The mood of the principals and chorus, of stagehands and wardrobe women, was one of joyful skepticism. Even after the Saturday-night audience duplicated the reaction of the matinée ladies, and the Monday-night crowd surpassed them both in enthusiasm—the entire house stood up to sing along at the curtain calls—there still was doubt. Cast members buttonholed theater ushers after each show to ask if the people really loved *No, No, Nanette* as much as they seemed to. If there weren't *some* negative comments.

On Tuesday afternoon, however, one person at the Shubert Theater knew—no matter what the critics would say after the "official opening" that evening—that *Nanette* was a hit. In the box office, the treasurer turned from the ringing telephones and line of people at the window and made a circular sign with his thumb and forefinger to publicist M. J. Boyer. Projecting ticket sales from years of experience, he matter-of-factly forecast that the show would sell out completely in its second week.

Financial and artistic success are entirely different things. And critical success, as indicated by approving notices from the newspaper and broadcast reviewers, is something else again. Before the official opening, the company worked to "fix" the show in order to win over the critics.

Donald Saddler solved the problem of the invisible "One-Step" dance by the simple expedient of junking the ultraviolet glow-in-the-dark idea. In full stage light, the customers not only could see the dancers' feet; they could admire Raoul Pène du Bois' beaded party gowns.

The "Always You" duet—Charles Gaynor's remaining contribution to the show—was eliminated. It left an over-long ten-minute stretch of plot lines and weak jokes immediately after the first song, but everyone agreed that the dullness was better than the disappointment that followed the duet.

One of the chorus girls practiced on her beach ball until she could scoot it fearlessly across the stage, and her co-walkers gained enough experience from the three preview performances that the odds were strong they could stay up throughout the routine.

An Election Eve audience—buzzing soberly, annoyed that the closed bars had kept them from enjoying an after-dinner drink—moved into the theater in formal gowns and black tie. Despite the presence of friends, such as the entire board of Sam Rubin's American Symphony Orchestra, the opening-night crowd was rich with skeptics. Yes, they had heard that *Nanette* was enjoyable. Fun. A hit. But just a few weeks ago, Bostonians had heard the same things about *Two by Two*; and then they had licked their lips in anticipation of a new David Merrick comedy with Carol Channing. Disappointed twice, the first-nighters were wary. They were prepared to resist, to make *No, No, Nanette* prove itself.

Backstage, Burt Shevelove assembled the cast as the audience grew quiet on the other side of the curtain. He delivered his Valentine's Day Speech, and ended with an exuberant, "Good luck, everybody." Handshakes . . . kisses . . . backslapping eased the performers' tension. Ruby's three daughters, who had flown in from Colorado and California to see for the first time their mother performing onstage, scurried through a side door to third-row seats on the aisle. Buster Davis slipped into the orchestra pit and lifted his baton . . .

And three hours later, the skepticism and doubt were gone. All of Boston and the entire *Nanette* company knew that the show was a rock-hard, can't miss, solid-gold HIT.

In the lavish suite of the Ritz-Carlton where wealthy Mrs. Crane hosted a party for the cast and friends, Burt Shevelove clapped his hands for silence and then mounted a chair. It was after midnight, and M. J. had just handed Merle Debuskey the reviews that she had rushed by cab from three newspaper offices around the city. Debuskey glanced at the headlines, smiled, and passed two of the papers to Shevelove. The crowd, which had been chattering with excitement, was suddenly still.

Slowly and deliberately, with great emphasis, Shevelove said, "From the *Boston Record-American: 'No, No, Nanette* is a Yes-Yes!' "

A roar of joyous relief rolled from the several hundred people jammed into the room. Laughter exploded, tears streamed down wide-smiling faces. Shevelove read on, with his robust tones turning each line of the review into a paean of praise—for Ruby, Bobby, Helen, Hiram, Susan, Roger, Buster, Patsy, Raoul, the chorus, *everyone*. Bursts of applause punctuated each loving appraisal.

Then, before he could stop himself, the director was reading about "flashes of his old directorial magic . . . from the grand old man of the really big, splashy movie musicals of the 1920s—" Shevelove slowed his words, lowered his voice, then plunged ahead with, "Busby Berkeley." An awkward silence cut through the gaiety as two or three scattered chorus people started to applaud, then stopped and sipped thirstily from their glasses of champagne. Ruby and Patsy looked up, half-frowning, but it was all right—Berkeley and his wife had left the party early, tired from the excitement.

Quickly, Shevelove began reading again. He turned to the other review and found a line about Ruby Keeler: "She is sweet, modest, entirely natural . . . a great star who is still a great star, and who works at it without apologies or concessions or without fuss." In the storm of applause, Ruby grinned in embarrassment as Patsy Kelly pounded her on the back and said loudly, "This is the most wonderful night in all my years in showbusiness—and, believe me, that covers a lot of years!"

Shevelove smoothed his beard patiently, waiting until the crowd stopped laughing. Then, with a grin, he said, "Now, I know there were some of you who had differences of opinion about the way I put *Nanette* together . . ."

Happily surrounded by her sister, her three daughters,

her son and his blonde, tanned fiancée from California, Ruby Keeler raised her voice.

"That was me, Burt," she said.

Then she started the applause as the room rocked with laughter.

There was another person who had differed—almost violently at times—with the director. Sick and exhausted, he was not present at the opening-night party. And the next morning, Chubby Sherman notified the producers that he was spitting blood . . . on the verge of a major illness . . . was working against his doctor's orders. And wanted out of the show. Wanted out at once. Wanted out so badly that he was willing to settle his run-of-the-show contract for two weeks' pay.

"There was no resistance on Cyma Rubin's part," Sherman said later. "She did not want to see another old man— me—collapsing and dying in her show."

But a replacement would have to be found before Sherman could be released, and Cyma knew that might be a problem. Besides, Shevelove and Harry and others did not want the actor who was so perfect for the role of Jimmy Smith to leave. The director suggested that Sherman consult a Boston doctor, an old friend. "Perhaps, if Hiram relaxed for a few days, took it easy while his understudy played the part . . ." The understudy, Ted Tiller, was an earnest performer, and although he lacked Hiram's warmth—well, people were coming to see *Ruby* anyway. The veteran actor agreed, but after Tiller played his part one evening, he showed up at the Shubert and insisted that he was feeling better, was feeling well enough to go on.

Over the director's protests, Sherman struggled into the costume that had already been cut down for the understudy. Then, Chubby Sherman—who had, according to one reviewer, "the bewildered air of a stoned March Hare"— proceeded to bewilder the cast and audience. Onstage, confused and ill, he started to make a simple exit that called for him to cross from one side of the stage to the other and go off. But, as Bobby Van gawked at his co-star in surprise,

Sherman walked up one staircase, across the balcony, and down the other side before exiting.

The next day, Hiram Sherman was released from his contract.

Despite Harry's protests, Cyma was glad to get rid of him. She had too many other things—better things—to think about. It had taken only moments for news of the show's rave reception in Boston to reach Broadway. Already, representatives of the choicest theaters were flying up to beg Rubin & Rigby Productions to rent their houses for *Nanette*. Cyma and the managers began negotiations with the 46th Street Theater, the Majestic, the St. James—and settled on the 46th Street. Record-company executives, who formerly had scoffed at the idea of an original-cast album that featured a *tap-dancer*, now were feverishly bidding for the right to put the show on wax.

Boston theatergoers, who had bought $70,000 worth of tickets for *Nanette*'s first week, made the second week a $100,000 sellout. In Toronto, Philadelphia, and Baltimore, the advance sale mounted rapidly.

Then, to top the good news, a replacement for Hiram Sherman proved to be close at hand. After a number of names had been suggested and discarded—"What about Jack Gilford?" asked Merle Debuskey, a close friend of the comedian. "Looks too Jewish," said Cyma—seventy-two-year-old Frank McHugh was found living in semiretirement in nearby Connecticut.

The round-faced Irish character actor seemed to be a natural for the part. A veteran stage performer who had played in countless Hollywood films of the Thirties, Forties, and Fifties, he possessed a lovable warmth similar to Hiram Sherman's, and he was well known to nostalgians. In *Going My Way*, he had portrayed a comical priest who counseled Bing Crosby, and in *Footlight Parade*, he had been a Busby Berkeley-type dance director who showed Ruby Keeler her routines. What was more, he had worked onstage with Ruby once before in *Show Girl*.

McHugh, mused Cyma, would be a bigger publicity and

marquee draw than Sherman. And he only wanted two-thirds as much money. Even with two weeks' salary going to terminate Sherman's contract, and the $50 per performance that she would have to pay Ted Tiller until McHugh was ready to go on, it would be a profitable deal. The aging Irishman auditioned his singing voice for Buster Davis, and then charmed everyone with a rapid sequence of stories about the golden days of movie-making, about how great it would be to work with Ruby again, about how marvelous the show was.

And he was signed to a one-year contract.

Cyma Rubin was glad that the contractual deal went easily. She was having enough problems with other principals' agreements.

Ruby's, for example.

Once the pressure of rehearsals was off, and the realization dawned on her that her presence in the show was of some importance, Ruby Keeler looked at her paycheck in surprise. It was smaller than she had thought it would be. Her first husband, Al Jolson, who had once remarked about his wife's casual ways with money, undoubtedly would have smiled knowingly. "I signed my contract without an agent," Ruby now said glumly. "It's been so long since I needed one. There used to be a man named Lastfogel at the William Morris office who helped me. Maybe if I'd called him—?"

At the giant William Morris Agency in Hollywood, Chairman Abe Lastfogel laughed when he heard the suggestion. Lovingly, he said, "Ruby always was a little—naïve."

At the heart of the problem was the star's "misunderstanding" of the percentage of the gross weekly receipts that was to be paid to her. After management wrote her, "We know of no moral justification for any change," Ruby turned to Gloria Safier, Patsy Kelly's strong-minded agent. Gloria promptly won a $1,000 weekly increase for her new client, who agreed to stay with *Nanette* two years.

Ruby won something else: a car and driver, furnished at the producer's expense, to transport her between the theater and her apartment—only. (When *Look* magazine noted that

"Broadway's newest toast" had a chauffeur-driven limousine at her disposal, it quoted Cyma Rubin as saying, *happily*, "I know how to protect my investment.")

As soon as Ruby's new contract had been settled to her satisfaction, Burt Shevelove demanded that Cyma give him a recount. He had been hired as a director, he informed her, and as a director, he had agreed to make such alterations in the script of *No, No, Nanette* as were needed to get the show onstage. He had not planned on writing an entirely new book for the show. For that, he wanted compensation.

When Cyma protested that his contract did not specify the amount of work that he would do—or not do—Shevelove angrily ordered his assistant to compare the original 1924 script with his new one. Beneath each line of the original that had been used intact, the assistant drew a red line. Beneath each line that had been rewritten went a blue line. And each line that appeared only in Shevelove's version, and not in the original at all, was marked in green.

"When we were through," the director said, "I was prepared to show that barely 5 percent of the original script remained, that 45 percent had been completely rewritten, and that 50 percent was entirely mine."

Armed with his factual evidence—and a threat to pull his script out and begin rehearsing Frank McHugh with the ancient 1924 *Nanette* book—Shevelove won his case. Cyma agreed that he would get a share of the production's subsidiary rights, the royalties that will pour in when the show is done by local stock companies, "little theater" groups, and so on.

"Everybody gets their money before the producers do" said an angry Cyma after the new contracts were drawn up. "It will take five months for the show to pay off on Broadway before any profits come in!"

She had minor worries, too—such as the one tall chorus boy who stuck out onstage like a sore thumb, and hairdressers who just could not seem to get the girls' hair the way she wanted it. One stylist had broken into tears when Cyma, comb in hand, insisted on standing backstage and "touching up" each chorine's hair after he finished with it.

But the big problem was Harry Rigby.

Harry had wanted to stay in Boston with the company throughout its two weeks there. Thank heavens, she had forced him to move from the $70-a-day suite he occupied at the Ritz-Carlton—"Oh, *heavens*, Cyma, the Ritz is the *only* place to stay in Boston!"—into a cheaper, $39-a-day room with his assistant. But, she thought, he had a lot of nerve staying there when she herself had moved to the Statler-Hilton, which was just as nice and had even better room service! Why, at the Ritz, his bill was going to come to almost $500!

By the time the company left for Toronto, on a Sunday afternoon at the end of a standing-room-only second week in Boston, Cyma and Harry were not speaking to each other.

And, after what happened at the Boston airport, virtually no one in the company was speaking to Cyma.

The night before the scheduled departure, a friend of one of the chorus boys had dropped backstage to say how much he had enjoyed the show. The young man also was a dancer, who had trekked from New York to Boston to see *Nanette*— and who was currently unemployed. Cyma had noticed the good-looking, youthful boy backstage.

"Get Donald Saddler over here," she ordered. "I've found a replacement for that tall one." But the choreographer could not be located, and even though Buster Davis and Burt Shevelove okayed the newcomer, he had to be consulted. It was not until the following morning that Saddler gave a quick audition to the dancer in the lobby of the hotel. Moments later, he arrived at the airport and nodded to the producer.

"Get that big one out of line," snapped Cyma to General Manager Peter Neufeld, gesturing toward the chattering crowd of chorus boys and girls at the airline departure gate.

Neufeld walked toward the happy group. He tapped lanky Jim Maher on the shoulder. The dark-haired performer, who only short hours before had danced as Ruby Keeler's partner in "Take a Little One-Step," looked up expectantly.

"Uh—here's your two weeks' pay and $22 for a plane ticket back to New York, Jim," Neufeld said. "You're not going to Toronto with us."

To the gypsies, it was as if one of their own family had been struck by lightning. The sudden dismissal of Carole Demas had hurt, but this was closer to home—a fist in the gut, a knife between the shoulder blades. Was this The Black Witch's revenge? A warning to them all?

"I tell you," said Maher, some weeks later, "you would have thought from the reaction that President Kennedy had been assassinated all over again."

Stunned, his fellow dancers and singers watched while he gathered his bags from the luggage cart that already was alongside the plane. Then, they lined up soberly, tearfully, to shake hands with their fallen comrade.

"Harry Rigby was crying," Maher recalls. "He carried on, saying, 'I didn't even *know* about it.' I almost was going to say to him, 'How can you possibly be a *producer*—with your name next to Mrs. Rubin's—and not know what's going on?'"

Busby Berkeley and Patsy Kelly, Maher recalls, shook their heads slowly as they reached for his hand.

"I'm sorry," Berkeley said, "but I tried very hard to do everything I could for you." Patsy asked if the dancer had enough money to get back to New York, if he would like to borrow some—?

Cyma did not look at him.

When the chartered plane lifted off the runway, the atmosphere was funereal. Finally, Patsy Kelly brightened spirits by noticing that the stewardess had slipped a luncheon tray in front of her.

"Wait a minute, wait a minute, wait a minute!" Patsy yelled, her brassy voice resounding over the *whoosh* of the jets. "What is this? *Lunch?*

"Without a drink first? Oh, *migawd!*"

**22** With one exception, the reviews for *No, No, Nanette* in Toronto were raves, as big as the raves the show had received in Boston after its opening two weeks earlier. And, since the musical that was presented in Toronto lacked the excitement and tension—not to mention the "Jimmy Smith"—that Boston audiences had witnessed, it began to dawn on the cast and production team that, somehow, they were in the right place at the right time. They could do no wrong.

There seemed to be no other explanation for the notices. The show's faults became vir-

> "Mrs. Rubin says she'll close the show before she puts Harry's name on it with hers as producer."
>
> JIM MENNEN,
> assistant company manager

tues in the eyes of the critics. ("Shevelove has even allowed the first act to drag, in establishing the right tempo," wrote Herbert Whittaker in the Toronto *Globe and Mail*.) To say a word against old-timers Ruby Keeler or Patsy Kelly suddenly seemed tantamount to burning the flag. Questioning the musical quality of the Youmans score was akin to denying Santa Claus. There was to be no room in America—or Canada, for that matter—for anyone who did not like *Nanette*. Or, at the very least, tolerate it as a kind of warm and amusing anachronism.

How seriously *Nanette*-lovers were to guard their own very special, very personal time machine showed up after the show opened in January on Broadway and *New York* magazine critic John Simon severely chastised it as being banal, trivial, and generally inept. Some months later, a bruised and battered Simon returned to the fray. Calling *Nanette* "mendacious and stupid beyond the rights of any show, however escapist, to be in this day and age," he noted that his previous blast had brought him "more hate letters . . . than for any other critical attack I ever launched." His mail, Simon went on, "ranged from one-word, anonymous obscenities to elaborate but no less hysterical anathemas, impugning everything from my virility to my religion."

Of all those who eventually saw and wrote about *Nanette*,

only one reviewer of note lent support to Simon's vitriolic, venomous vituperation. Nathan Cohen, longtime theater-watcher for the *Toronto Star*, similarly argued at length that in a world with so many problems to solve, the idea of escaping from reality via a mindless race into the past was nothing short of criminal. Yes, Cohen admitted, the tunes were pleasant, the dances eye-filling, the jokes weakly amusing, the performers talented—but does a remounting of a bit of 1924 fluff move the theater *forward*? (Three months after his unflattering notice was printed, the respected critic suffered a fatal heart attack. "We all wondered how Mrs. Rubin arranged that," half-jested one of the chorus boys.)

In Toronto, the cast of *No, No, Nanette* dismissed Cohen's blast along with the flowery notices of his rivals. In the 3,000-seat O'Keefe Center, the show came across to the audience with all the warmth and intimacy of a magician trying card tricks in Madison Square Garden. It seemed to take long minutes for a joke to make its feeble way from the stage to the last row of spectators, and minutes more for the hollow, echoing laughter to find its way back to the actors. Ruby's precise, machine-gun taps sounded muffled and slow in the huge theater, and the mood of nostalgic warmth that had enveloped the Boston audience would not materialize in Toronto's chilly November. The audiences, however, cheered, stamped, and sang along lustily, as if they were grateful that even this pale imitation of *Nanette* had come to town.

Standing behind the last row of seats, Burt Shevelove laughed at the idea of trying to catch any performing errors on the distant stage. "It's like seeing the show on a five-inch television set," he said.

Ordinarily, a musical trying out on the road undergoes extensive overhauling almost with each passing day. New songs are written, new dialogue and scenes are inserted, numbers are moved from one act to another. But when *No, No, Nanette* left Boston, one newspaperman noted that it seemed ready to go directly to New York. In his Valentine's Day speech to the company just before the Toronto opening, Shevelove tried to prevent overconfidence and win cooperation through the long weeks ahead: "We're *not* ready for Broadway. We're about 75 percent ready, and it's not enough. All I ask you is for the chance to get the other 25 percent ready."

The director knew what had to be done—some tighter lines here, a touch of "business" there, a new song for the dull stretch in the first act, and easing Frank McHugh into his role. But no major reworking was necessary. And some things did not have to be touched at all. Things like the simple, standstill staging of "Tea for Two," for example.

"One critic wrote how beautiful it was just to have those two young people stand and sing that song," Shevelove recalls. "I took the review, circled the paragraph, and handed it to Cyma. 'When you're finished reading this,' I said, 'pass it on to Berkeley.' "

The only thing that Cyma wanted to pass on to the legendary film director was a plane ticket for him and his wife back to California. Time and again she argued with Harry Rigby about the necessity of having Berkeley on hand—at $40 a day! And just as heatedly, Harry noted that Buz was showing up—promptly and ready to answer questions—at every interview that he was scheduled to make. "Well, all right," Cyma agreed, "it's cheaper than flying him in from the Coast for each opening, I guess."

Something else, something bigger, was on her mind. Harry himself did not want to return to New York, and begged that he be allowed to stay—*insisted* that he be allowed to stay—with the company, with Buz and Ruby and Patsy and Burt. He *should* be on hand, he said, in case there were *problems* or *trouble* or *who-knows-what*. Cyma, unsure of what Harry might do or *could* do in the event of any problems, was also unsure of what a producer's role should be once a show gets on the road. Reluctantly, she agreed that Harry could stay in Toronto a few days longer.

But if he did not come back to New York after that, she warned, she was going to cut off his . . . per diem.

Harry Rigby had personal reasons for wanting to stay

with the *Nanette* company. He enjoyed the theatrical magic, the accompanying applause and party invitations that came his way, the rounds of drinks and jokes and good feeling that followed each performance. But also, back in New York, he had told some friends that they might as well use the apartment on 17th Street—on which Cyma paid the rent —while he was out of town. Now, if he returned, he would have to evict them, and it would all be such a *bother*...

So Harry stayed on, even though some of the cast members were a bit bored with him. His inability to prevent the firing of Jim Maher, his humiliation in public by Cyma, caused the chorus kids to look at him differently now. They looked at the marquee and the first page of the program, where it said "Cyma Rubin and Harry Rigby present . . ." And they wondered.

New signs of dissension began to appear, now that individuals did not have to worry about the *show* itself. Bobby Van, who had been singled out for rave notices by the Toronto critics and audiences, stared at a headline on a full-page newspaper article: GALLAGHER AND VAN STOP SHOW. He folded the paper, and notified the publicity department that in the future he did not want to give any joint interviews with his co-star. " 'Gallagher and Van,' " he sniffed—"I'm not part of a vaudeville team." Curvaceous K. C. Townsend, convulsing the audiences nightly with her pillow-breasted, wide-eyed, Betty Boop-voiced performance, began staying up late to find fun and excitement—and once was said to have made her tired way back to the empty theater to sleep backstage rather than go to her hotel just in time to start getting up for a matinée.

The young starlet was not alone in trying to liven up the dull routine of daily rehearsal and nightly performance on the road. Eighteen attractive young girls were in the *Nanette* chorus, and they had a problem. Lodged in cramped hotel rooms, trying to save money, far away from their parents and friends (*husband,* in one case), they looked for ways to amuse themselves away from the theater. A day or two in a new city could be filled with window-shopping and postcard-writing—but two *weeks*? Where were some young men who might pay for a movie or a sandwich and cup of coffee after the show? ("Hell," said one girl, "we'll go Dutch.")

It is not easy to find casual dates during a brief working stopover in a strange city. Gone are the days of Stage Door Johnnies, the wealthy playboys who once waited outside every theater to escort chorines on wild night club sprees. Wealthy playboys were nonexistent in Boston, Toronto, and the other cities *Nanette* visited on tour—and night clubs in most of the towns were scarce, too. The closest thing any chorus member saw to a playboy was a handsome, but middle-aged, man who dropped backstage one night after the final curtain in Philadelphia and asked to meet "the charming girl in the blue dress and ribboned hat in the 'Tea for Two' number." After a lengthy consultation in the dressing room, the girls decided which of several blue-dressed, ribbon-hatted dancers best fitted his description, and sent the lucky young lady down to meet her admirer. He looked up, however, at a laconic teen-ager, wearing blue jeans and an old Navy pea jacket, who could have been his daughter. "I—uh—just wanted to tell you that—uh—you look—uh—very pretty—and *older*—onstage," he said as he backed out of the stage door.

After a week or two of enforced spinsterhood, the girls of *Nanette* were starved for masculine companionship. To be sure, there were a number of males traveling with the company—chorus boys, production staff, hairdressers, stagehands, and the like—but time spent with them meant talking about "the show"—and who wanted to do that night after night? And, besides, there was the other problem.

"I would say that if we all put our heads together," a blonde chorus girl whispered confidentially at the opening-night party in Toronto, "we could come up with the names of three men connected with the show who are 'straight.' " She cocked her head at the brunette standing next to her, who nodded and began enumerating slowly, "Well, there's John Lowe—but he's engaged . . ."

If the girls found themselves in little demand among the males of the company, a straight man ran the chance of being besieged by an entire harem of admiring females. But —and this could be unnerving—he also could be prized as a catch by any number of males. Should he fend off all entreaties from either side, and perhaps risk being called "stuck-up" by his fellow players? Should he accept only a *few* offers and foster jealous backstage squabbles? Or should he try to accommodate everybody, and let the chips fall where they may—even if it meant wearing himself out with fatigue? The straight male in a modern musical on the road might puzzle over such nearly unanswerable questions until he decides to chuck the whole damn thing.

Roger Rathburn was straight.

On the morning before *Nanette's* first Saturday matinée in Toronto, in a gesture reminiscent of Ruby Keeler's sudden flight from *Whoopee* some forty years earlier, Roger Rathburn left a note—and left the show. While his understudy rehearsed quickly to fill his part, the cast gossiped excitedly about what might have spurred his decision. A serious romantic entanglement with a girl he had left behind, perhaps? A realization that showbusiness—with all its petty rivalries and backbiting—was not the right world for a young man with a Master of Arts degree in American and English literature, who had shown promise as an instructor? Or was it just a nervous reaction to the decisions, *decisions,* DECISIONS that he was forced to worry about in his personal relationships with the company?

Back in New York, the handsome young baritone thought it over for a few days. Then—convinced by Cyma that he was vital to the show's success, and bolstered by her offer of financial assistance if he needed help to straighten out any personal problems—Roger Rathburn flew back to Toronto, where he disappointed his understudy by rejoining the show.

Roger's sudden departure produced one more twinge of post-partum pain for *Nanette's* mother, but Cyma took a certain pride in coping with it. After all, how impressive is a birth without great suffering?

298

Sam Rubin, too, was enjoying his new role of father to a Broadway-bound hit. A financial father, a foster father. But still a father. Once the Boston reviews were in, the camouflage of "many backers" that Cyma had devised to protect her husband's reputation in case of failure was promptly discarded. En route to New York by jet from Toronto after the show's initial success there, Sam pondered whether or not he should invest $1,000 for a special Masonite floor to make Ruby's taps sound louder in the huge O'Keefe Theater.

He decided not to bother. The show was a hit, without a special floor. Even if the floor was made portable, the other, older theaters where *Nanette* would play would not need it. And Sam Rubin did not like to spend money carelessly. On the jet, he flew tourist-class, while the show's brilliant lighting director, Jules Fisher, flew in the first-class section (at the production's—*Sam's*—expense).

"It's only an hour flight," Sam Rubin said with a shake of his gray mustache. "And both sections of the plane take off and land at the same time."

A shrewd man, a man with a zest for life, Sam always enjoyed dealing in the business world, challenging anyone to try to outsmart him. A good—but infrequent—loser, he delighted in telling a story about a neighborhood grocer who charged him $1.38 for two bottles of milk one morning. "As I handed him a five-dollar bill," Sam said, his eyes twinkling, "I said, 'Wait a minute. Isn't that *high* for milk these days?' The grocer slapped his forehead, and said, 'Excuse me, excuse me! I was thinking of the customer just before you. He bought some beer for $1.38.' Then he gave me my change. I was halfway down the block before I thought to count it. There was $3.62!"

Sam Rubin laughed. It was a hearty laugh, an honest laugh, a laugh of admiration for an opponent who could first apologize for overcharging him, then overcharge 'him anyway. That took brains. That took nerve.

Harry Rigby, Sam knew, had neither. Harry could be controlled. Why, in his way, Harry was probably dumber than Philippe, that damned Dalmatian who had been sent to obedience school, but refused to learn his lessons. Come to think of it, Sam thought, the dog was probably *more* dangerous than Harry. Left alone with only the servants while the Rubins attended the Boston opening, Philippe had shown his displeasure by nipping Sam on the hand upon his return. The wound had caused a severe infection.

But Harry? He would never have the courage to bite.

His wife agreed, even though she said the dog bite was Sam's own fault—"He frightened the dog," she stated flatly. "A dog or horse won't hurt you unless they're frightened." She knew that Harry was frightened. She had heard that he wanted to be booked onto radio and television programs as the co-producer of *Nanette* in order to cement his position in the public mind. But he would not fight harder. He still would take her orders—he *had* come back to New York from Toronto—and when the right moment came ...

First, though, she had to look into the problem of Frank McHugh.

*Problem?* Well, yes, sort of. It appeared that McHugh, who had been signed at $1,000 a week to play the chief male role in a musical, could not sing.

Burt Shevelove spoke with care as he explained the situation: "He did one chorus of 'I Want to Be Happy' at the piano for the audition and sang *perfectly*. It was very cute. But then he sang with an orchestra—and Buster, who is remarkable at teaching nonsingers (he taught Sidney Chaplin), just said, 'He's hopeless.' "

In Shevelove's version of *No, No, Nanette*, the character of Jimmy Smith sings only one chorus of "I Want to Be Happy," and a single line from the song at the end of the second and third acts. It is not much of a singing role, the writer-director admits. "But in a show this thin," he says, "the few lines must be done just *so*. They set the whole tone of the character."

To fill the slow spot in the first act that once held the Gaynor-Youmans number, "Always You," Shevelove and Davis wrote a new duet for Ruby and her new co-star. "Only a Moment Ago" was its title, and its idea was to refer nostalgically to the days when "Sue" and "Jimmy" had first met, just as Ruby Keeler and Frank McHugh had met in the long ago. In rehearsal, McHugh appeared to sing at least as well as Ruby.

When the worried Cyma caught a jet to Toronto where McHugh was being worked into the show during its second week—after he had received a considerable amount of publicity and had his photograph taken with Ruby for *Newsweek* —she saw other things that angered her. For one, the seventy-two-year-old performer had difficulty remembering his lines. When he forgot them, he tended to "fill" with hoary jokes and vaudeville patter (precisely as Skeet Gallagher had done in the original 1924 *Nanette*). Of more concern, however, was the actor's onstage appearance: that of a "dirty old man" cheating on his wife with three money-hungry chippies.

The innocence that Shevelove and Hiram Sherman had brought to *Nanette* was suddenly gone, according to observant members of the cast and production staff. The author had carefully removed all the original script's obvious innuendos of hanky-panky or deceit, but now Frank McHugh—without meaning to, or even knowing it—might raise an eyebrow or flash a smile that seemed to be a leer, and the fairy-tale charm vanished.

"I thought he was *terrible* in the part, but the fact of the matter is that he was not rehearsed," a performer who was on the scene said later. "I mean, he was *rehearsed,* but with a stage manager and with the *understudies.* He was not rehearsed with the full cast. He was not given direction by our supposed director. He was just thrown in—and made to sink or swim."

After performing in the role for three days, Frank McHugh sank.

Following the Saturday-night performance in Toronto, after Cyma had checked with the general managers to learn whether McHugh's year-long contract could be broken if he deviated from the script, the exuberant actor was sadly approached by his agent. The orchestra in the pit was still playing "I Want to Be Happy" to speed smiling theatergoers

**301**

on their way when the agent whispered something to Frank McHugh. Instantly, as if he had been shot, the round-faced Irishman's smile faded and his jolly, rotund body stiffened. "Wha—?" jumped from his lips. "I—I don't—"

"I'm sorry, Frank," the agent said. "We'll make them honor the contract on salary." He turned away.

A flood of tears began trickling down the actor's pink cheeks. He brushed the sleeve of his costume dinner jacket across his face, leaving a smear of make-up on the black fabric, and he stood there. Before the eyes of the chorus boys and girls who had stopped on their way to the dressing rooms, Frank McHugh grew visibly older. Only a moment ago, onstage, he had been a jocular white-haired leprechaun. Now, he was a tired old man. Slowly, fighting off his technicolor dreams of a triumphant return to Broadway, the old man began to walk toward his dressing room.

In his hand was an envelope. When he opened it hours later, he found a letter thanking him for his services—and a tiny fraction of the salary promised him for a year's run in the part.

"I won't pay another cent," Cyma said to Burt Shevelove, who was to notify a stricken Ruby and Patsy that their long-time friend was out of *Nanette* without warning, without notice. "The nerve of him, making us think he could sing! He breached his contract, and if he says different, he'll have to fight."

McHugh did. Quietly, without fanfare, he fought—and in August, 1971, at just about the time *Variety* reported that *No, No, Nanette* on Broadway had earned back its production cost, the paper carried another story: A check for approximately $25,000 in back pay had been sent to McHugh, and the actor was to receive his weekly salary for the duration of his contract. He had fulfilled his obligations, an arbitration board stated.

It was a major and angering defeat for Cyma and Sam Rubin, who reportedly had refused a settlement for half the amount. On Broadway, the word spread that Frank McHugh had been paid roughly $60,000 for a few days' work—which made him one of the highest-paid septuagenarian performers in the business. To the veteran actor, however, the money was small compensation for a moment of abject humiliation. Actors, like ordinary people, have pride—and dreams; and many actors of McHugh's age have little else. In one sudden stroke, Cyma Rubin had carried his pride and dreams to nearly forgotten heights, and then—as suddenly—shattered them. Was the taste of victory, even a victory that paid thousands of dollars, sweet enough to blot out the taste of his salty tears?

At the time of Frank McHugh's dismissal, however, Cyma saw no possibility of eventual defeat. "Get rid of him," she had ordered—and promptly forgot the matter. Besides . . . besides . . . besides, there were other problems to think of, other people to worry about.

Production Manager May Muth, for example. The grim-faced woman, who had worked effectively for David Merrick on a dozen shows, was becoming authoritarian on *Nanette*. She had actually suggested that Cyma had spent so much time shopping for lower bids on the construction of scenery that the builders had not had enough time to work. And she had dared to give Loni some critical notes on her performance!

And there was Patsy Kelly reminding people of Cyma's boast that she would not pick up lunch checks for the stars, and now telling them that she had been "trapped" into lunch with Cyma at the hotel cafeteria—and the producer had stuck her with the $4 check for them both.

And that exasperating Ruby Keeler! She had received a curt note from Cyma one evening at the first intermission. Delivered by Mary Ann Niles, the note read simply, "Fix your hair." What Ruby wrote in her return note to the producer was unknown to the cast, but it was something other than "Thanks." As if that were not enough, Ruby had asked that Loni not upstage Patsy Kelly in a scene—and had sent the young performer, almost in tears, angrily to her mother.

Burt . . . Raoul . . . the others who were not speaking to her? Cyma thought about them and shrugged. "All I need them for," she said, "is to get the show to New York. After that, I can get rid of all of them."

And Harry Rigby might not last that long.

Cyma had told Harry that he would not be allowed to fly up to Toronto and back down with the company when it moved to Philadelphia. At least, she would not pay his plane fare. She could shepherd the cast from city to city without his assistance. He could get from New York to Philadelphia by bus.

But Harry had friends in Philadelphia, his boyhood home. A wealthy society matron had promised to give a Sunday afternoon tea dance for the *Nanette* company, and on a crisp morning at the end of November, she sent her chauffeured limousine to New York to pick up Harry. Another member of the production staff rode along at Harry's invitation—and came up with a $10 tip for the chauffeur when the producer admitted that he was broke.

On the trip down, Harry appeared more nervous than usual. He chattered on excitedly, nonstop, about a party he would give that evening for Busby Berkeley's seventy-sixth birthday.

"I'm taking Buz and Etta, Ruby and Patsy, out for dinner," he announced proudly. "I'll pay for it *somehow*. Mrs. Rubin, y'know, has stopped my per diem. She says she'll pay for my room on the opening night in Philadelphia, but I just *have* to stay longer. It's my hometown, y'know, and this *is* my first show that's a big hit. There are so many people that will want to see me, so many that I'll want to see."

Harry's face clouded over momentarily. "I know *one* thing: If I'm not around, no one will know that I had anything to do with it. Y'know that Sam has *actually* been telling people the whole thing was Mrs. Rubin's idea? *Really!* And she and I were supposed to work together on some other things! That's all over, of course. Why, the author of one of the properties we had said that he was withdrawing it because he had agreed to work with *me*—not with Mrs. Rubin."

Suddenly, he cackled his familiar laughter. "I'll tell you this, I wouldn't treat a dog the way they treat me. But then, I've always been partial to dogs. Harry giggled softly and looked down at the tiny poodle on his lap, sleeping to the lullaby of the car's powerful engine. "Y' know, I've owned a lot of dogs in my life, but I *never* had one that bit me."

The *Nanette* company had moved hundreds of miles from Canada to the Cradle of Liberty, but the crowd that welcomed the production on Tuesday, December 1st, at the Forrest Theater in Philadelphia was a duplicate of the one that had bid it farewell in Toronto. Cheers, tears, standing ovations, swarms of autograph-seekers at the stage door waiting for Ruby, Patsy, Bobby, *everyone*—it was a familiar scene.

In the first-night audience, getting his initial look at the show, was a delighted Irving Caesar. "The pendulum has swung! The pendulum has swung!" he shouted over and over as he hurried up the aisle to shake hands with Busby Berkeley.

"I don't know why everyone keeps congratulating me," mumbled Berkeley. "I didn't do it all by myself." By this time, the entire cast had agreed on what would be said whenever interviewers asked how it felt to be directed by the legendary "Buz" Berkeley.

"He was marvelous, so kind and knowledgeable," went the typical reply. "His presence—all those years of creativity and imagination—it was just an inspiration to us all."

"Actually, we were all *sick* at the way he was treated," said Kevin Daley, a talented and good-looking chorus boy who eventually followed his friend, Hiram Sherman, and quit *No, No, Nanette* to seek opportunity and a less-wearing production elsewhere. "To have a man of his stature, his reputation, sit there day after day—and give him script pages and a punch so that he could make holes for the three-ring binders! Really, it was sickening."

By Philadelphia, the cast had become adept at concealing from the press—which would not have wanted to hear it, anyway, because nostalgia made "good copy"—how little the

305

fabled director had to do with the show. And when a reviewer wrote—as did Charles Petzold of the *Philadelphia Daily News*—that "director Busby Berkeley offers the perfect blend of age and youth . . . and has put together a solid evening of entertainment," the chorus kids smiled. "Let him have the glory," they said to one another. "He deserves it."

Director Burt Shevelove's attitude, however, was not quite so magnanimous. In some reviews, his name was left out completely—after all, "Berkeley" symbolized the whole nostalgia revival. In other reviews, the situation was even worse. The *Philadelphia Bulletin* critic, for example, wrote that "the 1925 musical had been recreated by Shevelove, with the help of Busby Berkeley, the old movie choreographer. . . ."

As if Burt Shevelove needed help! From that invalid! Weeks later, after Berkeley had returned to California, Shevelove ordered that the aged director's picture be taken down from outside the 46th Street Theater. "No one knows who that old man is," he said.

Angry as Shevelove was on the road, he had to set aside his personal problems. Cyma and Sam had canceled the scheduled two-week stand in Washington, and wanted to get *No, No, Nanette* to Broadway—where it could start making money—as quickly as possible. During the three-week run in Philadelphia, Shevelove had to find and rehearse a third Jimmy Smith so that he could play for two weeks in Baltimore before moving to New York. Finding someone *now*, three weeks before Christmas, would not be easy, Shevelove knew. There had been a long period of discussion before Hiram Sherman had been decided on—"we thought of Billy DeWolfe and a dozen others," Harry Rigby said. In Toronto, the sudden availability of Frank McHugh had seemed like an incredible stroke of luck. Now, pressed by time, the director would have to begin searching desperately.

A major worry, Cyma realized immediately, was that the actors who were right for the role would also be aware of the fact that someone *had* to be signed quickly. And they would demand sizable amounts of money since they knew, too, that the show loomed as a major hit. For a time, the producer toyed with the idea of leaving Ted Tiller in the role. He *was* improving with each performance, and his salary—even if she gave him a raise—would be considerably below that of any "star." Besides, Cyma argued, people came to see "the show"—not any individuals. Well, perhaps Patsy—she *was* funny. And Bobby and Helen *were* marvelous.

And Ruby? Well, she had *something*, Cyma had to admit. "She's an original," she said, "because she has no talent, but she's a star. She's a star because she represents all of the innocence that ever existed in America. With the face, the big eyes, the Irish nose—the whole thing—she *milks* the youth juices out of the audience! I've seen her do it. It's incredible. And if that is a quality that gives people pleasure, she's a star."

Cyma lowered her voice, and shook her head. "But as far as her personality goes . . . she's so *stupid!*"

On thinking it over, however, Cyma realized that her star was not so unintelligent that she would play happily on Broadway opposite the unheralded Ted Tiller. Ruby Keeler had wised up considerably to showbusiness ways in the last few months—she even had an agent—and some sort of "name" would have to be hired.

"How about Jack Gilford?" suggested Merle Debuskey once more. "He was great in *Forum,* and Burt wrote that. They'd work well together."

"He was great in *Cabaret,* too," Cyma snapped. "As a Jewish shopkeeper. How would it look if he tried to pass as a Bible publisher named Smith?"

Word went out to performers and agents that Burt Shevelove and Buster Davis would hold auditions in Philadelphia. Harry Rigby stayed on with the company, headquartering at the exclusive Barclay Hotel, while Cyma returned to New York to discover that the ancient heating unit in the 17th Street office had exploded. Angrily, she began placing calls to Harry to order him out of the building, but she had difficulty getting the message through.

Fuming now, Cyma contacted Shevelove to inquire about his search for a new Jimmy Smith. He had news—all bad. Jack Haley, a long-time Broadway and film star (best known as "The Tin Man" in *The Wizard of Oz*), was interested in the part. But Haley, an extremely wealthy man, could only be lured out of retirement by a huge salary and percentage of the gross. He was promptly eliminated.

Academy Award-winner Jack Albertson was another choice. Able to move easily from the heavy drama of *The Subject Was Roses* to song-and-dance vaudeville routines, the actor agreed to audition for Shevelove—but warned him that he was not really interested in playing such an unchallenging role. His audition—a warm and graceful rendition of "I Want to Be Happy"—almost drew applause from the businesslike production people. And then, having shown that he could play the part with one arm tied behind him, Albertson smiled, shook hands all around, and flew off to California to star in a television series.

A few other character actors were considered, auditioned, rejected. Then Shevelove suggested Iggie Wolfington, a jovial and rotund performer who had gotten laughs as Robert Preston's scheming sidekick in *The Music Man*. But Wolfington was in California and Cyma did not want to pay his fare to New York. Not after the Albertson incident.

"If you want to see him," she told Shevelove "you pay his way." Resentfully, Shevelove ordered an airplane ticket charged to the Nanette Company. (Several months later he received a bill for the amount of the fare.) For one reason or another, Wolfington was judged not right for the part.

The animosity between Shevelove and Cyma grew. It had to, she explained heatedly: "He wants money and power, and he hates me because I have both!"

It was getting more and more difficult to communicate, Cyma realized. So many people were not speaking to her— "It's the first time in my life I've ever had anything like that happen to me," she muttered one evening. She decided not to fight it any more. The business of auditioning actors and negotiating with them was taking too much time. There was another matter to be taken care of, as soon as a replacement was hired. Time was running out once more. What difference did it make who played Jimmy Smith?

"Let's talk to Jack Gilford," Cyma Rubin said.

The actor was located quickly, in the role of the wily Jewish furniture buyer in a stock production of Arthur Miller's drama, *The Price*. He would be unable to join *Nanette* until the very end of its Baltimore engagement, but that would be no problem for a professional. His terms were steep—considerably more money than Hiram Sherman had originally signed for, and slightly more than Ruby Keeler's original weekly salary. Cyma, who had long since given up all thought of bringing *No, No, Nanette* to Broadway for under a half-million dollars, reluctantly agreed.

And now she set about attending to her other business. The important business.

On the morning of December 10th, a registered letter arrived for Harry Rigby at the Barclay Hotel in Philadelphia. It was written on the stationery that bore the name of Rubin & Rigby Productions Ltd. With trembling fingers, almost as if he knew what the letter was going to say, Harry unfolded the two sheets of paper and began to read:

Dear Harry—

We have word from Peter Neufeld that you refused to respond to our telephone calls. It is regrettable that you have adopted this posture. You were authorized to remain in Philadelphia for the one night only and it is now over ten days. You extended your stay in Toronto with the emotional plea that the company is your life. You were informed then that your continued presence with the company was unnecessary and unauthorized and you ran up unapproved expenses which we had to pay and which have been charged to your account.

Since you refuse to communicate with us we must again remind you that you assumed responsibility for the proper maintenance of the 17th Street office. It is now a shambles. You were informed of our decision to vacate the premises since it became impossible to have it function properly. You agreed to remove your personal belongings but to this writing you have not done so. We are obliged to put you on notice that if they are not removed completely before the week is out, we will place them in a public warehouse at your risk and expense.

The owners of the building tell us you caused the heating unit to crack by running it on manual and without water. Assuming the unit was in bad repair you appear to have added the last straw to its final breakdown. All this has added to the chaos and has caused us endless grief and deep concern.

In addition to *Nanette*, the company has invested in other properties which you were and are obliged to help develop. These are at a standstill while you continue to stay with the show contrary to instructions.

Apparently you are unwilling to respond to our repeated efforts to have you comply with your employment contract. While we have no right or desire to interfere in your private life we continue to urge you to secure counsel to help guide you. We must insist that you return to New York to resume such duties as are assigned to you.

> Yours truly,
> Rubin & Rigby Productions Ltd.
> Cyma Rubin

Harry took it philosophically. He knew Cyma was angry —but that was nothing new. He was puzzled about her comment that Peter Neufeld said he "refused to respond" to the phone calls. He would have to check with the manager and see if any calls had been received for him. Harry did not remember any. A few days later, the general manager of the Barclay Hotel wrote a letter that said in part:

> Upon inquiring with our Chief Telephone operator and other operators about this matter, I have been informed by the Chief Telephone operator that neither she or her staff of telephone operators recollect having received any long distance telephone calls from Mr. and Mrs. Rubin to Mr. Rigby.

There were several phrases in Cyma's letter, however, that gave Harry a twinge of fear. He dug out a copy of his employment contract and studied it. Those "unapproved expenses" which had been charged to his account—well, that was what the account was *for*. And *Nanette* looked like such a certain hit that the Rubins would easily be repaid for his extravagance. Those "other properties" she said that he was obliged to help develop—well, if they still existed, they would be taken care of in a few weeks, just as soon as *Nanette* got to Broadway. Good *heavens*, didn't she realize that preparing a musical for New York was enough for nearly *any* producer to concentrate on at one time?

But there was that reference to his being "unwilling to respond to our repeated efforts to have you comply with your employment contract." He quickly found the line in the employment agreement that he remembered so vividly:

> This agreement may at any time after April 1, 1971 be terminated with or without cause and for any reason by either party and at the sole discretion of either party upon 180 days written notice by either party.

It seemed plain enough. *After* April 1, 1971, he could be fired. After April Fool's day. But *now* was early December, before Christmas. He had plenty of time. And soon, *Nanette* would be a big hit on Broadway, and there would be money coming in from his share of the profits, and authors and producers would be coming to him with ideas for future productions, and the world would be marvelous because Ruby and Patsy and Busby and all those wonderful boys and girls would be working right there on Broadway where he could see them! Perhaps he and Cyma—once she realized how *lucky* they all were to have brought the beautiful *Nanette* out of chaos—might even work together on some other things. But, if not, *let* her stop his weekly salary. *Let* her fire him.

After April 1, 1971.

On Christmas Day, 1970, while Patsy Kelly, in a Santa Claus suit and whiskers, passed out grab-bag gifts to Cyma and Ruby and the members of the *Nanette* company at a party in Baltimore, a Special Delivery letter arrived at the 17th Street address of Harry Rigby.

Dear Mr. Rigby [it began],

You are hereby notified that you are removed as a director of Rubin & Rigby Productions Ltd., effective as of this date.

Due to your continued failure to comply with the terms of your employment contract with Rubin & Rigby Productions Ltd., said contract is hereby terminated effective as of this date.

The letter was signed, "Sincerely yours, Cyma Rubin, President."

The next day, the light and heat were cut off in the building.

**23** The *Nanette company*—and Harry Rigby himself—had a warning of the downward-rushing guillotine blade a few days before it hit home and severed the co-producer's connection.

In mid-December, *New York Post* Fashion Editor Eugenia Sheppard reported an interview that she had with the fashion-conscious Mrs. Rubin. The article began with this sentence:

"No matter how gray I'm getting, I wouldn't have missed it," says Mrs. Samuel Rubin of *No, No, Nanette,* the giant musical she is producing virtually single-handed."

"Everybody in the business knows that Harry Rigby put the show together, and that Mrs. Rubin bankrolled it."

DAVID MERRICK

Mysteriously, since Stage Manager Bob Schear reportedly had refused to post it at Cyma's orders, the article found its way to the backstage bulletin board, where the cast gaped at it—and the production people fumed.

No one doubted that Cyma had given the writer the "single-handed" impression, or that she had led the fashion editor to believe also: "She created the American Symphony Orchestra for Leopold Stokowski and it seemed no less of a project to set up Busby Berkeley in a smash musical."

But no one believed that Cyma Rubin would do anything about another statement that she recently had made: "I refuse," she said, "to have Rigby's name associated with mine."

No one believed it—until Sam Rubin notified the publicity and advertising people that a new company had been formed to present *No, No, Nanette* on Broadway. The philanthropic financier ordered that a simple change be made on all posters, programs, and advertisements: "Take out 'Cyma Rubin and Harry Rigby present . . .' and put in 'Pyxidium, Ltd. presents . . .' "

"Pyxidium," explains the official *No, No, Nanette* souvenir book, means "a seed vessel that dehisces traversely, the top part acting as a lid, as in the purslane, a widely distributed yellow-flowered species of portulaca or any other tulacaceous plant."

To Harry Rigby, "pyxidium" meant disaster.

It was several days before he realized what had happened to him.

And realized that he would have to go to the American Arbitration Association in order to collect any profits from *Nanette* or reinstate his name as one of its producers. That would take lawyers. That would take time. That would take money.

And all that Harry had was shopping bag upon shopping bag filled with his few possessions, and a temporary room at Patsy Kelly's own temporary apartment.

He had one thing more: the consoling knowledge that, no matter how much she wanted to, Cyma Rubin had not dared list her name alone as the producer of *No, No, Nanette*. If she had, Harry understood, Ruby Keeler and Patsy Kelly both might have walked out of the show, whether or not the New York opening was two weeks away.

Unsteady from Cyma's blow, giggling less frequently now, Harry turned to Fitelson and Mayers, theatrical attorneys, and the firm promptly filed a demand for arbitration to settle (as Harry's employment contract said) "any controversy arising out of or in connection with this agreement." A date for the legal proceedings to begin was set for early spring.

All that Harry had to do, warned Attorney Clifford Forster, was to hang on through the long months of testimony and counter-testimony that lay ahead. The Rubins, to put it simply, had based their dismissal of him, and the removal of his name from the *Nanette* credits, on the grounds that he had breached his contract. Specifically, he had not lived up to the clause that said, "Rigby shall devote to the business of R&R and to the performance of his duties hereunder his full business time and attention and shall use his best efforts, skill and abilities to promote its interest." There was also, said Cyma, the fact that Harry frequently had used profanity and inappropriate language in her presence. (Patsy Kelly laughed when she heard the complaint: "I lived with Harry seven weeks while he looked for an apartment, and

**314**

he's a soft-spoken gentleman. Ruby wouldn't like him otherwise. Oh, he might have tapped Cyma on the wrist and said, 'Oooh, you witch,' but that's about it.")

The timing of the last-minute move on the part of Cyma and Sam Rubin was perfect. The production was about to leave Baltimore, where Jack Gilford had joined it for a brief period of rehearsal, and the cast was excited at the thought of getting to Broadway—finally—after the long months of rehearsal and tour. The Baltimore reviews once more had been raves, but the gypsies and long-time professionals knew that many a show that looked like a major hit out of town could fail in New York. With the activity and tension, the problems of packing clothes and finding a New York apartment, and continuing to rehearse by day and perform by night, the cast members had little time to puzzle over Harry Rigby's sudden disappearance.

The production moved into the 46th Street Theater on January 4th, and the rehearsal schedule that had eased up in Baltimore during the Christmas holidays was tightened. Dance routines that had worked well in the larger houses on the road had to be adjusted to fit the new stage. "When the girls go off in a line," said John Lowe in amusement, "they run into a brick wall a foot away." Jack Gilford and Ruby Keeler had to learn "Only a Moment Ago," which had been dropped with Frank McHugh's departure. Cyma wanted the girls' make-up lightened to avoid a garish appearance in the small theater. The first preview was set for January 7th, the show's opening for January 19th—and, suddenly, there were a million things to be done.

The record album, for example. RCA wanted to produce the original-cast recording—and Cyma thought of using the expensive color printing plates that RCA would have to make for the album jackets to print her own souvenir book. ("We'd save thousands of dollars that way," she told her husband.) But, then, the record company pulled out of the deal. "Ordinarily," said an executive, "you have *one* producer who is strong and can deliver all the rights, and even then the negotiations can be tough. Here, it was just a case of too many factions pulling different ways." Columbia Records, eventually convinced by Cyma and Sam that Harry Rigby had no control of *Nanette*, stepped into the picture.

For what seemed the tenth time, Cyma had the show's poster redesigned. The pink letters of *No, No, Nanette* were outlined in silver to make them stand out against the purple background.

High on the list of activities was the planning for an elaborate opening-night party that Mr. and Mrs. Rubin would give at the Hotel Pierre. On the road, the millionaire's wife had negotiated heatedly with various hotels and restaurants for "deals"—and she was ecstatic when persuasive M. J. Boyer talked Baltimore's Place-in-the-Alley restaurant into a low-cost party on Christmas Eve. In New York, however, and particularly at first-class hostelries and restaurants, "bargains" are harder to come by. Cyma's idea was to keep the bill as low as possible, through carefully controlled invitations. "I've got 325 acceptances," she announced with an exasperated shake of her head. "From everyone but Ruby—and she's the laughing stock of society because she's not coming."

Harry Rigby had not been sent an invitation to the party. So he planned his own, a smaller affair at a midtown restaurant that knew him and his friends well. It would not be as fancy as the Rubins' party, with a band for dancing and all, but it would have something special:

Ruby Keeler.

The day that *No, No, Nanette* opened on Broadway—January 19, 1971—began at 7:30 in the morning when Ruby appeared in a filmed interview on the *Today Show* on NBC-TV. Although interviewer Barbara Walters had heard that her guest would not talk about Al Jolson, the probing and poised hostess was delighted when Ruby made a passing reference to the singer and said, in all sincerity, "I really just do not know the lady who was married to Mr. Jolson." Elated, the interviewer turned the conversation in other directions and learned, along with hundreds of thousands of viewers, that: No, Ruby was not terribly excited about coming back to Broadway; yes, she was pleased with the reaction to the show out of town; and, yes, her children would all be on hand for the opening.

The first-night audience was studded with celebrities. Zero Mostel. Gwen Verdon. Marlene Dietrich. Harry Rigby was there, too, although he had not been given opening-night tickets. He attended the premiere as Busby Berkeley's guest.

With one glaring exception, what happened between 7:40 and 10:15 that evening was a repeat of the scenes that had been played regularly since that first Saturday afternoon in Boston. There were minor variations. Finally accepting Ruby's word that she could not sing, and did not *want* to sing, Shevelove had tossed out "Only a Moment Ago" at an early preview and reinstated the dull stretch of dialogue in the show's first fifteen minutes. Patsy Kelly, who comically topped "One-Step" with a soft-shoe of her own each evening ("Eat your heart out!" she called to Ruby), once more did an entirely different dance from the one Mary Ann Niles had tried to teach her for twelve weeks. ("She never does the same thing twice," laughed Mary Ann, watching in the wings.)

The audience did not care. From the moment Ruby Keeler eased her way into the "I Want to Be Happy" tap routine, then picked up the tempo—and an elderly woman in the audience, suffused with pleasure, shouted over the blare of the orchestra, "Attagirl, Ruby!"—the performers onstage knew they were "in."

As had happened so many times before, the audience was transported to an earlier time, a happier time, when girls were beautiful, jokes were funny, songs were lovely, and the biggest worry in life was whether or not it might rain during an Atlantic City holiday (and it never, never did).

As before, people in the theater saw things that were not on the stage. One reviewer later would praise the way Ruby Keeler "tapped up and down the twin staircases," although the performer did not leave the stage floor during the number. Walter Kerr, the perceptive critic of the *New*

*York Times,* told his readers that he had seen the original *Nanette* in the 1920s and complimented Burt Shevelove for his "admirably remembered" staging.

From the roars of "Bravo!" and thunder of applause that burst out during several numbers, from the standing ovation and lusty singing of "I Want to Be Happy" before the grinning audience consented to leave the theater, it appeared that the premiere performance in New York was a well-oiled, smooth-running time machine that took the spectators back . . . back . . . *back.*

In reality, the performance that night at the 46th Street Theater was fraught with an electrifying tension. Shevelove, Davis, Saddler, and the entire company had sweated blood to provide a momentary escape from reality, to make the audience forget every single worry of 1971. Like a bubble, *Nanette* was designed to float on air, shimmering and spinning in the warmth of the pink and blue floodlights. Let a suggestion of Vietnam, or crime in the streets, or drug addiction, or raw sex, for example, make its way into the theater, and the audience would be jerked back to reality. It would see *Nanette* for what it was—a foolish, mindless, momentary dream. The bubble would burst.

Blonde and buxom K. C. Townsend nearly stuck a pin into *Nanette's* gleaming surface that opening night.

The actress who was so perfect for the role of a scatter-brained gold digger, who had gotten so many laughs on the road with her comical delivery and bouncing figure, was "high" throughout the performance. Her timing was off. Her lines were blurred. And, at the end of the second act, when she swayed visibly during a chorus of "I Want to Be Happy," the performers behind her feared she was about to topple to the floor.

"My dancing partner and I were holding hands," a chorus boy said, "and she squeezed mine so tightly that her fingernails drew blood. We *knew* K. C. was going to fall."

But the actress stayed on her feet, insisting to the worried stage managers that she was all right, and she made it through the dialogue portions of the show. Then, during a heated exchange backstage just before the third-act curtain went up, Bobby Van refused to let her go on for "Telephone Girlie." When the act began, the audience saw Van sing and dance with only two gold diggers—although the playbill plainly listed three. As the trio cavorted and sang onstage, the missing performer was forcefully restrained behind the set.

There were explanations, of course—involving nerve pills and weight-control pills and gift bottles of liquor that Jack Gilford had passed out as opening-night presents—but the explanations came later. At the time, a frantic Mary Ann Niles, trying to calm the furious chorus kids, said, "That's why you get old in this business—we don't know what she's on, so we can't treat her for it."

"When the final curtain came down and we had taken our bows," a chorus member said later, "Bobby grabbed K. C. by the shoulders and began to shake her like a rag doll. He was so angry that, if Helen hadn't come over and put her arm around K. C. and calmly said, 'I'll take care of her, Bobby'— well, I think he might have killed her."

But the curtain was down and the audience was cheering out front.

*No, No, Nanette,* "the new 1925 musical," had weathered the first major crisis of what promised to be a long life on Broadway.

The next morning, on the heels of ecstatic reviews in the newspapers and on radio and television, a block-long line of ticket buyers stretched out from the theater box office, while two models dressed as maids served hot tea to ward off the January cold, and Irving Caesar tramped joyfully up and down, singing "Tea for Two" for his captive audience.

**24** The making of *No, No, Nanette* ended on that cold and snowy January evening. When the 46th Street Theater box office took in a record $35,000 the next day, it was apparent that *Nanette* was made.

As this is written in late September, the "survivors" of the original troupe that went into rehearsal exactly a year earlier marked the occasion with a congratulatory note to one another on the backstage bulletin board. It seems only just to note briefly what has happened to some of them, and some others whose lives were markedly affected by their association with the phenomenon that is *No, No, Nanette*.

> "The trouble with your book, Don, is that there are no heroes."
>
> LYLE STUART

\* \* \*

K. C. Townsend was brought before Actors Equity on charges of unprofessional conduct. The union agreed that her contract could be broken and she was dismissed, immediately taking her ample figure and comic ability to a stock production of *Scuba-Duba*.

\* \* \*

Bobby Van, nominated for a Tony Award as "best musical comedy star" of the season, worried that he might be beaten by Danny Kaye. The star of *Two by Two*, for some unfathomable reason, was not nominated—but the award went to Hal Linden of *The Rothschilds*.

Although Van reportedly had several offers (he was wanted for a musical biography of Jimmy Durante, among other deals) and had talked of going into television production after a year on Broadway, he signed for a second year with *Nanette*.

His young and pretty blonde wife—who waited patiently outside her husband's dressing room each night following the cancellation of the Don Knotts TV show—also had a number of offers. She took them. After playing in Otto Preminger's movie, *Such Good Friends*, Elaine Joyce landed the "plum" part of the 1971-72 theatrical season: She was signed by David Merrick to star in his musical version of *Some Like It Hot*, in the role Marilyn Monroe had played on the screen.

* * *

Loni Zoe Ackerman, rebelling against her mother's suggestions as to how and what she should sing and which young men she should see, moved out of the museumlike town house and into a small apartment. As she began to grow up emotionally and professionally, she worked hard to improve her performance—and did, to the point that when *Variety* re-reviewed *Nanette* some six months after the opening, she was singled out as having "interesting promise." Her effort and newly discovered individuality worked to win over her co-workers.

* * *

Helen Gallagher accepted her second Tony Award—her first one as a star—for her new-style, sophisticated performance, and signed for a second year in the show. Backstage, her calm and professional demeanor won admiration from the chorus kids—who showed it by becoming students in Helen's acting class, and even joining her group-therapy sessions to remain near her. After young Loni had taken some of her problems to Bobby Van (who advised her to "listen to your mother"), Helen Gallagher found herself with another new role, that of Loni's surrogate parent.

* * *

John Lowe performed efficiently in his backstage capacity and, after Cyma Rubin forced out both Production Manager May Muth and Stage Manager Robert Schear, he became *Nanette*'s stage manager. (Following the departure of the two managers, and a hairdresser, a gossip columnist tallied up the score and noted that thirty-five people had been fired by Mrs. Rubin since the show went into rehearsal.)

* * *

Donald Saddler accepted a Tony Award as "best choreographer" and staged the dances for a West Coast musical starring Burt Lancaster, before beginning work on the routines for a national touring company of *Nanette*.

* * *

Burt Shevelove signed for a slew of projects: As director of a West Coast version of *A Funny Thing Happened on the Way to the Forum*; director of a Broadway-bound musical called *Full Circle*; and author-director of a future show called *Vicky for President*. His schedule also included directing the *Nanette* road company.

\* \* \*

Hiram Sherman, in sound health, was in the midst of rehearsals for a revue based on the writings of Ogden Nash when the renowned poet died. The production was suspended.

\* \* \*

Gatchell and Neufeld, the fledgling managers who "lucked out" with their first Broadway effort, were suddenly "important people" on Broadway—so much so that they were chosen to serve as associate producers on the "super musical" of the 1971-72 season, *Jesus Christ Superstar*.

\* \* \*

Carole Demas, on her way in early fall to audition for a film, laughed when asked what she had done in the months following her dismissal. "I wish I could say something *marvelous*—but I can't," she said. "I've done a dozen TV commercials, and a few other things, including a new musical at Tom Jones and Harvey Schmidt's workshop. We sent about fifty pictures from it to *After Dark* magazine and they ran the *one* shot of me that showed my backside nude." Her saucer eyes laughed, too. "Imagine—sweet little Nanette, nude!" Then, musing, she said, "Funny, that magazine usually runs pictures of naked *boys*. But I've been told my backside looks like a boy's . . ."

\* \* \*

Susan Watson stayed with *Nanette* almost exactly one year, and then withdrew from the cast to concentrate on being a housewife and mother. Her replacement was a "fresh, delicious" newcomer named Barbara Heuman.

\* \* \*

Buster Davis, earning a salary of $550 weekly so long as he stayed with the show, stayed with the show. His original credit as musical director and vocal arranger was augmented some months after the opening when Cyma ordered him also listed as casting director and he was assigned the responsibility of assembling the cast of the *Nanette* road company. He also was announced as the composer of a new musical to be produced by Pyxidium, Ltd. At the arbitration proceedings, he testified as a highly-favorable witness for Cyma Rubin.

* * *

Merle Debuskey, on the heels of *Nanette*'s success and barrage of publicity, became the most sought-after press agent both on and off Broadway. Among the shows he handled during the succeeding season were *Jesus Christ Superstar*, the New York Shakespeare Festival's musical version of *Two Gentlemen of Verona*, and a collection of three one-act plays by Philip Roth. The surfeit of assignments—more than the union which he heads allows a member to accept—resulted in Debuskey's "rewarding" his young associate with a show of her own. M. J. Boyer took on the publicity chores for a musical adapted by Theodore Mann and G. Wood from *Member of the Wedding*, and produced at Off-Broadway's Circle in the Square. It closed in a week.

* * *

Ruby Keeler, taking a New York apartment not far from the neighborhood where she lived as a child, played nine months of *No, No, Nanette* without missing a performance, then flew to California to spend a two-week vacation with her children and grandchildren. A red-carpet reception by the cast greeted her return, and she settled down to work once more—earnestly and without enthusiasm, and counting the days until October, 1972, when her contract would expire and she could leave the show and showbusiness for good.

* * *

Patsy Kelly, winner of a Tony Award for her comic performance, signed for a second year in order to keep the money coming in and remain near her beloved Ruby and the others in the company. She announced open war with *Na-*

*nette*'s management by referring to "our producers, Harry Rigby and Mrs. Rubin" in her nationally televised acceptance speech at the Tony Awards show.

* * *

Jack Gilford, popular with audiences (especially the huge Jewish contingent), as well as with his fellow cast members and the critics, played a successful year with *Nanette*. During it, he was frequently called upon to perform his night club comedy routines and was a "regular" on the *David Frost Revue* on television. In December, preparing to ask for a salary increase as other principals received when they signed for a second year, Gilford was surprised to learn that his contract would not be renewed—and a long-time "second banana" performer, Benny Baker, had been hired (at a considerable saving) as the fifth "Jimmy Smith."

* * *

Busby Berkeley and his wife slept late the morning after they had attended Harry's opening-night party *and* Cyma's, and then they packed quickly for the return to California. Weary from the gray chill of New York in winter, they were anxious to get home. It had been a long, long six months for them.

Berkeley had one more publicity obligation to fulfill before he left: an appearance on *What's My Line?* as the mystery guest. A panelist recognized his distinctive growl after a few quick questions, and Berkeley returned to the dressing room with the audience's applause echoing behind him. As he slumped into a chair, another guest who was preparing to go onstage looked at him in alarm.

"Is there something wrong?" she asked Etta anxiously, pointing a nervous finger at Berkeley, whose head had dropped forward to his chest.

"Oh, no," said Etta as she held a glass of water out to her husband. "He's just resting."

With an intense effort, the aged director raised his head. "I'm—very—tired," he said.

Moments later, in the front seat of a limousine, while Etta rode in back with several suitcases, Berkeley was on his way to the plane. Nearly five months afterward, the couple passed through New York on their way home from Paris and Berlin, where Berkeley had been honored at a retrospective showing of his films. At the airport, he called Harry Rigby to say hello. While there, he collapsed and was taken to a nearby hospital for examination. He was promptly released, and returned to Palm Desert.

There, the fabled showman put final touches to his autobiography, and he and his wife relaxed comfortably on the weekly stipend from *Nanette*—which would be increased once the production sent out a touring company.

And in mid-August, *Daily Variety* reported that Jack Haley, Jr., had announced in Hollywood that he would produce a film about the career of Busby Berkeley. Apparently, he had neglected to tell Berkeley, who was quoted as saying, "I was quite surprised when I found out they were making a film of my life, so I came here from Palm Desert to wish them luck."

When Haley explained that the projected film would include clips of old musical numbers that Berkeley had staged, but also would have a new number for its finale, Berkeley told newsmen: "I haven't begun work on it yet. Some people think that I sit down and sketch my dance numbers in advance, but I have no more idea than the man in the moon of what I'm going to do until I actually get on the set with all the girls ready to go . . . .

"As soon as they're ready to start shooting, all they have to do is call me. I'll be there and put a number together with a snap of my fingers."

\* \* \*

Irving Caesar, basking in the glow of publicity and attention, enjoyed the new audiences that he found on every hand—enjoyed them far more than the money that came in from *Nanette*'s weekly grosses and the numerous airplays of "Tea for Two" and "I Want to Be Happy." A frequent visitor to the *David Frost Show* on TV, he began to talk seriously of the "one-man show" he intended to do Off-Broadway. The production money was volunteered by Lyle Stuart, as had been promised. But the deal was canceled when the songwriter insisted on doing his show without a script, without a rehearsal, without a guarantee that he would appear each night or perform for a prescribed period of time.

"I don't want to go on unless I know that every seat is filled," Caesar said with a Jolsonesque gleam in his magnified eyes. "I'll fill 'em, too. You just wait. I'll do my one-man show, maybe just for a month or so, at no salary, and then the offers will come in from Ed Sullivan and Vegas . . ."

\* \* \*

Harry Rigby, a little older, a little wiser, as impoverished as ever, plans to present a new version of the 1919 musical, *Irene*, on Broadway in the near future. A wealthy woman is involved as a backer, and among those who have been mentioned as possible stars are Patsy Kelly, Billy DeWolfe, and Debbie Reynolds.

Harry's legal battle with the Rubins had not been resolved by Labor Day, 1971, although he had won a preliminary victory when a New York Supreme Court judge ruled that the arbitration panel could decide whether or not he was entitled to billing as co-producer of *Nanette*.

The Rubins' newest lawyer—several others had been hired and fired during *Nanette*'s legal difficulties—had argued that, since the employment contract signed by Harry said nothing about billing, and since the arbitrators were to discuss only those controversies "arising out of or in connection" with the agreement, they could not legally discuss Harry's billing. But the judge noted that "a change of name from Rubin & Rigby Productions to Pyxidium, Ltd. goes to the issue of billing" and that Harry claimed "loss to his reputation for the refusal to credit him as co-producer." The court ruled against Pyxidium, Ltd.

"If they're waiting for me to *starve*," Harry Rigby said with a cackle of laughter, "they should know that I'm eating regularly. The arbitration? Oh, dear, I'm so busy I don't have time to think about it. I'm getting a fee up front to do *Irene*, and I'm being paid to do two other shows, so I don't have to worry. I've also been assured by several friends that if I need money, I can come to them. They know the kind of affidavits that Burt and Donald and Buz have given for me—testifying to all the ideas and work that I put into *Nanette.* And they are sure I'll come out all right.

"Meanwhile, I'm getting my new apartment fixed up. Raoul was going to decorate it for me, and he made all these beautiful sketches—and then I did a terrible thing! I left them all in a taxicab—and now I think Raoul is ready to just *kill* me . . ."

\* \* \*

Cyma Rubin gloried in her role as sole producer of *No, No, Nanette* . . . as the sole producer of a hit Broadway musical during the 1970-71 season . . . as the neophyte female producer who succeeded where experienced males failed. She gloried, too, in her equal-billing status with her husband: When Mayor William T. Somers of Atlantic City presented her with a plaque thanking her for the publicity that *Nanette* gave the New Jersey resort, Cyma stared at the shield of polished wood and gold in awe.

"Look," she said excitedly, "it says 'Mrs. Cyma Rubin'— not 'Mrs. Sam Rubin'! Sam's got a lot of these, but this one is *mine.*"

*No, No, Nanette* was all hers, too, Cyma Rubin firmly believed. *Hers.* Completely. Irrefutably. Undeniably. Irrevocably. Seated one midsummer afternoon beneath the framed caricatures of theatrical celebrities at Sardi's, Mrs. Rubin smiled politely at producers David Merrick and Joshua Logan at a nearby table, and then turned to the interviewer beside her.

"So you're writing a book about *Nanette?*" she said. "What would you like to know?"

Nearly three hours later, the writer turned off his tape recorder, thanked Mrs. Rubin, and left the restaurant. His head was swimming with isolated fragments of the Queeg-like monologue he had listened to for so long, with her words flowing faster than his pen could note them. He had listened in amusement . . . in disbelief . . . in wonder.

And then, to assuage his incredulity, he played back the tapes.

"I want you to know," Cyma's voice snapped out at him, "that I took that little house—Harry had no place to live—

327

I could have just rented an office, and I said, 'Look, we'll have nice offices and you can live there.' I had to spend five thousand dollars to fix it. I furnished it with things from the country house. I gave this sonuvabitch everything you can think of. He didn't move his ass one day! He never did a day's work! All he did was run up phone bills—and sashay around . . .

"He is a total phony . . . but he came to me and represented himself as a producer, that he knew *contracts*, that he knew *booking*. It's all fraud and misrepresentation. Then, when it finally came down to it, he didn't know *anything*. He can't even read a costume sketch. He can't even read a scenic-design plan. He doesn't know what an orchestration is. So that everything you see on the stage—and I have plenty of proof, not *only* from Buster who was there from the beginning—but all these . . . Even the *idea* of *Nanette*, and I tell the truth, this was *Raoul's* idea.

"He's a total faker! When he says *he* got Ruby—that was . . . Ruby was *my* idea. I was sitting in the living room, I let him *call* Busby Berkeley to find out about Ruby. What I did—I *used* him because he was supposed to be such an attraction. That's why I put his name in the company, because he told me how much money he raised for all these different shows. I *believed* him, like an idiot. I put his name in the company, I made him president—*I* didn't intend to work like this.

"So . . . there isn't a *thing* you see on that stage that belongs to Harry Rigby. Buster got Bobby Van. Buster got Patsy Kelly. Buster and I fought like banshees for Helen . . . The concept of the show is *Harry's* concept? There *was* no concept until Burt Shevelove came in . . . And we had no idea of where to go until I thought of Ruby.

"The costumes? *I* went to Paris to research the costumes. *I* worked with Raoul. And what Raoul started with is not what we have. I'm telling you because *I* saw the original sketches. He had an old-hat, campy 1922 look, and I said, 'Raoul, that's wrong, I don't want that. I want it young, fresh.'

"If you saw the girls that Harry picked in California, the

Berkeley girls, the nine girls that I had to pay off $5,000—you never saw such *dogs* in your *life*! There isn't anyth—The beach balls? That was Dick Barstow's idea . . . Harry claims the Dixieland in 'Telephone Girlie' was *his* idea? He came to me and said, 'Luther can't think of anything else. What do you think?' I said, 'Look, Harry, we have no Dixieland, and you know how crazy I am for banjos. Let's put it in Dixieland. We don't have that . . .' He walks out of the room, goes into the room where Luther and Buster are, and says, 'Gee, I've got a great idea . . .'

"I swear to God! He says the idea for the twin pianos was *his*? It was *Buster's*. I was *there*. The double staircase? *That* wasn't Harry's. I rememer how the whole thing came about. I was prodding Raoul on how we're gonna get people up and down. The *original* show had one staircase. I said, 'Then, if they go up one side, Raoul, how they gonna come down?' He said, 'They'll have to go down the platforms in the back.' I said, 'Well, that's no good.' I said, 'They should, you know, come down another way.' He said, 'Well, fine, then we'll have two staircases . . .' "

On the spinning tape, the sound of ice cubes clinking in a glass chimed through Cyma's harangue, and the interviewer remembered how she had swallowed thirstily from a water tumbler. Then, her throat soothed, she picked up the monologue again.

"If it was Harry's idea to put Ruby in the 'I Want to Be Happy' number, then what did we need Donald for? . . . *I* got Donald Saddler, you know . . . I let Harry call him up, do all of that, because he was *supposed* to. So Harry calls up Donald. Do you know that until about two months ago, Donald thought it was *Harry* who brought him into the show? . . . He went out to the Coast and he told Ruby and Patsy that he was the producer and he's got some 'lady with a checkbook.' Patsy *still* doesn't know that it's Buster who brought her into the show. Harry didn't want her. He said, 'Aw, she's on the sauce. Who wants her?' . . .

"So that's how we got Donald—and then Buster got Burt. And I tell you, he never lifted a *finger*. All he did was put me into a booking situation he should know from—because anybody who's been on one musical *knows* that you don't move around on two-week stands . . . Every time we moved, I dropped $40,000 . . .

"I never once spent *one* day working at the desk on 17th Street, because I could never get through the *filth*. He did things to harass me, and everybody! He kept birds, dogs . . .

"And as for Burt Shevelove—you think that sonuvabitch is easy? He's a *bastard*! He's *crazy*. He's a crazy bastard! He never had a hit in his life. Never! *Never!* . . . You know the real truth, who's the brains behind the whole thing? *Buster* . . . He *worked every line* with Shevelove. He and Shevelove—now, if he doesn't volunteer it, don't mention it—because he's very close with him; he thinks Shevelove is brilliant.

"And Shevelove does have a certain kind of—uh—ability, but emotionally he can't—he just can't make it. And that's why he's not on *Some Like It Hot*. They brought him over here to direct it, but they'd chew him up alive. He couldn't make it. ["Nonsense," says David Merrick, producer of the musical, which is now called *Sugar*. "All of the good choreographers insist on directing as well. Burt doesn't choreograph, so we got one of the top choreographer-directors (Gower Champion). I consider Shevelove a top director, completely reliable in every way. He should sue you for libel if you print that silly statement."] You see, Buster kept everybody away from him. But Buster wrote and wrote *every* line with him day and night . . .

"They wouldn't let Harry *near* the man. Harry's *concept?* . . . Harry was drinking all the time and taking pills. But Burt—he's a yellow-bellied coward of the worst—He'll *turn* on you! He has a *filthy* mouth. He had no reason to say anything against me. . . ."

The writer snapped off the tape recorder to study the affidavit that Burt Shevelove had submitted on Harry's behalf, testifying in writing in case he were in London during the arbitration proceedings. "I know that Harry Rigby initiated the production of *No, No, Nanette*—that it was his concept and idea," Shevelove had stated. "Mr. Rigby talked to me about a revival of the musical as long ago as

rehearsals of *Hallelujah, Baby* in January, 1967. . . . Mr.
Rigby was always a fine diplomat and did an excellent job.
. . . In short, Mr. Rigby has been most helpful in every way
in getting *No, No, Nanette* in the condition it now is. Mr.
Rigby . . . also created certain ideas for numbers in the
play which have contributed to its success. It was his idea
to use beach balls, the double staircase in Act One, the
song. . . ."

Small wonder that Mrs. Rubin had critical words to say
about the director. The writer pressed the recorder's "Play"
button, and her voice leaped out at him again.

"But *Buster*—! You cannot *imagine* how much of this
show is Buster's. If anybody should be getting the gold ring,
it should be Buster."

The producer had paused, taken another sip of water,
leaned closer.

"And as far as *Donald* is concerned, Mary Ann did *plenty*,
baby . . . You heard how I answered Logan when he asked
me about him. You heard how I answered. [Introduced to
Mrs. Rubin, a skeptical Josh Logan asked if Saddler
"really did all those beautiful things onstage." Cyma's
answer, delivered with a gracious smile, was, "Well, he
won a Tony Award."]

"Donald doesn't fight back . . . In this case, the chemistry
was good . . . But I can tell you that Bobby choreographed
*all* of his—The 'Happy' number? That was Ted Cappy and
Mary Ann. 'Tea for Two'? Mary Ann . . . The finale? That
was Mercedes Ellington, from the June Taylor bit. I mean,
the kids used to drop *dead* waiting for him to move . . . I'm
aware of it. But the chemistry at that point—He's a good
*editor* . . . 'Keep that in, or take that out.' He's a good editor,
that's what he is . . . It *worked*, in this case . . ."

The background noise of the restaurant blurred behind
Cyma Rubin's voice as she raised it like a knife.

"And the interesting thing is that all these people became
*stars*! When Bobby Van was doing with his hands like a
Bronx yenta, I was *screaming* at Burt Shevelove, 'Let's put
his hands in a vest! Let's do something with the hands.
Clean 'em up, Burt.' Because Burt won't direct. He's not a

director, you know . . . *Nothing*. Nothing! He moved them in and out of doors, and the excuse he used was that it was the style. That's crap! He didn't know what else to do . . . I saw him in action. He's not a *director* . . ."

She hurried on, compulsively, unable to stop, unable to think. Now she was talking about Ruby Keeler, and making faces of distaste as she said:

"Let her go out there and do her little tap-dance . . . but, remember, she alone is not the *show* . . . She's an interesting *addition*. It's like a freak show in a sense. For thirty years they didn't see her, and there she is! . . . 'Miss Modest.' "

There was more, much more, about other performers and production people, and then about her current film project and the fact that when she produced another musical, it would not be a revival. But then, she returned to her favorite subject:

Harry Rigby. Who once had dreamed.

"I *hired* him! He was just *hired*! He had a—you know—employment contract. That's *all*! And the only way he was entitled to get *anything*, a percentage of *Nanette*, was if he *worked*! At least until April first. He had to *work* for it to get it. But when the sonuvabitch breached the contract, refused to work, and wouldn't even come back when I *pleaded* with him to come back . . . He never *intended* to come back. He said he's got a contract, now screw her! And the whole thing with Ruby—! Ruby *knew* what she signed. Harry negotiated that contract. He started the whole thing . . .

"He's bulldozed the whole of Broadway, they think I'm such a *monster*!

"He was stupid. He just had to keep his goddamn mouth shut—you know, fake me along till April first. But now he couldn't convince the world of anything.

"Believe me, I have such evidence, you wouldn't believe it."

The writer reached out, shut off the machine. And played the line over in his mind. "You wouldn't believe it." It was a meaningful sentence.

He sat staring at the tape recorder, then changed the cartridge, searching for something that his incredulous ears thought Cyma Rubin had said later on—an hour later, near the end of the conversation. He found it:

"Tell me something, Don, do you work full time for *Business Week*? I mean, do you have time to do other things— free lance? We're going after something else where Harry's concerned, really beyond the employment thing—and that's fraud and misrepresentation. He's just gotten totally out of hand. I mean, the *damage* to my character and reputation is something I don't know how I'll ever repair. I never had a black word against me—that I knew of—in my life . . .

"Anyway, there's certain information which I know the source of, but it's a little difficult for *me* to go after. Now, what I'm saying to you is—would you be interested—of course, you know, you'd be *paid*—to dig out some of this stuff for me? . . . It might even mean a trip to England for you, to talk to a producer there . . . Now, if you're doing a book and talking to people *anyway* . . . I really want to get all the background on Harry that I can. I'm not interested in his sex life, but I am interested in what a phony he is . . . It could be kind of a special project for you . . ."

* * *

"You wouldn't believe it." The sentence stuck in the writer's consciousness for a long, long time.

As did something else, something said by Sam Rubin shortly after *No, No, Nanette* was clearly established as a multimillion-dollar property:

"You're writing a *book* about it? Marvelous! Cyma said when the show was in rehearsal that she just wished someone could write a book about what she had to go through to get it onstage."

**PLAY-OUT**     Some forty-eight hours before Christmas, 1971, almost exactly one year to the day that Cyma Rubin "fired" Harry Rigby, she instructed her lawyers to offer him a cash settlement— if he would discontinue the arbitration and court proceedings and withdraw his claim to the profits of *No, No, Nanette*.

As always, she had her reasons, and concessions were not necessarily among them. The long, drawn-out periods of testimony and rebuttal were boring her, and, besides, she was very, very busy. There was now a whole new *Nanette* to oversee—the road company scheduled to open in Cleveland on December 27, with June Allyson, Judy Canova ("Judy Canova?" was one startled reaction. "I thought she was—"), and Dennis Day. (At its premiere, the production drew *Nanette's* by-now-familiar raves). In addition, Mrs. Rubin was on a transcontinental shuttle in an effort to keep her eye on filmmaker Robert Downey, who was editing *Greaser's Palace* in California.

Harry Rigby, anxious to get on with his own revival of *Irene*, and without the financial resources to wage a court battle that he was warned might take several years, accepted the settlement. The amount was reported in *Variety* as $200,000—but it was actually closer to $300,000. Rigby agreed, somewhat fearfully, that the money could be paid in installments over a year's time. . . . and that he would not receive credit as co-producer of *No, No, Nanette*.